The Meaning of Life and Death

The Meaning of Life and Death

Ten Classic Thinkers on the Ultimate Question

MICHAEL HAUSKELLER

BLOOMSBURY ACADEMIC
LONDON • NEW YORK • OXFORD • NEW DELHI • SYDNEY

BLOOMSBURY ACADEMIC
Bloomsbury Publishing Plc
50 Bedford Square, London, WC1B 3DP, UK
1385 Broadway, New York, NY 10018, USA
29 Earlsfort Terrace, Dublin 2, Ireland

BLOOMSBURY, BLOOMSBURY ACADEMIC and the Diana logo are trademarks
of Bloomsbury Publishing Plc

First published in Great Britain 2020
Reprinted 2020 (twice), 2021 (twice), 2022

Cover design by Peter Somogyi
Cover image: Friedrich Justin Bertuch, Bilderbuch für Kinder, 1790–1830
(Eigenbesitz), Fabelwesen © Heidelberg University Library

A catalogue record for this book is available from the British Library.

A catalog record for this book is available from the Library of Congress.

ISBN: HB: 978-1-3500-7363-0
PB: 978-1-3500-7364-7
ePDF: 978-1-3500-7365-4
eBook: 978-1-3500-7366-1

Typeset by Deanta Global Publishing Services, Chennai, India
Printed and bound in Great Britain

To find out more about our authors and books visit www.bloomsbury.com
and sign up for our newsletters.

Dedicated to the memory of my father, Erich Arthur Hauskeller
(1905–74)

CONTENTS

ACKNOWLEDGEMENTS

None of the material used in this book has been published previously. However, drafts of individual chapters have been read and commented on by a great number of people. I am immensely grateful to all of them, but I would like to thank in particular those colleagues and friends whose continued interest and support has made me feel that when I was writing this book I was doing something that mattered, something meaningful: Drew Chastain, Lewis Coyne, Nikos Gkogkas, Simon Hailwood, Peter Herrisone-Kelly, Daniel Hill, Kyle McNease, Jelson Oliveira and Yiota Vassilopoulou. This book is for you.

PRELUDE

What is the point of living? If we are all going to die anyway, if nothing will remain of whatever we achieve in this life, why should we bother trying to achieve anything in the first place? Why does it matter what we do or not do? Or does it? Can we be mortal and still live a meaningful life? Questions such as these are not new. They have been asked for a long time. They are part of, or versions of, what is sometimes called the 'ultimate' question. The ultimate question concerns the meaning of life and death and is ultimate not only in the sense that it is the most fundamental question, reaching down to the very core of our existence, but also in the sense that it is the most difficult one to answer.

In Douglas Adams's *Hitchhiker's Guide to the Universe*, it takes the supercomputer Deep Thought several million years of calculations to come up with an answer to the 'ultimate question of life, the universe and everything'. That answer is, as many readers will know, 42. That is of course not much of an answer because it doesn't really tell us anything. If we had received no answer at all, that would have been just as instructive as this one. In the series, the cryptic nature of the answer is explained by the fact that those who programmed the computer had no clue what the question was that it was supposed to answer, and the vagueness and uncertainty of the question is indeed part of the problem. The 'ultimate question of life, the universe and everything' is, after all, not really a question at all. So what exactly is it that we want to know when we raise that question? Depending on what we are asking, the answer may not always be the same. And clearly there are questions to which '42' is a perfectly reasonable and indeed the correct answer, for instance, 'How much is six times seven?' except that it probably wouldn't occur to anyone that *this* might actually be the ultimate question of life. So what is it then?

One way of understanding the question is in terms of *purpose*. We can look at life, the universe and everything, and ask what all this is actually good for, what purpose it serves. When I recently asked my son Arthur (who is now ten years old and annoyingly smart), what he thought the meaning of life was, he did not have to think about it at all. Instead, he answered my question right away, without hesitation and with great confidence, as if he had already concluded his own personal calculations and then come up with the right answer (very much like Deep Thought, except much faster): 'The meaning of life, Dad', he said, 'is death.' When I asked why, he replied, 'Because everything dies in the end.' And then he added, 'But the meaning of death, Dad, is life, because there could be no life without death.'

This really happened. (Did I mention he is a smart kid?) Needless to say, I was quite impressed. But then again, it was not quite the answer I was looking for. His answer may have been right, but it is still wrong because what it answers is not really the question I meant to ask when I asked him about the meaning of life. Let me explain: the meaning of life is indeed death if we understand meaning as the natural endpoint of an event or process. As far as we know, all life ends in death. Not only we as individuals and everything else that lives will die one day, some sooner, some later, but also life itself (or at least life on earth) will one day come to an end even if that end may still lie millions of years in the future. But my son's answer actually suggested more than just that. There is an idea of purpose here, introduced in the second part of his response: if not only life but also death has a meaning, and if the meaning of death is life, then 'meaning' must mean more than just where something is headed. Death, after all, does not naturally end in life. There is, however, good reason to think that death is necessary for new life to arise. Not only do we all live off the death of others (the plants and animals we have to consume to be able to continue living); it is also difficult to see how there could ever be new life if the things that already are alive did not die at some stage. So perhaps that is *why* they die. Living beings would then come to an end to make room for new living beings. We may then answer the question 'Why do we have to die?' by saying that we have to die so that others can live. This would then be the *purpose* of our death, that which our death is good for. And if the meaning of death is life in *that* sense, then we must see death as the meaning of life in the *same* sense, namely, in the sense that we live *in order to* die, that the purpose of our living is our dying.

However, even if that were true, and even if we believed it was, it would still not provide us with a satisfactory answer to that elusive 'ultimate question' about life. If we live in order to die, and die so that more like us can live, what then is that whole cycle of living and dying, and living and dying again, good for? If life leads to death, and death leads to life, where does *that* lead? What is all this living and dying about? We may now know why we live and also know why we die, but we still don't know why we live *and* die.

Yet even if we found an explanation for all of this, an explanation for why there are living and dying things in the first place, it would still not give us the answer we seek. No purpose that we can think of can do that, no matter how big and all-encompassing it is. If I am told that x happens for the sake of y, and y happens for the sake of z, then I can still, independent of what z is, wonder what *that* is good for. If everything serves, say, the glory of God, then what end does that glory serve? And once we start considering not only life, but the whole 'universe and everything', wondering what *its* end or purpose is ('Why is there something rather than nothing?'), then the question is hardly intelligible anymore because we seem to be asking for something that simply cannot exist, namely, something that is somehow more than, or outside of, everything.

Clearly, questions about purpose ('What is it good for?') can only ever lead us so far. Whatever purpose we may come up with, it is always possible for us to ask what the point of that purpose is, and to be told that we live and die for the glory of God or in order to make the universe more colourful and varied, or whatever other purpose you may want to suggest here, is not necessarily more satisfactory than if we were told the purpose is 42. The problem is that we find it difficult to look at life and death, or at any rate our own life and death and (for most of us) the life and death of our loved ones, as just another fact in the world, a fact like any other. Death certainly is widely regarded as more than that: it is *morally* objectionable, something that ought not to be and yet is. So when we ask about the meaning of death we don't really want to know what death is good for. We are looking not for an explanation but for a *justification*. And since it is hardly possible for us to think of life and not also think of death, because we are well aware that there is no (or at least has never been so far) life without death, when we ask about the meaning of life we also want more than just an explanation in terms of an efficient or final cause of its existence. How it is possible that at some stage in the history of Earth life emerged from inanimate matter is an interesting scientific question, but answering it would not answer our ultimate question. Whether life has some purpose other than itself is also an interesting question, but answering it would not answer the ultimate question either, *unless* that purpose is so clearly worth all that was needed to realize it that the follow-up question 'And what is *that* good for?' simply no longer arises. In other words, we would need something that is not good for anything but itself (which means that it is not good *for* anything, but still undoubtedly *good*). Only such an intrinsic purpose (a means that is its own end) could conceivably allay or diffuse the moral scandal of our mortal lives. It would be something that helps us make sense of it all.

However, even if there were no death, even if we lived forever, we would probably still be asking the question, wondering what the point of life is. In any case, given how difficult it is even to figure out what exactly the questions is, it is hardly surprising that nobody seems to have found a conclusive answer yet. Many have tried, however, among them being some of the world's greatest writers and philosophers. It is their work that this book is about: Arthur Schopenhauer, Søren Kierkegaard, Herman Melville, Fyodor Dostoyevsky, Leo Tolstoy, Friedrich Nietzsche, William James, Marcel Proust, Ludwig Wittgenstein and Albert Camus. In the philosophical and literary work of these writers, the connection between death and meaning has taken centre stage. This book explores their ideas, weaving a rich tapestry of concepts, voices and images, helping the reader to understand the concerns at the heart of their work and uncovering common themes and stark contrasts in their understanding of what kind of world we live in, what role death plays in it and what really matters in life.

The reader should, however, not expect to get an ultimate answer to the ultimate question here or anywhere else. Perhaps it is just not the kind of question that somebody else can answer for us. Such answers can only ever be tentative, to be read and understood as suggestions how one might look at the world and our own place in it. The answers or viewpoints given in the following chapters are as deeply personal as the question is. What we find in these writers' work is not abstract theories: we find actual people, breathing, vulnerable individuals who when they reflect on life and death always also reflect on their *own* living and dying. We must see them as participant observers, fully immersed in the very reality they seek to understand. They did not merely have a theoretical, philosophical interest in the questions they explore, but an existential interest. They all lived, knowing that they were going to die. They all experienced the joys of living and the pain of living. And they are all dead now, just as we will be dead one day. *The Meaning of Life and Death* is just as much about those people as it is about their ideas and the way they expressed them.

For me, writing this book has been an extraordinary literary and intellectual adventure. Some of the authors featuring in it I hardly knew when I set out to write it. Others I hadn't read in a long time. But I knew enough to know that they all were likely to have interesting and important things to say about life and death, and I was not disappointed. I found reading their works and writing about them immensely rewarding. Here, there were whole worlds to discover, and for a little while I lived in these worlds, mining and savouring their hidden riches. Death should be a gloomy subject to read and write about, but it hasn't been for me. On the contrary, I felt uplifted by my engagement with all those wonderful writers. In their words, in the way they wrote about it, even death became a thing of beauty. Words matter. Thoughts cannot be fully abstracted from them. They not only reveal meaning but also create it. Words matter because they evoke images and tell stories that help us make sense of the world. That is why for me philosophy and literature seamlessly blend into one another. Words matter because the right words can capture and mirror the fragility and beauty of life, the tragedy of it and the comedy of it. And we all know there is plenty of both to be found in it. This book is about death, but it is also meant to be a celebration of life.

Note that the chapters that follow are exploratory, not critical. I do not engage with any of the vast literature that exists about the work of the authors I introduce and discuss. The reason for this is that I wanted to avoid all distractions, keeping my mind open for what I would find in their work, letting them speak for themselves. I do not try to assess their contribution either, only occasionally pointing out inconsistencies or worrisome implications, and being in any case more interested in *what* they have to say than in whether they are 'right' or 'wrong'. In fact, I strongly suspect there is no right and wrong when it comes to the ultimate question(s).

CHAPTER ONE

The worst of all possible worlds
Arthur Schopenhauer
(1788–1860)

The misery of life

What is the nature of the world in which we find ourselves? Is it, at its very core, a good place or a bad place, friendly or hostile, orderly or chaotic, controllable or uncontrollable, rational or irrational? And where should we look for an answer? Traditionally, philosophers have tended to emphasize the rational, human-friendly side of the world, arguing that there is a good reason for why the world is as it is, and that part of that reason is that it needs to suit our desires and needs. The world has a purpose, and we are, in one way or another, but always in a rather good way, at the centre of it. There is someone or something out there that makes sure of this, some kind of cosmic director or playbook that intends us to be the heroes of the story that is the history of the universe: a god perhaps, or a world spirit, or our own pure and transcendental, world-building self or 'I'. Yet if that is so, why do we have to encounter so much adversity and suffer so much? Why are there so many horrible diseases, epidemics and natural disasters that blight so many by all accounts innocent people's lives? Why do we keep fighting wars that maim and kill millions? Why can we not stop hurting each other? And why do we have to age and die? In short, why is there so much evil in the world, physical and moral, and how does all that fit into the alleged general purpose?

There is of course always a way to *make* things fit. Apparent contradictions are rarely so irreconcilable that a philosopher's speculative ingenuity cannot resolve them. Take for instance the German philosopher Gottfried Wilhelm Leibniz (1646–1716) who, in his *Theodicy* (1710), defended the common theological conception of God as a benevolent being whose power has no limits against the not unreasonable charge that if he really were both all-powerful and all-good, then the world could not possibly be as bad as it appears to be. The fact that there is so much evil and so much suffering in the world, much of it quite clearly undeserved, strongly suggests that either God is too weak to do anything about it (in which case he is not all-powerful) or he does not care (in which case he is not all-good). Leibniz, however, argued that such a conclusion would be unwarranted. For one thing because we know very little about why certain things are happening and what good may result from them, and for another because it stands to reason that even the most powerful being is constrained by what is logically possible. In other words, not even God can have his cake and eat it. He could not, for instance, have created a world whose inhabitants are both free and incapable of doing wrong, or a world in which people can prove their worth by overcoming their fears and resisting temptation if there is nothing to fear and nothing to be tempted by. Certain defects are simply necessary to allow the realization of certain greater goods, and since our understanding is limited it may not always be obvious to us *which* greater good an apparent evil serves. Accordingly, the reason why there are various evils in this world does not have to be that God could not have prevented them or did not want to prevent them. Perhaps the reason is simply that there was no other world possible that would have been *better*, all things considered, than the world we actually live in. We are, therefore, justified to continue to assume that God always wills the best and does the best, because even though this world is clearly not perfect, it may in fact be the best of all *possible* worlds. Some tough choices clearly had to be made, but even though we may not always be able to understand the rationale behind those choices, we can be sure that God made them with our best interest at heart. This means that we cannot reasonably expect a better world and therefore have no reason to complain, because all is well, or at least as well as things can possibly be.

The problem with Leibniz's optimistic interpretation of the world's obvious imperfections is that it requires a lot of faith to be persuaded by it. Clearly, if we begin our inquiry with the *assumption* that God is all-good and all-powerful, then we must indeed conclude that this world, despite its many flaws, has to be the best of all possible worlds, because nothing else makes sense. However, the world is such that we cannot really *infer* from what we know about it that it must have been created by an all-powerful and infinitely good being. Perhaps the world's evils can be reconciled with the existence of such a God, but nobody in their right mind could contemplate the various evils that plague our lives and the extent of human (and other creatures') suffering and then honestly conclude, *on that basis*, that an infinitely powerful and infinitely good being is responsible for it. This has to be assumed or inferred from something other than experience. Yet if we make no such faith-based assumptions and choose as the starting point of our inquiry into the nature of the world our *experience* of it, then a very different conclusion suggests itself: that this world is not at all the best of all possible worlds. Very far from it: it is, instead, in many ways a truly horrible place.

The grounds for that conclusion were laid by the French philosopher Voltaire (1694–1778), who in 1762 published his novel *Candide: Or, the Optimist*, which shows its naive hero stumbling from one calamity to the next, witnessing a broad spectrum of human misery that puts his belief in the essential goodness of the world to a very severe test. *Candide* relentlessly parodies Leibniz's attempt to rationalize away the very evilness of evil by declaring it to be necessary for the realization of the greater and indeed greatest good. In Voltaire's view it was preposterous, even dangerous, to believe that the world was basically fine, and even more so that it cannot possibly be any better than it is. Doing so just invites complacency and amounts to complicity with evil, since its existence is assumed to be necessary and hence inalterable. Voltaire refused to believe that things cannot be any better than they are. He believed in the possibility and desirability of improvement, of the human ability to make this world a better place. In that sense at least, Voltaire too was an optimist.

The German philosopher Arthur Schopenhauer on the other hand, whose work we will now turn to, was not an optimist. Not only did he despise and loathe those who attempt to persuade their reader that, ultimately, all is well, be it Leibniz with his best of all possible worlds or the post-Kantian German idealists of his own time, Fichte, Schelling and Hegel, who thought that reason – or what they took it to be, namely, some kind of autonomous, self-sufficient agent (Reason with a capital R) – was present and active in everything there is. He also did not, as Voltaire did, believe that we can actually change the world for the better. For Schopenhauer, the world was a very bad place indeed, but there is absolutely nothing we can do about it. The suffering and misery that people experience in their lives is, after all, not an accidental feature of life: it is all-pervasive and part of its very essence (which shows us very clearly what life really is, namely: something that ought not to be). Even if we are lucky enough to avoid major catastrophes in our life, even if we are not hit by disease, the death of loved ones, natural disasters, human exploitation or destitution, as so many are, our life will still be only marginally better than theirs. Living does not accidentally and avoidably involve suffering, but essentially and necessarily. All life is, by its very nature, suffering (W1, §56, 405) because it is characterized by permanent striving, a constitutional restlessness that is fuelled by the mechanics of human need and desire. Our existence is a constant wanting. Living is desiring, and all desires mark absences that are felt as such. As long as we do not get what we want we suffer from that absence, and once we do get it, we desire something else. The more and the more intensely we desire, the more we suffer. Yet not desiring is not a viable option either, first of all because it is not normally in our power not to desire and secondly because the absence of specific desires comes with its own kind of suffering. If there is nothing left to desire, then boredom sets in, which is even more painful than desires (which are always unfulfilled since a fulfilled desire is no longer a desire) because it confronts us with the emptiness of our existence, which we find unbearable. Ironically, although we desire nothing more than to exist and to continue to exist, as soon as we have managed to fully secure our existence so that there is nothing left wanting, we find that we don't really know what to do with our existence.

So we try to kill time, find distractions, for no other end than to make our existence, once again, unfelt (W1, §57, 408). Boredom is even worse than desire: it can easily lead to despair, even suicide. Between the pain of desire and the pain of boredom, the best we can hope for is a temporary, always very short-lived reprieve from any marked degree of suffering. This brief reprieve is what we call happiness, and all that happiness can ever be: the momentary comparative absence of suffering.

Since this is the situation we find ourselves in, the world really is a pretty bad place. One could even say that far from being the best of all possible worlds, as Leibniz would have us believe, the world is in fact the *worst* of all possible worlds, for if it were any worse than it already is, it would not be able to exist at all (W2, ch. 46, 678). Our existence is, after all, so precarious, dependent on so many conditions, that it would just take a few small changes (such as a few more degrees of global warming) to push us over the edge and make us disappear. We can only survive for a while by constantly fending off death. Life is always a struggle, a permanent fight against non-existence. Most importantly, it is a fight we cannot win. In the end, non-existence awaits all of us (although given what life is the fact that it will eventually end, and quite soon too, might actually be the best thing about it) (W1, §59, 422).

Because things are in fact so bad, it would be downright bizarre to fall in line with a common idealistic presumption and to claim that life is a desirable condition and that the purpose of human life is happiness. For Schopenhauer, it is quite obvious that we are not here to be happy. If we are here for anything at all, if there is a purpose to our life, then it is much more likely, and much more in accordance with our own personal experience of life and with what we know about it, that we are here to suffer as much as possible, and then die (W2, ch. 46, 680). The question is why.

The world as a problem

In my 17th year, lacking all scholarly education, I became as deeply moved by the misery of life as Buddha in his youth, when he caught sight of disease, old age, pain, and death. The truth that the world so very clearly revealed to me soon overcame the

Jewish dogmas that I too had engrained, and I concluded that this world could not be the work of an infinitely good being, but might very well be that of a devil who brought creatures into existence so he could revel in the spectacle of their agony. (HN IV/1, 96)

Schopenhauer believed that a keen sense of the misery of life (which, in its extent and relentlessness, seems almost purposeful) had turned his younger self, the son of a well-to-do merchant first in Danzig (now Gdansk) and then in the buzzing commercial town of Hamburg, into a philosopher. The initial plan had been that he follow in his father's footsteps and eventually take over his company, but when he was seventeen his father died (possibly through suicide), and Schopenhauer broke off his apprenticeship and went on to study philosophy instead, first in Göttingen with the Kant critic 'Aenesidemus' Schulze and then in Berlin with Johann Gottlieb Fichte – whom he later denounced as a 'windbag' (W1, Preface to second edition, 18) – and the theologian and the founder of hermeneutics Friedrich Schleiermacher. In 1818, at the age of thirty, he published his magnum opus, the magnificent *The World as Will and Representation*, one of the truly great books in the history of philosophy. Schopenhauer himself knew it, too. Unfortunately, nobody else did at the time: the splash its confident author fully expected the book to make failed to materialize. It took thirty years and a second volume of supplements, published in 1844, before people started to take notice. The public appreciation of his work and his genius came late for Schopenhauer. When it eventually did he was already a bitter, unsociable, self-opinionated and misanthropic old man. Yet being finally vindicated and revered by a new generation of thinkers, those last ten years or so may still have been the happiest period of his life because he no longer had to suffer from the lack of recognition that he had been craving in vain for such a long time.

In almost all other respects, Schopenhauer's life had not been at all a bad one. He inherited a large chunk of his father's money, which lasted him a lifetime and allowed him to spend his time as he pleased. He never had to work for a living, which was just as well because his repeated attempts to gain a paid academic position all failed. He made it unscathed through the Napoleonic Wars that ruined and destroyed so many. He survived the cholera epidemic that ravished Berlin in 1831 and that killed his arch nemesis Hegel, driving him away from Berlin to Frankfurt, where he spent the rest of his life quite comfortably. He may have occasionally feared for his life or his possessions, but in the end he always came out on top. Happy, however, he was not, which is a good thing because if he had been, *The World as Will and Representation* would never have been written. There would simply have been no reason to write it. According to Schopenhauer, all true philosophy starts with the knowledge of our mortality and the experience of suffering (W2, ch. 16, 180), either one's own or, if we are affected by it, that of others. The ones who are happy, those who take no issue with life and are largely oblivious to all the suffering in the world and the finiteness of our existence, do not philosophize. They do not ask why things are as they are. They just live their life without thinking much about it. There are certainly plenty of so-called philosophies out there that show little sign of any awareness that not all is well with the world, that some things, and indeed too many things in this life, are not as they ought to be, but for Schopenhauer such 'philosophies' are not really philosophies at all, but mere verbiage. 'A philosophy in which you cannot hear between the pages the tears, the wailing and gnashing of teeth, and the terrible uproar of the general mutual murder is not a philosophy' (Gespr, 337). Accordingly, philosophical wonder is at its core not a mere intellectual curiosity, but moral outrage. It stems from an awareness that things are not as they should be. All that suffering that people and indeed everything that is alive has to endure, not just occasionally, but on a regular basis, and all that killing and dying that never ends, blindly and stupidly repeated with every new generation, is not something we can just let stand. As philosophers, we must acknowledge the problem and seek to understand what is going on and what the *point* of all this is. Not to do so and instead to pretend that there is no problem, that all is well, is not only intellectually dishonest but also morally corrupt. The whole state of affairs is especially perplexing since most people's lives seem to be so banal and pointless that it is difficult to see how they should be worth all the trouble that it takes to live them.

It is really unbelievable how, looked at from the outside, empty and meaningless, and, felt from the inside, dull and unconscious the life of most people goes by. It is a weak longing and dragging oneself along, a dreamy tumble through the four stages of life towards death, accompanied by a series of trivial thoughts.

Those lives are like clockworks that have been wound up and that move without knowing why; and each time a human is conceived and born, the clock of human life is wound up anew, to repeat once again the same old story that has already been told countless times before.

And yet, each of those lives has to be paid for with many pains and a bitter death that has long been feared (W1, §58, 419). None of this makes any sense. Why invest so much in something that seems so utterly pointless? Such a sorry, nonsensical state of affairs certainly does not suggest that at the root of it all there is a wise and benevolent God or any other kind of rational conception and design. But if not that, what else can it be? What does the fact that all life is, by its very nature, condemned to suffering and death without offering much in return, tell us about the true nature of the world?

The true nature of the world

Schopenhauer starts his inquiry into the nature of the world with an endorsement of Immanuel Kant's critique of pure reason and what he sees as Kant's fundamental insight: that the world never appears to us the way it is in and by itself, but always in a mediated form. We are never directly with the things we perceive. The way we perceive things is determined by the way our perception and cognition works, so that what we end up perceiving is as much a reflection of our own nature as it is a reflection of the nature of things. In order for us to have knowledge of the world, it must appear to us in some way, so all we can ever be aware of and all we can ever talk and think about is the world *as it appears to us*. We can, therefore, never know what the world *really* is, beyond all appearance, except that it is something that appears to us the way it does. The thing-in-itself, as Kant called it, must remain unknown.

Schopenhauer seems to fully commit to this Kantian position in the very first sentence of *The World as Will and Representation*:

'The world is my representation:' – this is a truth that holds for every living and world-aware being, even though it is only man who can bring it to reflected abstract consciousness, and if he actually does, he has attained philosophical wisdom. He will then realize that he knows no sun and no earth, but always just an eye that sees the sun, a hand that feels the earth, and that the world surrounding him only exists as representation, that is, always just in relation to something else, that which represents, which is he himself. (W1, §1, 31)

Now if we look at the way the world presents itself to us, we can easily see that there are some features that are so pervasive that they are common not only to all actual but also to all possible representations of the world: whatever we look at, it is always in time, in space and in some way causally connected to other objects and events, and we cannot even imagine an object that is not. Kant argued, and Schopenhauer fully agrees with him, that we must therefore assume that those most general features of our experience are not really *objects* of our experience at all, but rather the subjective conditions that allow those objects to appear in the first place. In other words, time, space and causality are not part of the *content* of our experience, not things or aspects of things that we find 'out there', in the supposedly external world. Instead, they pertain to the *form* of experience. This means, however, that we must assume that whatever the world really is, in and by itself, it is not subject to those conditions. Accordingly, the real world must be considered free of all causal relations, not spatially extended and, most importantly, timeless. Kant, of course, would not have put it this way. For him the world of appearances *was*, for all theoretical and most[1] practical purposes, the real world. It is, after all, the only knowable world and hence the only world that needs to concern us. In contrast, Schopenhauer makes it very clear that how the world appears to us is not how the world really is. Appearances deceive us; they foster an illusion. Our life – the life we *think* we live – is very much like a dream, except it is one we do not usually wake from.

Yet once we have understood that the world is our representation, once we have understood that it is not the ultimate reality, we quite naturally want to know what the *meaning* of the whole spectacle is. Kant, apparently, was not very much interested in that question. Schopenhauer certainly was. In fact, for him it was the only question that really mattered. And we have good reason to ask that question, not only because of the unsatisfactory nature of our lives, all the pain and suffering, but also because we feel that this cannot possibly be the last word about what the world is. If what we used to think of as the real world is in fact just representation, why then do we take things so seriously? Why does it feel so real if it isn't? Might it have something to do with what the world is *beside* representation? 'We want to know what those representations mean. We ask whether this world is nothing but representation, in which case it would have to pass by us like an unsubstantial dream or a ghostlike apparition, not worthy of our attention, or whether it is not also something else, something beyond that, and what it might then be' (W1, §17, 150). Yet the problem is that it seems impossible to go beyond the way things appear to us. There may very well be 'something else', but we can never know what it is. That is the position that Kant adopted. Schopenhauer, however, believed that there is a way we can get around this problem. It is true that we can never get any closer to the hidden nature of the world if we continue to look at things from the outside, which is what we normally do, mostly because there is no other way to look at the vast majority of objects. However, there is one object that we have access to in a different, namely, non-representational, way: one object that we know not merely from the outside but also from the inside. We know what it is to *be* that object. That object is our own body, which we know not only as an object, as a thing among things, but also as the seat of our own being. We have a body, but we also *are* that body,[2] and it is through our body that we gain knowledge of the world and are in this world in the first place. So what is it we, living in and through this body, discover ourselves to be? Not a thinking thing, as Descartes had claimed, at least not primarily, but a thing that is motivated to everything it does by a variety of drives and urges, by hunger and thirst and lust; by fears and hopes; by affections and disaffections; by love and hate; by the desire to avoid pain and to find pleasure; and, last but not least, by the sheer desire to exist, to sustain itself and to postpone death as long as possible. These existential drives are the very core of our being, to which all thinking, all conscious reflection, is literally an afterthought. And what is all this? Schopenhauer names it 'will to life' or simply 'will' (W1, §54, 362). So we are part of the representational world, but we are also, and more fundamentally, will. The body is nothing but the external representation of the will: it is what the will looks like from the outside, just as the will is what the body looks like from the inside. Yet if that is what we are, in addition to being representations, then should we not use this knowledge of our own true essence as a key for the understanding of the true nature of all other things as well? If *we* are essentially will, then perhaps all *other* things are essentially will too. What else could they be? There is, after all, nothing other than will and representation that we have any knowledge of, nor can there ever be. So that is what the world is, *will and representation*, but in its inner essence it is nothing but will.

Making sense of the world

We shall not here concern ourselves with the question whether Schopenhauer's identification of the thing-in-itself with the will is entirely consistent. There is certainly a problem here because clearly the will can also only be known to us as a representation and not as it is in itself. Schopenhauer is of course aware of that and assures us that the real will is different from how it appears to us, but even though that helps explain how the blind forces active in the natural world (such as gravity) can also be 'will', it doesn't quite solve the problem: for if the will that we know, even if it is the will that we know ourselves to be, is not the will as it is in itself, then how can we be sure it is still will, or for that matter anything else that we may understand and give a name to?

Yet even if Schopenhauer's move is a bit dubious, it certainly helps explain why our lives ultimately appear so pointless, and that is precisely what it is meant to do. Our lives appear pointless because they *are* pointless, because there is no master plan, no rational conception that is reflected and actualized by what happens in the world. There is, instead, some blind, powerful, but entirely dumb and purposeless striving at the heart of the universe, something that wills, but does not know what it wills, except that it continue to exist, and this fact is reflected in the world as we know it. This hypothesis does a good job at explaining why our life is as it is and why things work as they do, which is all the verification it has and all the verification it needs. Once we have understood that the restless striving of the will is at the heart of all things everything begins to make sense. It is as if we had been puzzled by a message in an unknown language that we have now finally found the key to, and we know that it is the right key because we can now read the message and understand everything perfectly (W2, ch. 17, 214–15).

All suffering springs from the fact that the will wills and that it wills without rhyme or reason, never resting, never content, fighting unwittingly against itself for survival and dominance, like a mad dog mauling its own tail. Our being, then, has no purpose. It does not serve any higher goals. It is not meant to go anywhere. It just is. No wonder we cannot figure out what we are here for. We are here because the will wills, and because we are one of its many representations, one way in which the will comes to be aware of itself. That is all there is to it.

Unfortunately, however, even though we have now found an answer to the question how it is possible that the world is such an unreasonable place and one that contains so much suffering for those who have the misfortune of being born into it, it does nothing to appease the *moral outrage* that the state of the world incites in us. We may now understand why the world is as it is and why it contains so much suffering, but that does not change the fact that the world is still not as it *ought* to be. It is still a bad place, and we need it to be a good place, or at least a *just* place, a place that makes *moral* sense to us, one that is not entirely hopeless and that does have *some* point. The seemingly endless cycle of life and death, creation and destruction, is something 'so obviously absurd that it can never be the true order of things, but must be a shell that conceals it, or more precisely a phenomenon caused by the constitution of our intellect' (W2, ch. 41, 551). What is required here is not just a plausible explanation for why the world is as it is, or appears as it does. The hypothesis of the will does provide such an explanation (while the alternative hypothesis of a wise and benevolent creator or rational world spirit does not). What it does not do, however, is make the absurdity go away. It is still absurd that we spend our whole life trying to stay alive and then die anyway. It is absurd that nature puts so much effort into something that will not last, not once, but over and over again, like a deranged cosmic Sisyphus. It is absurd that the world is full of living beings who want nothing more than to live and who *for this very reason* fight each other to the death. All this is so absurd, so nonsensical, so morally obnoxious, that it simply cannot be what is really happening. To make sense of all this we need more than just an explanation for why things are as they are. What we need instead is some assurance that the world is *not* what it appears to be, that the things we regard as real and that cause us so much suffering, like death or the fragmentation of being into separate individuals that compete with each other and hurt each other in the process, are in fact not real, and that it is not completely impossible for us to step out of this illusory world that contains so much suffering and find a foothold and perhaps even a home in the truly real, which does not.

For Schopenhauer, philosophy, or more precisely metaphysics (which is the part of philosophy that deals with the true nature of the world), has to do more than just to provide a complete description[3] of the world. Its role is not merely theoretical but also, and perhaps even primarily, practical. It is meant to give people hope and 'unfailing solace in suffering and in death' (PP, ch. 15, 302). In this respect it is not so different from religion, except that religion provides solace by telling lies and is therefore unreliable, whereas metaphysics is more dependable because it soothes our existential anxieties with something far more solid: the 'indestructible diamond' (PP, ch. 15, 305) of truth.

Temporal immortality

So how exactly does metaphysical truth make things better for us? For one thing, it teaches us that death, which we fear more than anything else and which for this reason causes a lot of suffering, is not real, and if it is not real there is no reason to fear it. It is not real because there can be no death without time, and we know that time is only one of the forms in which things appear to us. It does not rule over or affect in any way the true nature of the world, which includes our own true nature. The will, which is what we really are, is timeless and therefore indestructible. But the world as we know it is nothing but the objectification of the will: it is the form in which the will becomes aware of itself. Since we are will and as such are also timeless and indestructible, and since the world only exists for us (the subject to whom it is an object), the world has always been there for us and will always be there for us.

> Since the will is the thing-in-itself, the inner content, the essence of the world, while life, the visible world, appearance, is only the will's reflection, it will accompany the will as inseparably as the shadow accompanies the body: and when will is there, there

will also be life and world. To the will to life, therefore, life is certain, and as long as we are filled with the will to life, we do not need to fear for our existence, not even in the face of death. (W1, §54, 362)

Individuals are born and die, of course, but individual people, as all individual things, are only phenomena. They only *appear* to exist: they are there for us only because that is how we represent the world to ourselves. As representation, the world is subject to the *principium individuationis*, the principle of individuation, which fragments the world both spatially and temporally. Nature itself, however, already gives us a good indication of how unreal the individual actually is by showing very little interest in its well-being and survival. Once individuals have reproduced and thus assured the survival of their species, nature is entirely indifferent to their destruction (W1, §60, 429). We should take our hint from that and treat the individual with equal indifference. Schopenhauer compares the event of death with the process of excretion: in both cases matter is discarded, without any great consequence, and we should be as indifferent to the individual body that we leave behind in death as we are to the waste products that we remove from our body on a daily basis (W1, §54, 365). In other words, when we die, the species is having a bowel movement.

We cannot lose the present. In a way we already know that. Even though we are used to the idea that our life has a temporal duration: that it started in the past and will continue in future until one day it ends, so that sometime in the future our life will be past, we in fact only ever live in the present, never in the past and never in the future. Schopenhauer insists that this will not and cannot change.

Nobody has ever lived in the past, and nobody will ever live in the future. The *present* alone is the form of all life, and it is also its certain possession, which cannot be snatched away from it. The present is always there, as is its content: both stand fast without fail, like the rainbow on the waterfall. For life is certain to the will, and the present to life. (W1, §54, 366)

The past is gone precisely because it never really existed in the first place. Only the present moment is real, the will and its expression, which is the world of representation. We may marvel at how fortunate we are to still exist at this very moment while billions of others, many of them greater than we, have already passed away, but there is nothing fortunate about it. We are here right now for the simple reason that we cannot *not* be here. If we could ever not be, we would already not be. There is, therefore, no reason to fear death. To fear death because it supposedly snatches the present away from us is just as silly as to fear that one might slide off the globe when it turns and we are no longer on top (W1, §54, 368). This also means, however, that we cannot escape a bad life by committing suicide. As long as we affirm our own existence, and that means as long as we are will (because the will, as will, can do nothing else but affirm its own existence), we are, for better or worse, tied to this world. The present can neither be lost nor be cast away. This is the reason why, while we acknowledge our own mortality in an abstract way, we are all at the same time secretly convinced that our life will never end, that we will always be. We know that we will have to die, like everyone else, but at the same time, in our heart of hearts, we don't really believe we will. And we are right not to believe it, for if the world is our representation, then the end of our existence would necessarily spell the end of the world. We do not doubt, however, that the world will continue after our death. Therefore we will too.

   This does of course not mean that the individual that we are is not going to die. In the temporally extended world of representation we appear, to ourselves and to others, as separate individuals. We usually think that is *all* we are, that this separation between beings reflects ultimate reality. In that world, death is the point in time when a particular individual representation of the will comes to an end. But other individual representations will continue to exist, and I am actually they as much as I am I. The difference between me and them, between me and you, is only apparent, for the same will lives and becomes reflective in both of us. Each of us, in our temporal form, is just an eye with which the will becomes an object to itself. But the one who looks at the world through this eye is the same being. I am you, and you are me, so when I die I live on in you, and when you die you live on in me, and both of us live on in future generations. We are forever reborn in each other. Schopenhauer calls this 'temporal immortality' (W2, ch. 41, 556). This is how things appear from the perspective of the temporal world. The ultimate reality, however, knows no death (and therefore no rebirth) because it knows no change. Time is an image of eternity, says Schopenhauer, quoting Plotinus.

This is good news if we appreciate being alive. If we don't, not so much. But if reason has any power over the way we feel (and for Schopenhauer that's a *big* if), then it can help those in whom the will to live is strong to shed their fear of death and live their life more fully and positively. They will, however, have to ignore the fact that all life is still, by its very nature, suffering and that for this reason living forever and never having to die is not at all desirable because it just prolongs the pain of living into eternity.

> A person who had fully absorbed into his disposition the truths so far expounded, but had not also come to realize, through his own experience or more extensive insight, that ongoing suffering is essential to all life, who instead found satisfaction in life and felt perfectly fine with it, and who, after careful consideration, desired his life, as he has experienced it so far, to be of endless duration or eternally recurring, and whose appetite for life was so great that he was willing and happy to accept, in exchange for life's pleasures, all the sorrow and pain that life is subject to, such a person would stand 'with firm, solid bones on the well-rounded lasting earth'[4] and would have nothing to be afraid of: armed with the knowledge that we attribute to him, he would face death, which comes rushing towards him on the wings of time, with indifference, regarding it as a false appearance, an impotent spectre, fit to scare the weak, but holding no sway over the one who knows that he himself is that will whose objectification or image the world is, so that life is certain to him for all time, and so is the present, which is the proper, sole form of the will's appearance, who therefore cannot be frightened by an unending past or future in which he does not exist, since he regards it as the vacuous mirage and veil of Maya, and who therefore has as little reason to fear death as the sun to fear the night. (W1, §54, 372–3)

This is the unreservedly positive attitude towards life and death that (as we shall see in Chapter 6) Nietzsche later endorses and commends: a complete affirmation of the will to life in all its forms, an unhesitant willingness to welcome and embrace even the eternal recurrence of this life, with everything that it contains, the good and the bad. For Schopenhauer, however, such a complete affirmation of life requires the suppression of the truth that all life is essentially and unavoidably suffering and that for this very reason life is ultimately not worth living. The complete affirmation of the will to life rests on an important insight: that appearances deceive us and that death is not real, that it cannot harm us because we exist in everything that is, so that as long as the world exists we also exist. However, it also rests on the mistaken belief that life is a *good* thing so that it is desirable for it to never end, while in fact the opposite is true: life is irredeemably bad, and not being is infinitely more desirable than being. But if we cannot cease to be by dying, if suicide is no option (not because it is in any way morally wrong – it is not – but simply because it does not achieve what it is meant to achieve: the desired transition into nothingness), then it seems that we are condemned to eternal suffering. There is, however, one way out. Schopenhauer calls it the 'negation of the will'.

How not to be: The negation of the will

Everyone fears death. We tend to regard it as the greatest of all evils. However, this fear is not based on a rational assessment, but simply results from our nature: we *are* the will to live, so the prospect of extinction is diametrically opposed to what we are. This is why we fear death. We have, however, no good reason to fear death because there *is* no death, or more precisely, death is not what we think it is. Crucially, it does not lead to our non-existence. Yet even if it did, we would still have nothing to fear because non-existence, which we mistakenly expect from death, is not an evil, let alone the greatest of all evils. Schopenhauer echoes Epicurus's argument that death (which here means ceasing to exist) is nothing to us because when death is, we are not, and when we are, death is not (W2, ch. 41, 542), and then goes even further: non-existence, absolute nothingness, is not only not an evil; it is actually *preferable* to life. One clear indication of this is that our existence is only ever properly felt when we suffer. Happiness is the absence of suffering, or in other words an absence of the sense of existence. We are happiest when we are least aware of our being, from which we can infer that it would be better for us not to be (W2, ch. 46, 669).

Nature, too, in its indifference to the individual teaches us, not only that death is not real but also that life, or at any rate the life of the individual, has no value. It is not worth having. Schopenhauer approvingly cites Mephistopheles's speech in Goethe's *Faust*: 'I am the spirit of perpetual negation, and rightly so, for all that comes to be deserves to perish, much better thus if nothing came to be.' Obviously, however, we have already come to be, so it is now too late to never have been born. The only option is to return to non-existence (or rather to achieve non-existence for the first time because we have in fact never not been before). But how can we accomplish that if we cannot do it by ending our individual life? Schopenhauer assures us that it is difficult, but possible. In fact, his whole philosophy culminates in the exploration and commendation of that very possibility. Essentially, what we need to do is say no and really mean it when we say it. The first part is easy, the second very, very hard. Everything that exists continues to exist, endlessly, except for a person who 'eventually said to this game, from the bottom of their heart: "I don't want this anymore"' (W2, ch. 41, 556). If that happens, if we manage to turn our backs on the world and become completely detached from it for good, then, and only then, we will be saved. The will then turns against itself and annihilates itself.

There are two ways to accomplish this negation and subsequent transition to nothingness. Both depend on there being an excess of suffering in one's life. If we are particularly unfortunate, if our individual life contains so much suffering that we simply cannot bear it anymore, then we may find ourselves taking the leap from affirmation to negation. Schopenhauer calls this the 'second best way' (*deuteros plous*, literally second sailing).[5] The first and foremost way is the way of compassion. Compassion, for Schopenhauer, is primarily not an emotion, but a veiled insight. All morality stems from it. When we feel compassion for someone – another human or animal – we have intuitively understood that the difference between ourselves and the other is merely apparent. We are no longer blinded by the principle of individuation that rules the world of representation. We recognize ourselves in the other. It is then that the suffering of the other becomes real to us; it becomes our own suffering. As a consequence, however, our suffering multiplies, with potentially dramatic consequences. If we are truly compassionate, our compassion will not be confined to this person or that. What we have now understood, after all, on an intuitive level, is that *everyone* else – every human and every living being – is in fact us. This means that we become painfully aware of *all* the suffering in the world, which we now feel as our own. This is such an overwhelming experience that a continued affirmation of the will to life becomes all but impossible. 'How could he, with such knowledge of the world, affirm life through his acts of will and thereby tie himself to it ever more firmly, press it ever more firmly to himself?' (W1, §68, 488). If we find that we cannot, the opposite takes place: 'The will now turns away from life: it is now repulsed by its joys, in which it recognizes its affirmation. Man thus reaches the state of voluntary renouncement, of resignation, of true calm and complete will-lessness' (W1, §68, 488–9). Thoroughly disgusted by the whole sorry state of affairs, we turn against the will that is responsible for it. We start working against the will by becoming ascetics. We stop wanting things, no longer seek pleasure, refuse to get attached to anything and basically become completely indifferent to the world and to our own physical existence in it. We elect to fast and to live in voluntary poverty, and, most importantly, we refuse to ever again satisfy our sexual drive (which is the clearest and most intense expression of the will), thus staying chaste at all times. We will then become a pure mirror of the world which is no longer affected by anything that happens, because everything is just like a feeble dream to us, without significance. If we carry on with these self-denying practices until our life comes to an end, we will find not only peace and happiness in this life but also salvation at the moment of our death, for 'what ends with it is not just the phenomenon, as is the case with others, but the essence itself is annulled, which here had kept only weak ties to existence through and in the world of phenomena, which last brittle bond now also rips for good. For the one who ends like this, the world has also ended' (W1, §68, 492).

Naturally, if *everyone* acted this way and consistently negated the will, then humanity would go extinct. This is not very surprising since there would then no longer be any sexual intercourse. However, according to Schopenhauer, this is not all that is most likely going to happen. Should humanity go extinct, then all non-human animals would *also* at once disappear (as the weaker reflection of the will depends on the stronger), and once *that* happens, the *whole* world will disappear with them because the world as we know it is object to a subject and nothing else, so that when there are no subjects left, there will not be any objects left either. It is therefore up to humanity, which alone can turn its back on the will, to bring salvation to the whole of creation (W1, §68, 490).

Life's true purpose

This entire doctrine of the negation of the will is of course quite odd and hardly consistent. Frankly, it is difficult to make sense of it. First of all, it is unclear how it should ever become possible for the will to deny itself. Schopenhauer insists that the will is free, that it is bound by no law, but still: the will is the will, which means that by its very nature it cannot do anything but will. Will is always the will to be, and since there is no other power in the world (reason being powerless on its own, without the will), there is nothing that could work against it, which is why it is a complete mystery how the will can ever be denied by anyone. How can the will to be suddenly become the will not to be?

Perhaps an even more serious problem with the idea is that it does not seem to be possible to achieve a transition into nothingness just for ourselves. If I do what Schopenhauer suggests, in response to some great suffering of my own, or to my unlimited compassion for all suffering creatures, then my life is supposed to end for good when I die. But *my* life would have ended with my death anyway. Death *always* ends the life of the individual, the particular person that I am. So what has changed? What have I gained by negating the will? It seems that as long as there are other people around, as long as the world continues to exist, I will also continue to exist, namely, in the form of those other people and what is really real in them: the undivided eternal subject to the object that is the world. Nothingness, therefore, seems only achievable if it is complete, if *everything*, and not just this particular, individual expression of the will, disappears. Obviously this has not happened yet, because if it did, then we would not exist anymore and would not be thinking about it. We and the whole world with us would already be saved.

Finally, if time does not exist on the ultimate level of existence, the level of the will, then how can the will ever turn against itself? This would seem to involve a change in the fabric of the world, and there can only be change if there is time. A timeless being cannot change and can therefore not end its own existence either. If there is no time, then whatever is, is, and whatever is not, is not. There can be no transition from being to non-being, or from non-being to being.

But perhaps all this is ultimately not very important. Philosophy's purpose is, after all, to reflect on the existence and experience of suffering and to provide some solace in an accurate (or conceivably accurate) description of the nature of things. To satisfy our metaphysical desire, we need to believe that the negation of the will is possible because we need to believe that there is a way out of the misery of life, even though we cannot quite understand how that should be possible. It is a mystery, somewhat like the Christian doctrine of the Trinity, which surpasses our understanding, but is still central to a particular vision of the world. If the negation of the will were not possible, then we would be stuck in this world forever. This cannot be because the world is clearly something that ought not to be. It would simply be wrong for it to persist in all eternity. The world must make sense, not only in such a way that there is an intelligible fit between what the world is and how we experience it, but also in the more existential way of providing us with a sense of significance, direction and purpose. We expect a complete philosophy to tell us what this – our life, our existence – is all about, what the point is of being here, and such an account is what Schopenhauer attempts to provide. In the first instance his answer to our demands for an ethically or existentially satisfactory metaphysics is that there is no point to life. It is in fact, at its very core, utterly pointless, which explains why things are the way they are. Yet out of this very pointlessness of our existence suddenly a point emerges. The world may be a hellish place, but as it turns out, precisely for this reason we have an important job to do. We have to literally save the world by leading and paving the way to nothingness and thus to salvation. And the world actually helps us to fulfil our destiny by pushing us hard in the right direction.

At the beginning of this chapter we wondered how we can, in a world that has so much evil in it, nonetheless hold on to the idea that there is a purpose to the way the world is organized and a purpose to our own existence in it. We now have an answer to that question: the suffering *is* the purpose. To realize this is strangely comforting. We can now at least take solace in the fact that our suffering is good for something: if there is enough of it, it pushes us over the edge by making us realize that nothing in this world is of any value. Our suffering, then, is not pointless at all. There is a purpose to it.

> Life, with its hourly, daily, weekly and yearly, small, big and bigger tribulations, with its deceived hopes and its accidents that defy all calculations, so clearly bears the imprint of something that is meant to put us off that it is hard to understand how this could have been overlooked and how people could have let themselves be persuaded that life is there to be enjoyed gratefully, and humans to be happy. (W2, ch. 46, 667)

It is very clear that the purpose of existence is not happiness. If it were, then the world would look very different. To believe that we are here to be happy is not only a fundamental error of judgement; it also creates even more suffering for us, for when we, inevitably, fail at being happy we feel that we have failed life's purpose, which makes us unhappier still (W2, ch. 49, 738).

The penultimate chapter of the second volume of *The World as Will and Representation* is entitled 'The Order of Salvation'. It is here that Schopenhauer – the atheist, anti-rationalist and metaphysician of the will – brings his vision of the world as the worst of all possible worlds to its final, quasi-teleological conclusion:

> So everything in life is indeed suited to free us from that initial error and to convince us that the purpose of our existence is not that we are happy. When we look at it more closely and without bias, life presents itself as if it were directly intended to make us *not* feel happy, since it bears, through its whole constitution, the character of something that we are meant to get sick of and to renounce as a mistake, so that our heart be healed from its addiction to pleasure, and indeed to life, and be turned away from the world. (W2, ch. 49, 738)

Life's true purpose is to enable the negation of the will. The world appears to be perfectly designed for the attainment of this goal, almost as if the will had through the creation of the world cunningly and purposefully orchestrated its own final destruction.

It would appear then that Leibniz was right after all: the world is indeed the best of all possible worlds, if only because it is perfectly suited to its final end, which is an escape from being, or total annihilation.

CHAPTER TWO

The despair of not being oneself
Søren Kierkegaard
(1813–1855)

I cannot endure my life any longer. I loathe existence; it is insipid, without salt or meaning. ... One sticks his finger in the ground to judge where one is. I stick my finger in existence – it feels like nothing. Where am I? What is the 'world'? What does this word mean? Who has duped me into the whole thing, and now leaves me standing there? Who am I? How did I come into the world; why was I not asked, why was I not informed of the rules and regulations ...? How did I come to be involved in this great enterprise called actuality? Why should I be involved in it? Am I not free to decide? Am I forced to be part of it? Where is the manager, I would like to make a complaint! (R, 60)

Kierkegaard is a strange, difficult and elusive author. His writing is excursive, unsystematic, fragmented,[1] contradictory, polemical, often convoluted and dense, sometimes playful and witty. His most important works were published under various pseudonyms (or, as Kierkegaard referred to them, 'poetical characters'), not (or not primarily) in order to conceal his identity but to allow him to adopt different personas for different purposes and to experiment with different styles and viewpoints. As a consequence, the reader can never be entirely sure to what extent the views they find expressed in Kierkegaard's pseudonymous writings can really be attributed to Kierkegaard himself. Yet even though Kierkegaard, especially in his later years, very much resented being identified with his fictional authors and editors, the ideas we find articulated in his writings are what they are: they can, to a large extent, be understood on their own terms and assessed according to their merit and interest, irrespective of intended authorship or explicit authorization.

Kierkegaard is also very much a Christian author, which makes it hard, if not downright impossible, to untangle his philosophy from his theology and his Christian faith. As Kierkegaard points out in his autobiographical *The Point of View for My Work as an Author* (1848, published posthumously in 1859), his whole work is essentially concerned with one issue and one issue only, namely, how to become a real, *genuine* Christian. That is more interesting than it may sound. For Kierkegaard, becoming a Christian is not about acquiring certain beliefs. One can have all the requisite 'Christian' beliefs, go to church every Sunday and do all the things that a good Christian is supposed to do, without actually *being* a Christian. Most people who think of themselves as Christians and whom we would normally not hesitate to call Christians are not really Christians at all. In fact, even the highest church dignitaries, and *especially* they, were not proper Christians in Kierkegaard's eyes.[2] Christianity, *real* Christianity, 'is spirit; spirit is inwardness; inwardness is subjectivity, subjectivity in its essential passion, at its maximum an infinitely, personally interested passion for one's eternal happiness' (CUP, 29). One can only become a true Christian through a radical transformation of one's inner life or 'spirit', by acquiring a certain manner of relating to oneself: a certain – let's call it 'authentic' – mode of existence, which the vast majority of people lack.[3] For Kierkegaard, there is no real difference between becoming a Christian and 'becoming what one is', and one can only become what one is by learning 'what it means to be an individual human being' (EK, 469). This question, however, seems relevant even for those of us who are not (in a religious sense) Christians and do not aspire to become one. For to ask what it means to be an individual human being is to ask not merely what it means to be *a* human being, but what it means to be *me*. It is not so much about *our* place in the world, but about *my* place, and only by answering this question, by reflecting on what it means to be this *particular* individual human being that *I* am, I can eventually hope to become what I am and thus be myself.

The aesthetic mode of life

Being oneself is far from easy. What is easy is *not* being oneself. That is why not being oneself is the rule rather than the exception. The most common and also most natural way of not being oneself is living one's life only *aesthetically*. To live one's life aesthetically means to pursue pleasure and to avoid pain, to follow one's desires and passions wherever they may lead, to seek both physical and mental satisfaction, to enjoy all the thrills that life can offer us, enriching our subjective experience, indulging our senses. The aesthetic conception of life's meaning and aim is this: 'That one must enjoy life' (E/O, 493). Naturally, the aesthetic life can appear well worth living. It is a good life, surely, if you are lucky and know how to play it. But it has its drawbacks. *Serious* drawbacks. For one thing, it won't last. It never does. Pain is sure to come sometime. Death will end it all. Living aesthetically, we may believe ourselves to be self-sufficient, but in fact we rely very much on the circumstances, both internal (having the right kind of desires and moods at the right time) and external (the non-appearance of events that prevent the satisfaction of our desires). If those circumstances change the wrong way, the good life can very quickly turn into a bad one. Yet it will also turn bad if the circumstances do *not* change. Things usually interest and amuse us only for a while. To keep up our interest, to continue to be amused, we need variation. Repetition is the enemy of passion. Living aesthetically, we get bored quickly, and we must constantly seek out new attractions to prevent ourselves from having nothing left to live for. 'How terrible is tedium – how terribly tedious. ... I lie stretched out, inert; all I see is emptiness, all I live on is emptiness, all I move in is emptiness' (E/O, 53).

Boredom is not just a particular emotion or mental state. It is an *insight*, a realization of the state one is in, not only while one is bored but also while one is *not* bored. The emptiness we feel when we are bored is always there, even when we are not aware of it. This is why, for Kierkegaard, the aesthetic view of life is essentially 'despair': 'Everyone who lives aesthetically is in despair whether he knows it or not' (E/O, 502), 'since it is always despair to have one's life centred in something whose nature it is to cease to be' (E/O, 531). We try to ignore our despair, the emptiness beneath, by keeping ourselves busy,[4] but that does nothing to defeat it. It only works as a distraction. Idleness is more in keeping with the aesthetic way of life, but it is difficult to stay idle for long without getting bored. Boredom is in fact a hallmark of (natural) humanity. 'The gods were bored so they created man. Adam was bored because he was alone, so Eve was created. From that time boredom entered the world. ... Adam was bored alone, then Adam and Eve were bored in union, then Adam and Eve and Cain and Abel were bored *en famille*, then population increased and the people were bored *en masse*' (E/O, 228). In a word, we do things in order to stave off boredom. Once we stop doing things, boredom at once returns. We also seek the company of others to stave off boredom. Alone with ourselves, boredom overcomes us again. Boredom is the natural, foundational condition of the aesthetic man, his secret driving force, that which to escape from we do everything we do. Within the aesthetic way of life, however, there is no way to banish the emptiness that lies beneath. It is, after all, an emptiness that we encounter also in ourselves. Thrown back onto ourselves we find there is nothing there either, nothing to hold on to, no identifiable self at all. Living aesthetically, we define ourselves mostly by what we happen to be doing, and when there is nothing to do, the self that we thought we were evaporates. The aesthetic self is fickle. It is sometimes this, and sometimes that, and therefore neither this nor that. The aesthetic self can be anything because it is, at bottom, nothing. Kierkegaard would say that it is not really a self at all. Being a real self is being a 'relation which relates to itself' (SD, 43). The aesthetic way of life does not allow for such a relation because the aesthetic self is and remains pure possibility, in which it becomes lost because it never gains actuality. 'The [aesthetic] individual has no actual shape, but is a mere shadow. ... The individual has a multiplicity of shadows, all of which resemble him and each of which is, at least fleetingly, equally justified as being his self. Personality has not yet been discovered, its energy announces itself only in the passion of possibility' (R, 24). That is why the aesthetic way of existing is not really existence at all. It is, rather, an 'existence-possibility in the direction of existence' (CUP, 212).

Living aesthetically, we seek constant amusement in one form or another. Yet even when we amuse ourselves we sense the shallowness of it all, feel dimly that right beneath the glittery surface there is only emptiness. 'Boredom rests upon the nothingness that winds its way through existence' (E/O, 232). And when boredom becomes reflective, when it becomes all-encompassing, then it transforms into a strong sense of meaninglessness and pointlessness. We become world-weary (as, eventually, Kierkegaard himself seems to have done).[5] The world no longer interests us because all that has ever interested us in it has been revealed in its essential pointlessness.

> How empty life is and without meaning. – We bury a man, we follow him to the grave, we throw three spades of earth on him, we ride out in a coach, we ride home in a coach, we take comfort in the thought that a long life awaits us. But how long is threescore years and ten? Why not finish it at once? Why not stay out there and step down into the grave with him, and draw lots for who should have the misfortune to be the last alive to throw the last three spades of earth on the last of the dead? Wretched fate! (E/O, 49)

We are also essentially alone when we live aesthetically, being cut off from the world, which we only know as a means for our enjoyment and which we therefore only have a fleeting, superficial acquaintance with. In the aesthetic mode of existence we are like a sailor in a small jolly boat, all by ourselves, skimming 'along with the infinite speed of restless thoughts' over the surface (but only the *surface*) of the sea of life, 'alone on the infinite ocean, alone with the infinite heaven' (E/O, 426). This can be fun for a while, but ultimately it is painful, sad and humiliating because it just confirms our status as 'a stranger and an alien in the world' (E/O, 426). This is because in order to live life to the fullest aesthetically, we need to always preserve a certain reservation and detachment. We should not get too passionate about any one thing. All in good measure. The trick is not to get carried away and to treat everything as if it were equally important, equally memorable and forgettable (E/O, 234). It is a question of staying in control. One needs to stay in control in order to live well aesthetically. Once we have managed to perfect these arts, the art of forgetting and the art of remembering, we are where we want to be and need to be in order to be able to make the most of life. We are 'in a position to play battledore and shuttlecock with the whole of existence' (E/O, 234). Such a playful attitude towards life obviously requires staying independent. We must therefore guard ourselves against all close relationships, such as friendship (E/O, 236) and marriage (and especially against having children!), because that only serves to constrain us by tying us to other people. 'One must always be careful not to enter into any life-relation in which one can become several. ... When you are several you have lost your freedom' (E/O, 237). Such are the blessings of remaining single.

Yet again, those blessings cannot be relied on. For those who build their life around the satisfaction of their desires (which is most of us most of the time), unhappiness is never far away. In the end, the world, despite being full of pleasures, almost always disappoints. That is why the aesthetic mode of existence can also give rise to a renunciation of life as a miserable thing that is not worth having. It is Schopenhauer's reaction, the reaction of the spurned lover. This renunciation is still aesthetic in nature. Precisely because one still seeks the satisfaction of one's desires, a world that does not live up to one's expectations can only be denounced and rejected. Death now seems to be the more attractive option, more likely to give us what we desire. 'A', the 'author' of the first part of Kierkegaard's first major work, *Either/Or* (1843), whose aesthetic perspective we have by and large followed so far, treats the reader with an address delivered to a society of people who call themselves the *Symparanekromenoi* (roughly: the dead people's club). The Symparanekromenoi 'believe in nothing but misfortune' (E/O, 212). They do not fear death because they know of a greater misfortune: life. According to 'A', there is a grave somewhere in England, whose stone bears the inscription 'The Unhappiest One'. No other name is given, and when the grave was opened it was discovered that the grave is empty. 'A' suggests that the grave is, and must forever remain, empty because the unhappiest one would be the one who cannot die. It is, after all, only the prospect of death that makes life bearable: 'Happy the one who died in his old age, happier the

one who died at birth, happiest of all the one who was never born'
(E/O, 212). Given life's misery, if there were someone who did not
die, then they would clearly be the unhappiest. Yet death is our
common lot. So who is unhappiest among *mortals*? To this question
'A' gives an answer that already points beyond the aesthetic: 'The
unhappy person is he who has his ideal, the content of his life … ,
his real nature in some way or other outside himself. The unhappy
man is always absent from himself' (E/O, 214). From this it would
follow that happiness consists in, or results from, my being present
to myself, which amounts to being myself, properly understood: I
am *being* myself by being *present* to myself, that is, by my *relating*
to myself and thus taking hold of myself.

Kierkegaard did not think that this was possible within the
aesthetic sphere of existence. To truly be ourselves, we need more
than that. We need to transcend the aesthetic and move on to the
ethical and religious sphere.

Kierkegaard's poetic character 'A', however, appears to have a
different view, when he explains how even within the aesthetic
sphere of existence we can be more or less present to ourselves
(E/O, 214–18). (This might not be real or full presence yet, but it
may be a step in the right direction, or perhaps even, for some of
us, good enough.) According to 'A', we are absent from ourselves
when we live in the future or in the past. We do this mostly through
hope and memory. Those who live only in their memories, or only
in their hopes, and while hoping or remembering forget to live
in the present, are unhappy because they don't have themselves.
But they are not *entirely* or *genuinely* unhappy if they are at least
present to themselves *in* the future or in the past. The unhappiest
are those who do not even have this kind of delayed presence,
because they know already that the future they are hoping for
will never happen and thus will 'have no reality' for them (their
hopes will be disappointed), or that the past they remember did
in fact have no reality for them when it was still the present,
because the past they remember or wish to remember is not the
past they actually had. The unhappiest one is the one who keeps
hoping without having anything to hope for, or the one who keeps
remembering without having anything (worthwhile) to remember.
However, since the future is yet to come (so we cannot know for
sure what is going to happen), while the past is gone and can no
longer be changed, genuine unhappiness resides mostly in the loss

of past presence rather than that of future presence. Imagine for instance 'a person who has never had a childhood himself, this age having passed him by without acquiring significance for him, but who now … discovered all the beauty that lies in childhood, and would now remember his own childhood, always look back upon it' (E/O, 216). Such a person, along with everyone else who has 'lived without appreciating the joy of life', should surely count among the unhappiest. Being absent from oneself in this manner is what constitutes a meaningless life: one in which, as it were, the future is already over (because what we hope for lies already behind us) and the past has not arrived yet (because what we remember lies before us) (E/O, 217). Someone like this 'cannot become old, for he has never been young; he cannot become young, for he has already become old; in a way he cannot die, for he has never lived; in a way he cannot live, for he is already dead' (E/O, 217).

The ethical mode of life

'There are', writes Kierkegaard in *Stages on Life's Way* (1845), 'three existence-spheres: the esthetic, the ethical, the religious. … The esthetic sphere is the sphere of immediacy; the ethical the sphere of requirement …, the religious the sphere of fulfilment' (EK, 182).

The ethical sphere of existence or mode of life is given a strong voice in the second part of *Either/Or*. Despite the book's title, however, the ethical mode of life is not conceived as a strict alternative to the aesthetic mode. Rather, it is meant to supplement it.[6] The retired judge Vilhelm (another of Kierkegaard's poetic characters), who defends the ethical viewpoint in a series of letters to 'A', suggests that those who live their lives (only or predominantly) aesthetically play a game of hide-and-seek with existence, and may do that so successfully that their 'true nature' will never reveal itself, not even to them. Their nature then dissolves 'into a multitude, with your really becoming many …, and in that way losing the innermost, the most holy thing in a man, the unifying power of personality' (E/O, 479).[7] This is a most serious matter, warns Vilhelm, a truly terrifying possibility, for there 'is, in every person, something which to some degree prevents him from being completely transparent to himself; and this can be on such a scale that he is so inexplicably woven into the circumstances of life which lie outside him that he is almost unable to reveal himself. But he who cannot reveal himself cannot love, and he who cannot love is the unhappiest of all' (E/O, 479–80). Love is here distinguished from the desire to conquer, which is what the aesthetic lover, immortalized in the figure of Don Juan, mistakes for love (E/O, 464). Love, in the ethical sphere, entails commitment. It also entails, precisely for this reason, *making choices*, and it is by making choices, by consciously deciding for something (or someone) and against something else, that we do what Vilhelm claims is 'the main thing in life: to win yourself, to take possession of yourself' (E/O, 482). The choice in question is *not* the choice between the aesthetic and the ethical. In the aesthetic mode of life we do not make choices, not really. Instead, we let our choices be made by others (or by the circumstances), and thus lose ourselves (E/O, 483). Or if we do seem to choose for ourselves, we choose what we choose for the moment, and thus we may choose something else the next instant. This is not choosing proper because it lacks commitment. Aesthetic choices are not in any way binding. Real choice means taking possession of ourselves. Making the choice says 'This is me'. Choice defines the ethical because the 'only absolute either/or there is, is the choice between good and evil' (E/O, 485). Ethically, we take the choices we make *seriously*. There is of course also a choice (or quasi-choice) of some sort between the (merely) aesthetic and the (also) ethical. This 'choice' is not between good and evil but between good-and-evil on the one hand and not-good-and-evil on the other. One could also say, it is a choice between choosing and not-choosing. The aesthetic mode of existence, on its own, 'is not evil but indifference' (E/O, 486).

Choosing the ethical does not mean that we have to renounce the aesthetic. On the contrary, once we have made this choice, 'the whole of the aesthetic returns, and you shall see that only then is life beautiful, and that only in this way can a person succeed in saving his soul and gaining the whole world' (E/O, 492). The ethical does not replace the aesthetic. It *transfigures* it. From Vilhelm's perspective the 'choice' is thus not really an either-or at all. It is a both-and. But perhaps instead of 'choice' we should better say 'transition': a transition from one sphere of existence or 'stage on life's way' (the aesthetic) to the next (the ethical). Despair plays an important role here. The transition from the aesthetic to the ethical occurs, or can occur, when one has 'tasted the bitterness of despair' and that despair is not a despair over something in particular (some kind of misfortune that has happened to us), but is found to be a despair of the *self*, so that it does not lead to a misguided hatred of the world (which is blameless), but still allows for, or even reinforces, our loving the world 'for being the world that it is' (E/O, 511). So despair is not all bad. On the contrary, it can become 'the true point of departure for finding the absolute' (E/O, 515). The absolute, Vilhelm explains, is 'myself in my eternal validity' (E/O, 517). And what is that? It is 'the most abstract thing of all which yet, at the same time, is the most concrete thing of all – it is freedom' (E/O, 516).

Living ethically, we do not rely on the world so much because we always have sovereignty over ourselves. It is not the circumstances of our life that make us what we are. Unlike the aesthetic self (or non-self), the ethical self can do well in *any* life situation. 'He knows that everywhere there is a dance floor, that … his dance can be just as beautiful, just as graceful, just as expressive, just as moving as that of those who have been assigned a place in history' (E/O, 544). Unlike the aesthetic self, the ethical self is free.

> To the person who lives aesthetically the old saying, 'to be or not to be', applies and the more aesthetically he is allowed to live, the more demands his life exacts, and if only the least of them is not fulfilled he is dead; the person who lives ethically always has a way out even when everything goes against him, … there is always a point he keeps hold of, and it is – himself. (E/O, 544)

It is precisely because, living ethically, we always have a hold of and in ourselves, we do not permanently have to chase the new to keep us entertained and hold boredom (and the nothingness that it reveals) at bay. We make our choices, and we stand by them. This naturally leads to some repetition in our lives (which, as we saw earlier, is, aesthetically speaking, the enemy of passion). Yet while the aesthetic self cannot endure repetition, the ethical self thrives off it and positively embraces it. Kierkegaard wrote a whole (short) book in which his aptly named poetic author, Constantine Constantius, praises the virtues of repetition. 'He who chooses repetition, he lives. He does not chase after butterflies like a child, or stand on tiptoe in order to glimpse the wonders of the world. He knows them. … He goes calmly about his life, happy in repetition' (R, 4).

The ethical life is usually associated with the notion of 'duty'. Kierkegaard goes along with this when he calls the ethical the 'sphere of requirement'. However, duty is normally conceived as something that we relate to externally, as something that (we are told) must be done, universally and without taking into account the particular circumstances of one's life and who one is. All of this makes the ethical life appear rather unappealing, not the least because it seems to require that we distance ourselves from ourselves. This, however, is, according to Kierkegaard (or at any rate *Either/Or*'s Vilhelm), a misunderstanding of what duty is (or ideally should be). Duty needs to become an 'expression of our inmost nature' (E/O, 546). It needs to be not just duty, but essentially *my* duty. Only then have we entered the ethical sphere of existence, thereby realizing the universal in the particular, the ideal self in the actual self, which is 'the true art of living' (E/O, 548). And because ethical duty is always essentially *my* duty, only I can tell what my duty is, as only you can tell what yours is. I have my task in life, and you have yours. Every person has a specific vocation, and each person knows best what their vocation is.

Kierkegaard thus equips the ethical with a strong subjective perspective, which is exactly as it should be. Pure objectivity is neither possible nor desirable in ethics. We are so used to externalize the ethical that we tend to forget that questions about how to live one's life can never be asked and answered in the abstract, from an objective, disinterested, observational point of view. The whole point of the ethical way of life is the realization that this (whatever this is) concerns *me*, and whatever choices I make I am the one who has to live and die by them. Therefore, when we reflect on whether life is worth living, whether death is an evil, or what it actually means to die (and to live), it would be a serious mistake to ignore the fact that the one posing those questions is alive and will himself have to die, and more importantly, that the one who is alive and posing those questions is *me* and that *I* am also the one who is going to die. The question therefore can, or should, never be 'What is *one* to do?' but always 'What am *I* to do?' Not only do I, this particular single individual, matter, it is, namely, for me, I that matters and should matter most of all. 'Ethically, the individual subject is infinitely important' (CUP, 123).

The religious mode of life

The religious mode of life is an extension or perhaps an intensification or radicalization of the ethical. This is because the ethical is anchored in the religious. Living ethically, we are already in touch with the divine (perhaps not quite face to face yet but certainly back to back). The ethical is 'the breath of the eternal and, in the midst of solitude, the reconciling fellowship with every human being' (CUP, 126). But for Kierkegaard our fellowship with every human being is less important than our fellowship with God. By embracing the ethical mode of life, we put ourselves in 'co-consciousness with God' (CUP, 129). In making an ethical choice we not only take possession of ourselves (and thus become, for the first time, what we are, this particular self) but also bind ourselves for eternity to an eternal power (E/O, 509). As *Either/Or*'s Judge Vilhelm puts it, 'Inasmuch as the choice is undertaken with all the personality's inwardness, his nature is purified and he himself is brought into immediate relation to the eternal power whose omnipotence interpenetrates the whole of existence' (E/O, 486). Being fully myself and being with or before God is, for Kierkegaard, one and the same thing. However, this relationship to God is not a cosy one. It entails a lot of 'fear and trembling' and therefore requires plenty of courage. One who commits to the ethical must 'dare to become nothing at all, to become a single individual of whom God ethically asks everything' (CUP, 124). Living ethically, we must be willing to take huge risks. We must be willing to sacrifice everything, even our own life, even that of the ones we love, even the recognition and approval of other people. We must, if necessary, go against 'the crowd',[8] against what is commonly thought to be right and wrong, good and evil. Nothing good comes from the crowd. The single individual needs to stand on his own feet. Ethics is not about being nice. It is not about pleasing everyone (or anyone) either. As it is usually practised, Christianity is very much about being part of the herd, whose reassurance we crave. But this is not really Christianity, or at any rate not the Christianity that we should emulate. What we should seek to emulate is the Christianity of the New Testament, which 'is precisely designed for relating itself to this isolation of a person of spirit. In the New Testament, Christianity means to love God in hatred of humankind, in hatred of oneself and thus of all other people, hating father, mother, one's own child, spouse, et cetera – the most powerful expression of the most painful isolation.'[9] Ethically, we stand alone (with God), potentially against the whole world.

In *Repetition*, the 'Young Man', whose love affair has stimulated the 'author' Constantine Constantius's reflections on the nature and value of repetition, praises the heroism of someone who acts in such a way that he is a hero 'not in the eyes of the world, but in one's own eyes', marvelling over what it must be like 'to be unable to appeal to human beings, living within the walls of one's own personality, to be one's own witness, one's own judge, one's own accuser, one's only accuser!' (R, 53). This is the challenge of the ethical. What makes it so challenging is that it requires us to act in possible defiance of all human reason.

In *Fear and Trembling* (1843) Kierkegaard lets yet another 'author', Johannes de silentio, reflect on the biblical story of Abraham and Isaac (Genesis 22). Here Abraham emerges as the paradigmatic ethical (or perhaps post-ethical) hero, the kind of hero that the Young Man in *Repetition* describes. Johannes calls people like him 'knights of faith'. According to the biblical account, Abraham is told by God to sacrifice his only son Isaac. He is given no reason, and Abraham does not ask. When he proceeds to kill Isaac, an angel appears and tells him to stop. The sacrifice is no longer necessary. God just wanted to test him, to see whether he would obey him. Because he did, he and his descendants are now forever blessed. This is all we learn from the biblical account of the story. It does not tell us anything about how Abraham felt about the whole thing. For all we know, he did not feel anything at all. In *Fear and Trembling*, Kierkegaard imagines what it must have been like for Abraham to be asked to kill his only son. First of all, he had to bear the full moral weight of his decision to obey the divine command all by himself. In 'cosmic isolation' he 'walks alone with his dreadful responsibility' (FT, 107). He could not tell anyone, not his son, not his wife, not anybody else, because nobody would have understood. There is nothing he could have said to justify before them what he was about to do. So he was condemned to silence. Because humanly speaking, it was not justifiable, and certainly not *ethically* justifiable. Ethically, a father should love and protect his son. 'The ethical expression of what Abraham did is that he was willing to murder Isaac' (FT, 60). Johannes concludes that Abraham, in agreeing to kill Isaac, 'overstepped the ethical altogether, and had a higher *telos* outside it, in relation to which he suspended it'

(FT, 88). He could not claim that he had to do it in order to save the nation or for the sake of some other higher good (like for instance the tragic hero Agamemnon when he was forced to sacrifice his daughter Iphigenia). 'The tragic hero renounces himself in order to express the universal; the knight of faith renounces the universal in order to be the particular' (FT, 103).

However, here we are talking about human ethics or what is ordinarily understood as ethical in terms of what counts as an acceptable justification for somebody's actions. Human ethics is all concerned with the following of rules or adherence to the universal. But the *real* ethical (or at any rate the highest duty) reveals itself in the exceptional. What Abraham was willing to do was not ethical in the usual understanding of the word. But in a different, Kierkegaardian (self- and God-affirming) sense, which sets the individual high above the universal, it was. 'The ethical is the universal and as such, in turn, the divine. It is therefore correct to say that all duty is ultimately duty to God' (FT, 96). So we may say that although it certainly isn't generally a father's duty to sacrifice his son, it certainly was *Abraham's* duty. Abraham's story shows that 'living as the individual', which is 'thought to be the easiest thing of all' is in fact 'the most terrifying thing of all'. It also happens to be the greatest (FT, 102).

His departure from what is commonly understood as morally required partially explains Abraham's anguish, which Johannes de silentio vividly describes. But his anguish is also due to the fact that he *loves* his son, that his son means everything to him. He knows that the demanded sacrifice of Isaac would make his life meaningless. In spite of this, he is still going to carry out his plan, not because he thinks that obeying God is more important than his own happiness but because he trusts that God, somehow, will fix it. Not in an afterlife, but in *this* life. He believes that he will have to kill his son, that his son will die, and at the same time that Abraham will not lose him, that, somehow, he will not die. This is clearly absurd. It does not make any sense. But this is exactly what religious *faith* is: to believe that all is good or will be good, even in the face of complete failure, when clearly and undeniably everything is lost. Faith defies understanding, precisely because God defies all understanding. Aesthetically, we expect the possible. Ethically, we expect the eternal. Religiously, however, we expect the *impossible* (FT, 50), which would find its justification in the fact that for God, being God, nothing is impossible, except that the existence of God cannot be proven and must itself be taken on faith (since God himself is impossible). For Abraham, his faithful submission to the will of God worked out: 'He resigned everything infinitely, and then took everything back on the strength of the absurd' (FT, 70).

Despair and the sickness unto death

Key to Kierkegaard's understanding of life and how to live it are the twin notions of 'despair' and 'faith'. Only faith can save us from despair.

> If there were no eternal consciousness in a man, if at the bottom of everything there were only a wild ferment, a power that twisting in dark passions produced everything great or inconsequential: if an unfathomable, insatiable emptiness lay hid beneath everything, what then would life be but despair? ... If one generation succeeded the other as the songs of birds in the woods, if the human race passed through the world as a ship through the sea or the wind through the desert, a thoughtless and fruitless whim, if an eternal oblivion always lurked hungrily for its prey and there were no power strong enough to wrest it from its clutches – how empty and devoid of comfort would life be! (FT, 48)

Fortunately, there *is* an eternal consciousness in man. The challenge is to reach it and take possession of it. To become what we are, namely *spirit*. As long as we have not done that, we live in despair. The possibility of despair distinguishes us from non-human animals. It is in fact an advantage we have over them. Despair is an advantage because it articulates the need for a change, the possibility of there being more to life than this (the life of the natural man qua animal, the aesthetic perspective). Even though it is a disease, precisely for this reason it points to a state of health that lies beyond it. The disease itself is perhaps 'the greatest misfortune' (SD, 45), but acknowledging the disease *as* a disease is the first crucial step on the way to a cure. You cannot cure something that you don't know is there in the first place. In *The Sickness unto Death* (1846), Kierkegaard (in the guise of 'Anti-Climacus') defines despair as the 'sickness unto death', not because it *ends* in death (which it does not) but because it consists in *believing* that death is the end of everything. The effect is that one experiences one's life as a form of prolonged dying. Despair is defined by an inner contradiction. In despair, we live our life as if we were already dead. It can also be understood (quite literally) as a failing act of suicide: as an unsuccessful, impotent 'consumption of the *self*' (SD, 48). That one wants to annihilate oneself (or one's self) is already despair, but it is heightened by the despairer's inability to do so: that he 'cannot consume himself, cannot be rid of himself, cannot become nothing' (SD, 49). We want to be something that we are not (say, a Premier League footballer or a top banker)[10] and we do not want to be what we are (*not* a Premier League footballer and *not* a top banker). The one who despairs over not having become what he wanted to become really despairs over himself, for not *being* the one that he wanted to be. But he only wanted to become whatever it is he wanted to become because he wanted to be *himself* (by, as it were, finding the self that suited him best). So he wants to be himself and at the same time not be himself. But neither the self that he wants to be nor the self that he does not want to be is his real, *spiritual* self, the eternal consciousness that he truly is. To want to be *that* self, the one that he truly is, is in fact 'the very opposite of despair' (SD, 50). This, however, is extremely rare. Despair, the sickness unto death, is in fact the most common of all diseases:

> There is not a single human being who does not despair at least a little, in whose innermost being there does not dwell an uneasiness, an unquiet, a discordance, an anxiety in the face of an unknown something, or a something he doesn't even dare strike up acquaintance with, an anxiety about a possibility in life or an anxiety about himself, so that as a physician speaks of one's going about with an illness in the body, he ... goes about weighed down with a sickness of the spirit, which only now and then reveals its presence within, in glimpses, and with what is for him an inexplicable anxiety. (SD, 52)

Only someone who is truly and wholly Christian (if there is such a one) is entirely without despair. We may not even be aware of our despair and imagine ourselves to be completely healthy, while in fact we are not. Despair is exactly man's unconsciousness of being characterized as spirit. Even what humanly speaking is the most beautiful and loveliest thing of all – a womanly youthfulness which is sheer peace and harmony and joy – is nevertheless despair. For while it can be counted the greatest happiness,[11] happiness is not a specification of spirit, and deep, deep inside, deep within happiness's most hidden recesses, there dwells also the dread that is despair. (SD, 55)

We waste our lives if we spend it focused on life's pleasures and sorrows, ascribing 'infinite value to the indifferent' (SD, 63), without ever becoming conscious of ourselves as spirit, or, which is the same, becoming 'grounded transparently in God' (SD, 60). Often we fail to be ourselves by trying to be like other people, which appears a lot easier and safer than being ourselves. We hide and disappear in the crowd, gladly letting ourselves become 'a cipher, one more person, one more repetition of this perpetual Einerlei' (SD, 63). Since being part of 'the crowd' allows us to fit in, and fitting in generally makes it easier for us to flourish in human society, we hardly notice the price we pay, namely, that we lose our selves. This ignorance of our own situation and of this loss of selfhood marks the worst kind of despair.

In order to be ourselves we need to strike a balance between possibility and necessity. The self loses itself not only if it is all possibility with no actuality, and the individual has 'become nothing but an atmospheric illusion' (SD, 66) but also if it is all necessity, leaving no room for development and choice, faith and redemption (remember: for God *nothing* is impossible), thus suffocating the self. 'The person who gets lost in possibility soars with the boldness of despair; but the person for whom all has become necessary strains his back on life, bent down with the weight of despair' (SD, 72). We cannot become something that we are not (meaning that our possibilities of self-creation are limited), but we can still *become* what we are (meaning that a spiritual transformation of our existence is far from impossible). Being truly oneself is different from being one's own master (as the Stoics may have understood it). Because we are not our own master, and we cannot create or reshape our self any way we like. Our identity ultimately rests in God who made us what we are and who is the ground of our being. It rests in the eternal. Being truly ourselves means having God as our standard. It means being conscious of being 'before God'.

What *that* means, however, is not at all clear, given that the divine standard is supposed to be utterly incomprehensible. Christianity 'wants to make man into something so extraordinary that he cannot grasp the thought of it' (SD, 116). It 'goes a huge gigantic stride … into the absurd' (SD, 119).

Learning to be silent

So how do we get there? How do we find and relate properly to our eternal selves and thus to God? How do we become true Christians? In *The Lily in the Field, the Bird of the Air: Three Godly Discourses* (1849), which Kierkegaard published under his own name, it is suggested that above all we need to learn to be silent. Silence is the beginning of the fear of God, which is the beginning of wisdom (EK, 334). Naturally we tend to be silent before God because we don't know what to say, because, overcome by fear and trembling in the face of his incomprehensible power, words fail us. Our wishes and desires, our gratitude, our complaints, all of that becomes silent. But learning to be silent means more than just not saying anything. It means learning to *listen*. Listening (and not talking, not asking, not pleading) is the essence of prayer. To find ourselves, we need to drown out all human voices, the buzz of the busy world with its many distractions. We need to concentrate. We can learn how to do that from the natural world, from the lilies in the field and the birds of the air of which the gospel of Matthew speaks (Matt. 6:26). They are all silent, listening patiently, respectfully. In nature's silence we become aware of God's voice.

> The forest is silent; even when it whispers it nevertheless is silent. The trees, even where they stand in thickest growth, keep their word, something human beings rarely do despite a promise given: This will remain between us. The sea is silent; even when it rages uproariously it is silent. … In the evening, when silence rests over the land and you hear the distant bellowing from the meadow, or from the farmer's house in the distance you hear the familiar voice of the dog, you cannot say that this bellowing or this voice disturbs the silence. No, this belongs to the silence, is in a mysterious and thus in turn silent harmony with the silence; this increases it. (EK, 335)

The silence of nature makes us aware that we are *before God*, 'who says eternally: Today' and who 'is eternally and infinitely present to himself in being today'. And so are the lily and the bird and all the rest of nature 'with their silence and unconditional obedience'. From them we can learn how to live our own lives in similar self-presence:

> What is joy, or what is it to be joyful? It is truly to be present to oneself. But truly to be present to oneself is this *today*, this *to be* today, truly *to be today*. And the more true it is that you are today, the more you are entirely present to yourself in being today, the less the sorrows of tomorrow exist for you. Joy is the present time, with the entire emphasis upon: the present time.[12]

CHAPTER THREE

The interlinked terrors and wonders of God
Herman Melville (1819–1891)

The ungraspable phantom of life

When Herman Melville wrote his sixth novel, *Moby-Dick* (1851) – that powerful, stunningly original tale of one crazed man's obsessive hunt for the ferocious white sperm whale that ripped off one of his legs in a previous encounter – he was only thirty years old. Yet even though he had been quite successful so far, especially with his first two novels, the semi-autobiographical South Sea adventure novels *Typee* (1846) and *Omoo* (1847), the new book's reception was at best lukewarm. Many critics and readers could not make head or tail of it. It was too wordy, too philosophical, too morbid. When he followed up with an even stranger novel, the psychological study *Pierre* (1852), which was widely perceived as incomprehensible and morally repulsive, Melville's literary reputation was in tatters and his career as a writer over, even though it took him a few more years to realize it. His last novel, *The Confidence-Man*, was published in 1857. When it, too, sold poorly and attracted little critical attention, Melville finally gave up on his ambition to make his living as a professional writer and became a customs inspector instead. During the last thirty and some years of his life he wrote very little and published even less (mostly poetry). When he died in

1891, he was virtually forgotten. His work was only rediscovered shortly after the end of the Great War, aided by the republication of *Moby-Dick* by Oxford University Press in their World's Classics series in 1920. After all the horrors of that war, readers were finally ready for Melville and his dark vision of a world plagued by radical uncertainty (and, just possibly, much worse).

This was not so seventy years earlier when Melville wrote *Moby-Dick*. Melville's style was certainly unusual for his time and not what contemporary readers expected from what was, on the face of it, supposed to be an adventure novel. But what really nettled them was Melville's pessimistic philosophy. *Moby-Dick* was published in 1851, the same year in which London hosted the *Great Exhibition of the Works of Industry of All Nations*, which attracted millions of visitors. The Great Exhibition was a celebration of industrial capitalism, reflecting and reinforcing a common belief in the power of science, technology and commerce to increase the wealth of the nations, bringing prosperity and happiness to all. The general mood of the time was optimistic: people widely believed in the necessity of progress. They thought that industry was virtue, and that a divine providence was busily at work behind the scenes, making sure that our efforts would always be rewarded and things would continue to improve.[1] Melville did not share this optimism. He knew early on that the world could not be trusted and that behind its glittery surface there may well be not a benevolent God looking out for us, but either nothing at all or, even worse, a positively malign power intent on hurting and destroying us and everything we care for and hold dear. The world is a con man and we are his dupes. Or perhaps it isn't. The point is, we don't know and have no way of knowing what is really going on, whether or not there is a godlike being controlling or influencing events, and if there is, what this being's nature and intentions are. 'Mystery is in the morning, and mystery in the night, and the beauty of mystery is everywhere' (CM, 264). Beauty there is, no doubt, and plenty of it, but the question is how deep it goes. Is the world's beauty really a reflection of an underlying goodness that reaches all the way down to the very core of things, or is it, rather, a mask the world is wearing to make us drop our guard and give us a false sense of security? Is the trust that beauty inspires justified, or is it part of the con? Is whatever it is that rules the universe sympathetic to our struggles, our hopes and cares, or are the gods just having their fun with us?

This metaphysical uncertainty would not necessarily be a problem if we did not care so much about what lies beneath the surface. Unfortunately we do. We are human. On the one hand we want things to *mean* something because the thought that nothing means anything, that things just *are* what they are, without any higher purpose or goal, is unbearable: 'And some certain significance lurks in all things, else all things are of little worth, and the round world itself but an empty cipher, except to sell by the cartload, as they do hills about Boston, to fill up some morass in the Milky Way' (MD, 512). On the other hand, however, it is quite possible that if they *do* mean something, we may not like *what* they mean. In any case, we are almost certainly unable to understand their meaning. We see the signs, or what looks like signs, but cannot read them. We live in a world in which what happens and what we do *seems* to matter in some way, but we cannot figure out in what way exactly, no matter how hard we try. When, in *Moby-Dick*, Captain Ahab nails a richly illustrated gold doubloon to the top mast, promising it to the first of his men who catches sight of the whale they are chasing, various characters take a closer look at the coin and the image it shows, each coming to a different interpretation of what it signifies. What they see is not what is there, but what they want to see, or more precisely what, being the kind of person that they are, they are conditioned to see. And that is exactly how we look at the world: we think we see the world as it is, but in fact we see only a reflection of our own hopes and fears, interests and preoccupations: 'This round gold is but the image of the rounder globe, which, like a magician's glass, to each and every man in turn but mirrors back his own mysterious self. Great pains, small gains for those who ask the world to solve them; it cannot solve itself' (MD, 513). The real nature of the world remains a mystery. What is revealed to us is a cipher to which nobody has found the key yet. Or perhaps the key has been lost. The genial cannibal Queequeg in *Moby-Dick*, an accomplished harpooner and loyal friend to the story's narrator, Ishmael, is said to have his whole body covered with tattoos and hieroglyphic marks. These marks are the work of a seer who engraved onto Queequeg's body a 'complete theory of the heavens and the earth, and a mystical treatise on the art of attaining truth' (MD, 571). Unfortunately, however, the seer is dead now, and Queequeg himself cannot read and does not know what the seer intended to say, so that when he dies, Queequeg will take the secrets entrusted to his skin with him to the grave, and nobody will ever know the truth about the world we live in.

We do, in fact, not even fully understand ourselves. We are part of the mystery, and perhaps the greatest mystery. When we look at ourselves, we are, after all, confronted with 'the ungraspable phantom of life', which, according to Ishmael, is 'the key to it all' (MD, 15), which is a strange, seemingly contradictory thing to say. How can something that is 'ungraspable' be the key to everything? Unless it is precisely the ungraspability of life that we need to grasp in order to understand what life is, and hence what we are. When Ishmael begins his journey as a common sailor on that ill-fated whaling ship, the *Pequod*, he is full of curiosity, eager to see the world, to experience its wonders, welcoming both the good and the bad, both joy and pain, all that life has to offer. When the Pequod leaves the harbour of Nantucket, he feels that 'the great flood-gates of the wonder-world' are finally swinging open (MD, 19), and indeed they are. Yet the real wonders are quickly exhausted and are no match for the wonders we imagined there to be. The world is, after all, round, so that we always end up where we started.

> Were this world an endless plain, and by sailing eastward we could for ever reach new distances, and discover sights more sweet and strange than any Cyclades or Islands of King Solomon, then there were promise in the voyage. But in pursuit of those far mysteries we dream of, or in tormented chase of that demon phantom that, some time or other, swims before all human hearts; while chasing such over this round globe, they either lead us on in barren mazes or midway leave us whelmed. (MD, 286)

We feel that there must be more than what the real world, or what appears to be the real world, can offer us. And perhaps there is. But it keeps eluding us, leads us around in circles and forever taunts us from an unreachable beyond. We are searching, without quite knowing for what. Where do we come from, where do we go? We long for an answer, but do not get any, at least not as long as we are alive. Perhaps death will give it to us. 'Our souls are like those orphans whose unwedded mothers die in bearing them: the secret of our paternity lies in their grave, and we must there to learn it' (MD, 582).

No hearts above the snow line

There is a lot we don't know about the world we live in. What we do know, however, is that the world is a dangerous place. There are monsters under the bed, and monsters in the closet. 'Though in many of its aspects this visible world seems formed in love, the invisible spheres were formed in fright' (MD, 235). Of course we usually do our best to ignore them. We normally don't 'realize the silent, subtle, ever-present perils of life', unless we are directly threatened by imminent death (MD, 339). Yet the visible and tangible dangers of this world are manageable. At least we understand what we are up against. There are weapons we can use against them. We can put up a good fight, and may even win it. However, not all perils are of that kind. Some are deeply embedded in the very fabric of this world, and there is no escape from them. To us, those perils are much more fearsome and threatening than the things we can understand: 'What are the comprehensible terrors of man compared with the interlinked terrors and wonders of God!' (MD, 135). Even the pious first mate of the Pequod, Starbuck, feels 'the latent horror' in life (MD, 205), and he is right to do so. Even though he stubbornly refuses to let go of his faith (in a good God and a benign providence), in the end he perishes like all the rest of the Pequod crew (with the one exception of Ishmael, the story's narrator), killed by the whale they had all sworn to bring down. In the end, the whale always wins, because the whale is more than just an animal. Moby-Dick, the white whale, represents the evil undercurrent of this world. Among the seafaring folk he is widely believed to be ubiquitous and immortal (MD, 220), a godlike being, but thoroughly lacking in any sympathy. With his actions revealing an 'intelligent malignity' (220), he is something like 'the gliding great demon of the seas of life' (MD, 226). His demonic nature is indicated by his whiteness, which appals Ishmael more than anything else about him (MD, 226). Melville devotes a whole chapter to 'the whiteness of the whale', one of the longest and most memorable chapters in the book. There is, we learn, an 'elusive something' about the colour white, 'which causes the thought of whiteness, when divorced from more kindly associations, and coupled with any object terrible in itself, to heighten that terror to the furthest bounds' (MD, 228). The whiteness of the whale not only is reminiscent of the marble pallor of the dead but also, 'by its indefiniteness', 'shadows forth the heartless voids and immensities of the universe, and thus stabs us from behind with the thought of annihilation, when beholding the white depths of the milky way' (MD, 235). For this very reason, white, which is not really a colour at all and which signals an absence, is also the 'colorless, all-color of atheism' (MD, 236).

Moby-Dick is the spectre of annihilation. He is an avatar of death. We will all find him eventually, however long the chase, or else he will find us. There is no escape. Death really *is* death, the end of everything. And what is more, we know it. That is why religion is a sham. If we really believed in heaven and an afterlife, we would not mourn the dead. We do because we know, deep down, that there is no coming back. Paradoxically, however, because we find the idea of total annihilation so unbearable, the experience of death is also what makes us seek solace in religious belief. 'But Faith, like a jackal, feeds among the tombs, and from these dead doubts she gathers her most vital hope' (MD, 55). *Moby-Dick* features a conversation between the second mate Stubb and the black cook Fleece about what happens to us after death. The naively religious Fleece is convinced that an angel is going to come and take him 'up there', but the cynical Stubb ridicules the idea. Up where? The main-top, you mean? No, that is not what Fleece means, but he cannot really say what he does mean, and Stubb has the last word on the matter: 'But don't you know the higher you climb the colder it gets?' (MD, 357). In other words, 'up there' is not a place where you'd want to be. Captain Ahab later makes the same point, overcome by compassion for the unfortunate boy-sailor Pip who lost his sanity when he was briefly abandoned by his shipmates in the middle of the ocean: 'There can be no hearts above the snow-line. Oh, ye frozen heavens! look down here' (MD, 614). We don't know *what* is 'up there', but we do know that it is freezing cold up there. Either there is no God up there or else he has no heart to feel for us. There is too much evil and too much suffering down here to allow for any other possibility. When the ship's crew manages to hunt down a sperm whale (*not* Moby-Dick), Ahab addresses the whale's severed head: 'Thou hast seen enough to split the planets and make an infidel of Abraham' (MD, 374), and when he later watches another whale turning on its back and looking towards the sun, as whales do when they are about to die, he muses: 'Life dies sunwards, full of faith; but see! no sooner dead, then death whirls round the corpse, and it heads some other way' (MD, 586). The dying whale looks upwards, but the dead whale turns back on its stomach, looking down, and is soon eaten by sharks. Faith comes easy to us, especially when death approaches. We are hopeful creatures. But when death comes, it sets us straight. Nobody and nothing is coming to the rescue. The sun gives life only once, and once we are dead nothing remains of us, all things going 'down, down, to dumbest dust' (MD, 591). This is the reality, the truth that we are too scared and too weak to face. When we are happy, when we feel joy, we ignore the truth about our condition. All is vanity. *All*! We have yet to understand that. 'This wilful world hath not got hold of unchristian Solomon's wisdom yet' (MD, 506).

That we lack Solomon's unchristian wisdom is, however, not entirely our fault. There is, undoubtedly, something demonic at work in the world, but it remains largely hidden. We sense it, although we are usually unable to perceive it clearly and distinctly. Monsters lurk in the shadows, rarely in the light. Moby-Dick remains invisible most of the time, concealed by the impenetrable depths of the ocean. But we know he is there, somewhere. He could be anywhere. Even animals have 'the instinct of the knowledge of the demonism in the world' (MD, 235). In *Moby-Dick*, the ocean itself has something uncanny about it. It represents the power of destruction the world has over us, as well as its 'demoniac indifference' (MD, 628). We often forget that power because we flatter ourselves to be able, with the help of science and technology, to master nature, 'yet for ever and for ever, to the crack of doom, the sea will insult and murder him' (MD, 331). But the threat is not merely physical. Even in our own minds we are surrounded by a vast ocean of lurking horrors, and we live in the midst of that ocean on a small island of sanity, where there alone is peace and joy. We need to take great care to protect and never to leave that island because we may not find our way back to it (MD, 332), and then we will be lost forever like little Pip who falls off the boat and is left by his mates. Being exposed to that 'awful lonesomeness' of the shoreless ocean is 'intolerable'. Unable to bear the 'intense concentration of self in the middle of such a heartless immensity' (MD, 494), Pip loses his mind. The reason: he left the island and met the monsters of the invisible world.

> The sea had jeeringly kept his finite body up, but drowned the infinite of his soul. Not drowned entirely, though. Rather carried down alive to wondrous depths, where strange shapes of the unwarped primal world glided to and fro before his passive eyes; and the miser-merman, Wisdom, revealed his horded heaps; and among the joyous, heartless, ever-juvenile eternities, Pip saw the multitudinous, God-omnipresent, coral insects, that out of the firmament of waters heaved the colossal orbs. (MD, 495)

As a result, Pip becomes 'indifferent as his God' (MD, 495) and mad like the German poet Friedrich Schiller's youth at Sais who despite warnings lifted the veil of the goddess Isis and saw, for the first time ever, the naked truth, which no one can bear (MD, 405). Perhaps, under the circumstances, madness is a blessing, though. It is the last protection we have, so that staying sane would be the real curse. As Ahab says to Perth, the ship's carpenter, 'How can'st thou endure without being mad? Do the heavens yet hate thee, that thou can'st not go mad?' (MD, 577).

The tiger heart that pants beneath the ocean's skin

That we do not all go mad like Pip is largely due to the fact that the world is very good at hiding its true nature. On the surface, everything is bright and shiny and immensely colourful, but if you dig a little deeper, it all disappears. Appearances are misleading. The Emperor Nature is, even though most of us never become aware of it, quite naked under all his fancy clothes. The light gives us beautiful colours, but they are fake, because the light itself is white or colourless. That is why white is the only colour that reflects how things truly are:

> All the other earthly hues – every stately or lovely emblazoning – the sweet tinges of sunset skies and woods; yea, and the gilded velvets of butterflies, and the butterfly cheeks of young girls; all

these are but subtile deceits, not actually inherent in substances, but only laid on from without; so that all deified Nature absolutely paints like the harlot, whose allurements cover nothing but the charnel-house within. (MD, 236)

Nature appears here as an active agent intent to deceive and seduce us, like a 'harlot', dolling herself up to appear younger and prettier than she really is. Yet once we have seen through the masquerade, 'the palsied universe lies before us a leper' (MD, 236), which is a horrible thing to see. No wonder then that the white whale, who stands for all this, for the true nature of things, is hunted so obsessively by Ahab and his crew. It is an act of defiance.

Nothing about the chase would make sense if Moby-Dick were only a whale, because there is nothing to be gained really by his relentless pursuit. It is not profitable, and it is dangerous. But Moby-Dick is more than just a whale. When Starbuck admonishes Ahab for his irrational quest, thinking it madness to try to cast 'vengeance on a dumb brute', Ahab corrects Starbuck's fundamental error (and indeed delusion):

All visible objects ... are but as pasteboard masks. But in each event – in the living act, the undoubted deed – there, some unknown but still reasoning thing puts forth the mouldings of its features from behind the unreasoning mask. If man will strike, strike through the mask! How can the prisoner reach outside except by thrusting through the wall? To me, the white whale is that wall, shoved near to me. Sometimes I think there's naught beyond. But 'tis enough. He tasks me; he heaps me; I see in him outrageous strength, with an inscrutable malice sinewing it. That inscrutable thing is chiefly what I hate; and be the white whale agent, or be the white whale principal, I will wreak that hate upon him. (MD, 199)

The wall, however, is strong, the mask persistent, almost as if it was held up by a powerful will. The true nature of things is not merely well hidden; it is actively hiding. The beauty of the natural world is complicit in the grand deceit. It lulls us into thinking that all is well and nothing bad can happen to us. It makes us drop our guard and sets a trap for us, like the deceptive tranquillity of the ocean in calm weather: 'These are the times of dreamy quietude, when beholding the tranquil beauty and brilliancy of the ocean's skin, one forgets the tiger heart that pants beneath it; and would not willingly remember, that this velvet paw but conceals a remorseless fang' (MD, 581). Contemplating nature's beauty we are easily persuaded to believe that there is an intimate connection between ourselves and the world around us, that we are, somehow, an integral part of a larger whole, that we truly belong, that we are, on some level, one with the universe, which, accordingly, can never harm us. If, however, we really believe that, we are in for a rude awakening, because in truth our holistic reveries make it so much easier for the cosmic tiger to get us. It can be fatal to let oneself be enthralled by the tiger's velvet paw and to forget its remorseless fang. According to Ishmael, when seamen on a whaler's ship are on masthead duty, spending a couple of hours precariously poised on two thin parallel sticks at the top of the mast to look out for whales and other ships, they are often, having nothing much else to do, overcome by what Sigmund Freud would later call an 'oceanic feeling'. The man on the lookout then takes 'the mystic ocean at his feet for the visible image of that deep, blue, bottomless soul, pervading mankind and nature' (MD, 193). He becomes one with the movement of the waves, the movement of the ship, which is a highly dangerous thing to do because he may easily lose his grip and foothold and then plunge to his death.

> But while this sleep, this dream is on ye, move your foot or hand an inch, slip your hold at all; and your identity comes back in horror. Over Descartian vortices you hover. And perhaps, at midday, in the fairest weather, with one half-throttled shriek you drop through that transparent air into the summer sea, no more to rise for ever. Heed it well, ye Pantheists! (MD, 194).

When that happens, the sea will be just as blue and peaceful as before. We will be dead and gone, but the sun will go on shining and others will go on living, which can easily feel like mockery (MD, 221). Destruction and suffering do not register with nature: its beauty is essentially heartless. Where the heart of things should be, there is nothing, or if there is something, it is, at best, indifferent to us. The gods don't care about us. In fact, let us *hope* they don't. For if they really are as they appeared to Pip, heartless, insect-like, inhuman, we do not want to attract their attention. H.P. Lovecraft may have learnt his trade from Edgar Allen Poe, but his nightmare world, haunted by strange gods, horrible beyond comprehension, he inherited from Melville. Melville's universe is not a good place to be in. The only goodness anywhere to be found is in the human heart. 'Lo! ye believers in gods all goodness, and in man all ill, lo you! see the omniscient oblivious of suffering man; and man, though idiotic, and knowing not what he does, yet full of the sweet things of love and gratitude' (MD, 614). Yet even the human heart is treacherous. Often enough what looks like a human from the outside turns out to be a monster inside. The inhuman is hiding in the human form, and it is qualities like love and gratitude as well as our trust in the basic decency and goodness of other people – the very qualities that make us human – that make us so vulnerable to it.

That beautiful creature, the rattlesnake

In Melville's late, posthumously published novella *Billy Budd, Sailor*, it is precisely Billy's innocence that prevents him from suspecting the evil behind the friendly facade of the ship's devious master-at-arms, John Claggart. His 'innocence was his blinder' (BB, 441). When Claggart accuses him to the captain of the ship, falsely claiming that he had conspired to start a mutiny, he is literally speechless, numbed and paralysed by his 'generous young heart's virgin experience of the diabolical incarnate' (BB, 467). Unable to speak and defend himself, he strikes out at Claggart. Claggart goes down, hits his head and dies. It was an accident, and everybody knows it. Nor does anyone believe that Billy really committed the crime that Claggart accused him of. However, since he did attack a superior officer and discipline needs to be maintained, Billy is quickly sentenced to death and, the next morning, hanged. Yet before he strikes Claggart, looking into his eyes, he catches a brief glimpse into the true nature of the other (and perhaps, with that, also the true nature of the world). A transformation takes place right before him, similar to the one experienced by the hero of John Carpenter's 1988 film *They Live*, when he first puts on the sunglasses that reveal the skull-faced aliens masquerading as humans: 'The accuser's eyes', writes Melville, 'underwent a phenomenal change, their wonted rich violet color blurring into a muddy purple. Those lights of human intelligence, losing human expression, were gelidly protruding like the alien eyes of certain uncatalogued creatures of the deep. The first mesmeristic glance was one of serpent fascination; the last was as the paralyzing lurch of the torpedo fish' (BB, 449).

Several other works of Melville provide variations of the same theme of deception and the blinding effects of trust and basic human decency. When in *Benito Cereno* (1855) the kindly, good-natured Amasa Delano, captain of an American trading ship, encounters, off the coast of Chile, a Spanish slave ship that appears to be in distress, he offers his help, not knowing that the slaves have taken control of the ship, holding the captain, Don Benito Cereno, and what remains of his crew hostage. Delano senses that something is not quite right, but for a long time, almost right to the very end, he does not understand what is really going on. This is partly due to his prejudices: the deeply held conviction that black people are simply not capable of an uprising. They are just not smart enough, also too full of natural conviviality, and therefore essentially harmless. 'Captain Delano took to negroes, not philanthropically, but genially, just as other men to Newfoundland dogs' (BC, 91). This is why he does not really consider what turns out to be the true explanation for the Spanish ship's crew's strange behaviour. But it is also because he is too generous and pious to be able to suspect that 'such wickedness' could be possible (BC, 122). In fact, he firmly believes that since he is a good person (which he is, in his own conceited and patronizing way), God will surely protect him from all evil. It would simply be too unjust if he didn't. Still he knows, something is wrong, but he cannot put his finger on it. So he doubts, then reassures himself, doubts again, reassures himself again and so on, many times. Ultimately his trust, or his unwillingness to let himself be guided by doubt, maintains the upper hand, not the least because nature itself conspires with the mutineers to deceive him. He is betrayed by the semblance of peacefulness of the scene:

> He saw the benign aspect of nature, taking her innocent repose in the evening; the screened sun in the quiet camp of the west shining out like the mild light from Abraham's tent. ... Once again he smiled at the phantom which had mocked him, and felt something like a tinge of remorse, that, by harboring them even for a moment, he should, by implication, have betrayed an almost atheistic doubt of the ever-watchful Providence above. (BC, 105)

However, as the events show, he is mistaken. His 'almost atheistic doubt' was justified: nobody has been watching. Providence must have looked the other way. It turns out that the ship's pious owner, Don Joaquin, was murdered, his faith obviously had not afforded him protection against evil, and Don Benito himself, after the plot is finally discovered and all the mutineers killed or apprehended, does not recover and dies soon after the events. He does not die because of any fatal physical injuries, of which he had none. He dies because his trust in the world has been shattered for good. After what he went through, he sees deception everywhere, and the genial, stubbornly optimistic Delano, despite trying his best, cannot talk him out of it. The veil has been removed, once and for all. When the ever forward- and upwards-looking Delano tells him to forget it and not to moralize upon it because 'the past is passed' and even the 'bright sun has forgotten it all, and the blue sea, and the blue sky; these have turned over new leaves', Don Benito replies: 'Because they have no memory, … because they are not human' (BC, 125), and when Delano suggests that the mild winds 'that now fan your cheek' come 'with a human-like healing' and are warm and steadfast friends to them, Don Benito is having none of it: 'With their steadfastness they but waft me to my tomb, senor.' But you are saved, cries the increasingly exasperated and still uncomprehending Delano: 'You are saved; what has cast such a shadow upon you?' – to which Don Benito replies (most likely referring to Babo, the deadly, pitiless leader of the slave revolt who pretended to be his loyal servant): 'The negro' (BC, 125–6).

Melville's perspective here is not political, but metaphysical. Just like the white whale in *Moby-Dick*, the black man in *Benito Cereno* is an avatar of the demoniac, which both disguises itself in and acts through certain natural forms, animal and human. Melville's focus in *Benito Cereno* is not on the political and ethical issue of slavery, as his focus in *Moby-Dick* is not on the brutal butchery of the whaling industry, even though he is very well aware of the ethical dubiousness of either practice. In both cases, the main focus is on the question to what extent we can and should trust appearances, and on the discrepancy between the way the world presents itself to us and the way the world really is.

The problem of radical uncertainty takes centre stage in Melville's last novel, *The Confidence-Man: His Masquerade* (1857), which confronts the reader with a dazzling parade of characters, none of whom we can be sure really is what they appear or pretend to be. In ever new disguises the confidence man (if it is indeed one and the same man) tests the trust of the people he meets on a steamboat travelling down the Mississippi. What he is really up to we do not know. We only know what he does, namely, encourage people to trust their fellowmen, but it is not entirely clear whether this is done to take advantage of them or because he is really convinced that it would be good for us to trust each other. After all, trust builds bridges between people. The good person trusts others. Friendship requires trust, and love does. We reach out to others by trusting them. However, trust is also dangerous. It can easily be abused, and when it is, then trust becomes mere gullibility.

The Confidence-Man is set on April Fools' Day 1857, which is also, not coincidentally of course, the year and day the novel was published, which suggests that a practical joke is being played, except that it is not clear on whom (or what exactly the joke is). On the face of it, the novel makes a strong case against trusting appearances. Neither the reader nor any of the characters in the book can ever be sure that things really are as they appear to be. Who is who? Do they really mean what they are saying, or are they lying? What are their true intentions? Who is fooling whom? The masquerade is inscrutable. What is clear, though, is that there is a crucial difference between the outside and the inside, appearance and reality. They *may* match, but there is no guarantee that they do, and since there is only one way to be the one that you appear to be, but many different ways *not* to be what you appear to be, it is considerably more likely that there is indeed a difference between what you appear to be and what you really are. When one of the characters in *The Confidence-Man* starts a conversation with another passenger (referred to as 'the Cosmopolitan', who later introduces himself as 'Frank Goodman' and who may or may not be an incarnation of the confidence man), claiming that he must be a beautiful soul because of his winning, genial appearance, the other replies that this is exactly why he has 'confidence in the latent benignity of that beautiful creature, the rattlesnake, whose lithe neck and burnished maze of tawny gold, as he sleekly curls aloft in the sun, who on the prairie can behold without wonder?' (CM, 251). The mockery is unmistakable. The Cosmopolitan makes fun of the idea that you could figure out what kind of person someone is just by their looks and the way they dress. Monsters are not always ugly, and you cannot judge the book by its cover (or by its title), no matter how pretty it is. This holds true both for other people and the world in general. It is even suggested that humanity itself can occasionally be but a mask: when the barber calls the Cosmopolitan a 'man', he replies, 'You can conclude nothing absolute from the human form, barber' (CM, 300). There have, after all, been devils in human form (like Claggart in *Billy Budd*), and there have also been angels (like Billy Budd himself). The problem is that we often cannot tell which is which. The confidence man could be either (as could each one of us).

Yet it is not only that people are not always (and not even usually) what they appear to be. It is also that they *change* all the time. Sometimes there is a greater difference between two incarnations of the same person at different times in their life than there is between completely different persons. People, just like the rest of the world, are in permanent flux, so that there is really nothing we can fully rely on (CM, 295). This leads to a situation of radical uncertainty, where even our own personal identity remains elusive and permanently in doubt: 'What are you? What am I? Nobody knows who anybody is' (CM, 255). Accordingly, we could be an angel one day and a devil the next. Friends can quickly turn into enemies when circumstances change. When the Cosmopolitan becomes quite chummy with a fellow passenger who calls himself 'Charlie Noble' and asks him for a loan, he has no luck. Noble refuses, and to explain why he tells him the story of the candle maker China Aster (CM, 276–93) who trusted an old friend who convinced him to accept a loan from him, no strings attached, to make his modest business more lucrative. Unsurprisingly, the story ends badly: things do not go as planned, the so-called friend suddenly insists on getting his money back, plus interest, and the candle maker is ruined and dies an early, ignominious death. His wife follows him to the grave shortly after, and the children end up in an alms house. The story (or its narrator, Charlie Noble) makes it very clear that China Aster's sad fate directly resulted from, for one thing, his unwavering honesty, and, for another, his trust, not only in people, but generally in life. He showed too much confidence and so quite naturally got conned big time. He used to believe that by working hard and staying brave and true one could make sure that things will turn out well, but he learnt the hard way that this is not how it works. People cannot be trusted. *Life* cannot be trusted. And it certainly isn't fair. The inscription on Aster's gravestone neatly captures the lesson to be learnt here:

> Here lie the remains of China Aster the candle-maker, whose career was an example of the truth of scripture, as found in the sober philosophy of Solomon the Wise; for he was ruined by allowing himself to be persuaded against his better sense, into the free indulgence of confidence, and an ardently bright view of life to the exclusion of that counsel which comes by heeding the opposite view. (CM, 292)

Heeding the opposite view, however, is more easily said than done. Obviously, China Aster should not have trusted his friend. But if you cannot even trust your friends, then you cannot really trust anybody. Yet if you generally don't trust people, then you have actually lost your trust in the universe and that means God. If you don't trust the creature, then you are clearly not trusting the Creator (CM, 325). Misanthropy and atheism are in fact closely related. They spring from the same root. As the Cosmopolitan points out, 'What is an atheist, but one who does not, or will not, see in the universe a ruling principle of love; and what a misanthrope, but one who does not, or will not, see in man a ruling principle of kindness? ... In either case the vice consists in a want of confidence' (CM, 211). The Cosmopolitan can, of course, not be trusted if nobody can be trusted, especially not if he himself is one of the incarnations of the confidence man, in which case we would of course expect him to sing the praises of trust because he can only con us if we trust him. And why would a want of confidence be a vice anyway if it clearly makes us less gullible? On the other hand, what are we without confidence? Can we imagine human life without it? Can we imagine a *good* human life without it? It may well be that a life that is completely, or even largely, lacking in trust is a life that is not worth living. This is what Melville seems to be suggesting, or at least hinting at, in *The Confidence-Man*. As, once again, the Cosmopolitan puts it, 'The traveller who has not this trust, what miserable misgivings must be his' (CM, 334). So we cannot and should not trust (because if we do we are almost certainly going to be duped), and yet we *need* to trust in order to live well. An impossible situation. So what are we to do?

Like a true child of fire

One way of dealing with an untrustworthy world is to rebel against it, to refuse to accept the rules of the game and to confront the roaring tiger head-on. This is Captain Ahab's way in *Moby-Dick*. He fights back against an unfeeling, cold and heartless world. But for that he needs a concrete target, something he can actually lay hands on, something that can be physically attacked. The whale is a surrogate. In him, the intangible becomes tangible. 'The White Whale swam before him as the monomaniac incarnation of all those malicious agencies which some deep men feel eating in them, till they are left living on with half a heart and half a lung' (MD, 222). Moby-Dick, for Ahab, is the cancer eating away at the heart of the world, the devil incarnate. 'All that most maddens and torments; all that stirs up the lees of things; all truth with malice in it; all that cracks the sinews and cakes the brain; all the subtle demonisms of life and thought; all evil, to crazy Ahab, were visibly personified, and made practically assailable in Moby Dick' (MD, 222). When the pious Starbuck suggests to him that the whole endeavour smacks of blasphemy, Ahab is defiant. He does not care if his actions offend the gods, because he feels that it is the gods who have offended him. He sees no reason for gratitude or reverence, and refuses to be impressed by sheer power. 'If you hurt me, then I hurt you' is his precept. An eye for an eye, no matter whose eye it is, and be it the eye of God himself. 'Talk not to me of blasphemy, man; I'd strike the sun if it insulted me' (MD, 199). This is the angel Lucifer raging against an unjust world order and demanding equal rights. In Ahab's mind, he is doing no more than what every decent and proud person would or should do: fight back against the schoolyard bully (MD, 204). The only right worship of the world spirit, if there is one, is defiance, even though we stand no chance of victory. Better die fighting than not to fight at all.

> To neither love nor reverence wilt thou be kind; and e'en for hate thou canst but kill; and all are killed. No fearless fool now fronts thee. I own thy speechless, placeless power; but to the last gasp of my earthquake life will dispute its unconditional, unintegral mastery in me. In the midst of the personified impersonal, a personality stands here. Though but a point at best; whencesoe'er

I came, wheresoe'er I go; yet while I earthly live, the queenly
personality lives in me, and feels her royal rights. ... Oh, thou
clear spirit, of thy fire thou madest me, and like a true child of
fire, I breathe it back to thee. (MD, 597–8)

Unfortunately we already know that appearances cannot be trusted.
Things are not always as they seem, so when it seems to Ahab that
he is defying the gods, that he uses his own free will to oppose
them and the fate that they have assigned to him and humanity in
general, it is quite possible that this is yet another delusion. The
novel certainly suggests as much. Already in the very first chapter
Ishmael remarks that we are all slaves (MD, 17), and looking back
at everything that came to pass and how it did, it seems to him that
his decision to go on that whaling voyage 'formed part of the grand
programme of Providence that was drawn up a long time ago' (MD,
18). Wasn't Providence supposed to ensure a good outcome? In this
case it certainly did not. And bad omens there were plenty once
the journey started, warning of or rather predicting a calamitous
ending. Yet those predictions are 'not so much predictions from
without, as verifications of the foregoing things within'. We are
driven on by 'the innermost necessities in our being' (MD, 200).
Towards the end of the book, before the final showdown with the
white whale, Starbuck almost manages to talk sense into Ahab.
Forty years has he already wasted 'to make war on the horrors of
the deep', is it not time now to reconsider his priorities, give up
the crazy chase and start living again (MD, 636)? For a moment
Starbuck seems to get through to Ahab. He realizes what a fool
he has been. Looking into his first mate's human eyes, he sees his
wife and child at home, waiting for him. But Starbuck's hopes are
disappointed. Ahab cannot stop. He has to go on, despite himself.
Some hidden power directs his actions.

What is it, what nameless, inscrutable, unearthly thing is it;
what cozening, hidden lord and master, and cruel, remorseless
emperor commands me; that against all natural lovings and
longings, I so keep pushing, and crowding, and jamming myself
on all the time; recklessly making me ready to do what in my
own proper, natural heart, I durst not so much as dare? ... By
heaven, man, we are turned round and round in this world, like
yonder windlass, and Fate is the handspike. (MD, 639)

So the hunt continues, the arms of the wind, invisible and irresistible, rushing them on, a symbol of the unseen agency that enslaves not only Ahab but also everyone on the ship to the race (MD, 653). Ahab, then, does not really defy the gods at all. The 'cruel, remorseless emperor' is still in charge, so he does exactly what he is supposed to do, both his effort and his failure all part of the plan. As always, the gods seem to be having the last laugh.

However, there are other ways to defy the gods. A very different kind of rebel Melville portrays in his marvellous, enigmatic short story 'Bartleby, the Scrivener: A Story of Wall Street' (1853). Bartleby is hired by a lawyer to copy legal documents. At first Bartleby does a fine job, until one day, to the consternation of his employer, he refuses, without apparent reason, to comply with a request to examine a document. Instead of doing what he is asked to, he states, mildly and firmly, that he would 'prefer not to'. The baffled lawyer decides to let it go, but when it happens again and again until Bartleby eventually refuses to do any work at all, preferring to spend his time looking at a brick wall, he feels he must take action and tells him he no longer requires his services. Bartleby, however, prefers to stay. So the lawyer moves out himself to get rid of him, and Bartleby goes on to haunt the lawyer's former offices, which are now occupied by somebody else. Eventually Bartleby is forcefully removed and imprisoned, where he dies shortly after of starvation, not because he was mistreated but because he preferred not to eat.

It is unclear why Bartleby does all that. No definite explanation is offered. Surely there is nothing inappropriate or demeaning about what he is asked to do, and people are throughout unusually accommodating to his eccentric behaviour. Bartleby's actions are simply inexplicable. It makes no sense at all. The only clue the story offers to a possible motivation is a rumour that comes to the lawyer's attention after Bartleby's death. Apparently Bartleby used to work as a clerk at a dead letter office, taking care of letters that could not be delivered to the intended recipient, in most cases because they were no longer alive. Perhaps, the lawyer speculates, this was simply too depressing for someone who probably was 'by nature and misfortune prone to a pallid hopelessness' already (BS, 51). The story ends with the lawyer's puzzled sigh 'Ah Bartleby! Ah humanity!', which seems to suggest that Bartleby's fate is somehow *our* fate, that each one of us works in some kind of cosmic dead letter office. Whatever this means exactly, it can't be good. The lawyer (who is also our narrator) notices how alone Bartleby seemed, 'absolutely alone in the universe. A bit of wreck in the mid Atlantic' (BS, 38). In *The Confidence-Man*, the first incarnation of the confidence man is introduced to us as 'in the extremest sense of the word, a stranger' (CM, 1), and even though the Cosmopolitan claims that 'no man is a stranger' (CM, 177), the novel itself suggests that, on the contrary, we are *all* strangers all the time and everywhere 'in this strange universe' (CM, 260). Bartleby, too, is a stranger 'in the extremest sense of the word', meaning that by his very nature he does not belong. He is a stranger in an indifferent or hostile universe, another cosmic orphan, as we all are. He is of course *also* an incarnation of that very universe that we try in vain to make sense of. He is both the wall that Ahab (as well as, though far less obsessively, the unnamed lawyer in 'Bartleby') is determined to thrust through and someone confronting the wall *without* trying to thrust through. He just faces it for a while and then quietly takes his leave.

Both Ahab and Bartleby refuse to accept the rules of the game. They are both, each in their own way, rebels. Yet while Ahab tries in vain to change the rules, Bartleby simply refuses to play. Ahab's resistance is active, Bartleby's passive, but Bartleby seems to succeed where Ahab fails. In truth, however, his success is at best comparative. What he has clearly not managed to do is find a way to live with confidence without letting himself be duped. After all, both Ahab and Bartleby end up dead. Neither of the two provides much of an example of how to live one's life. For that we need to look at the one who lived, the only survivor of the hunt for the White Whale: the one who asks to be called Ishmael.

Playing the fool in a sensible way

Ahab made a mistake: he resented the laughter of the gods. Instead, he should have laughed along with them. 'There are certain queer times and occasions in this strange mixed affair we call life when a man takes this whole universe for a vast practical joke, though the wit thereof he but dimly discerns, and more than suspects that the joke is at nobody's expense but his own' (MD, 273). But what if it is? Let the whole thing be a joke and let us be the butt of it, there is no need to take offence and go all nuclear like Ahab, or to turn one's back on the world like Bartleby. Ishmael, who is playing his part in the events but is present to us almost purely as an observer, becoming all but invisible in the course of the narrative, takes a very different approach. He feels strangely liberated by the idea that all the things that happen to us, including all the bad stuff and even death itself, may actually be nothing but 'good-natured hits, and jolly punches in the side bestowed by the unseen and unaccountable old joker' (MD, 273). Ishmael welcomes and endorses the cheerful indifference that such a way of looking at things may inspire, that 'free and easy sort of genial, desperado philosophy' (MD, 273), and resolves to look at the whole chasing-the-White-Whale adventure in precisely this light. If you cannot change it, the best strategy is to play along. *The Confidence-Man* encourages a similar philosophy: 'Life is a picnic en costume; one must take a part, assume a character, stand ready in a sensible way to play the fool' (CM, 178). Charlie Noble cites Shakespeare's 'All the world's a stage', a stage on which we may have to play many different parts (CM, 298), and while we may not be able to choose which part we want to play, as all the roles are being assigned by somebody else, there is no reason not to enjoy the ride as long as it lasts and to play our part as best we can. There is, after all, plenty to enjoy along the way, starting with everything Ahab renounces in his obstinate pursuit of metaphysical revenge. While Ahab chases his whale, Ishmael discovers, or rediscovers, the simple pleasures of smell and touch and the company of fellow humans when he is tasked with squeezing a dead whale's spermaceti to make it fluid again, which makes him feel 'divinely free from all ill-will, or petulance, or malice, of any sort whatsoever', as he imagines 'long rows of angels in paradise, each with his hands in a jar of spermaceti' (MD, 497–8). It does not need much for us to be happy. We simply need to look for it in the right places, 'not placing it anywhere in the intellect or the fancy; but in the wife, the heart, the bed, the table, the saddle, the fire-side, the country' (MD, 497), also keeping in mind what the whalers say, 'when cruising in an empty ship, if you can get nothing better out of the world, get a good dinner out of it, at least' (MD, 532).

Of course such a relaxed, ironic attitude to life requires the ability to develop a certain detachment, not only from the world but also, and even more so, from one's own instinctive reactions to it.

Ishmael advises that we model ourselves after the whale and remain warm among ice, live in the world without being of it and retain in all seasons a temperature of our own. Like the whale, we need thick walls and a spacious interior, none of which is easy for a human to acquire (MD, 369), but this is no reason not to try it. Ishmael seems to have managed something like it: 'Amid the tornadoed Atlantic of my being, do I myself still for ever centrally disport in mute calm; and while ponderous planets of unwaning woe revolve around me, deep down and deep inland there I still bathe me in eternal mildness of joy' (MD, 464). The stranger thus becomes the master, precisely because he is a stranger. He does not fully belong to this world. He is an actor who plays his role, and plays it well, but the role he plays does not exhaust who he is. Monsters there may be, but they are made of papier mâché. They can hurt the character, but not the player. And when his character dies, he may still live on to play another role and to fight another whale.

> There is no steady unretracing progress in this life; we do not advance through fixed gradations, and at the last one pause: – through infancy's unconscious spell, boyhood's thoughtless faith, adolescence's doubt (the common doom), then scepticism, then disbelief, resting at last in manhood's pondering repose of If. But once gone through, we trace the round again; and are infants, boys, and men, and Ifs eternally. (MD, 582)

CHAPTER FOUR

The hell of no longer being able to love
Fyodor Dostoyevsky
(1821–1881)

Nothing matters

The plotlines of Dostoyevsky's stories frequently revolve around suicides and murders. Various characters end up killing either themselves or others. Some try, but fail or change their mind. Many consider the option. All of Dostoyevsky's great novels feature at least one suicide or suicide attempt and one murder. In *Crime and Punishment* (1866) the former student Raskolnikov murders a pawnbroker and her mentally challenged sister, and the rich, morally challenged Svridrigailov commits suicide after being rejected by Raskolnikov's sister Dunya. In *The Idiot* (1869) the young Ippolit Terentyev who is dying of consumption unsuccessfully tries to shoot himself, and Rogozhin stabs Natassya to death, the woman he supposedly loves. In *Demons* (1872) Pyotr Verkhovensky and his gang of would-be revolutionaries kill their former ally Shatov, while Shatov's neighbour, Kirillov, puts a bullet in his brain, and the novel's warped anti-hero Stavrogin hangs himself. In *The Brothers Karamazov* (1880) the old father Karamazov is killed by his servant and (as rumour has it) illegitimate son Smerdyakov, who then hangs himself, not out of remorse but (most likely) out of spite.

What is odd about all these murders and suicides is that they do not really happen for any pressing reason. Dostoyevsky's characters do not kill themselves because they are unable to pay their debts, because they face public humiliation, because they are wrecked with guilt, or because they have lost their loved ones. Rather, Dostoyevsky's characters kill themselves because, largely independent of their personal circumstances, they no longer see a point in living. Similarly, when they kill not themselves but others, they do so mostly because they no longer see a point in not killing. It is true that sometimes a pretext is used: both Raskolnikov and Smerdyakov rob the ones they kill. However, once they have done so, they no longer care about the money, clearly showing that it was never very important to them in the first place. For the most part, Dostoyevsky's characters kill simply because they can, and in order to prove (to themselves and others) that they can. They are making the point that there is no point in not doing it. It is an assertion of power, a declaration of independence. By killing others they declare their independence from the moral laws that govern ordinary people's lives and that most of us have been raised to accept as binding. By killing themselves they declare their independence from the fear of death and the common and very natural appreciation of life. Murder and suicide are two different ways of making the point that nothing really matters, including whether we live or die or who lives and dies. Ultimately, it makes no difference.

For Dostoyevsky, this kind of evaluative nihilism, which became popular in Russia in the 1860s, poses a serious threat to our ability to live a meaningful life, and he tried hard to refute it in his novels, not through rational argument but by presenting his readers with the practical consequences of such a world view and thus demonstrating the unliveability of nihilism. However, for those who adopted and supported this new world view, it promised liberation and a chance for us to assume the role of God, to finally become a creator of worlds, or at least to shape this world in our image, unhampered by the traditional moral-religious prejudices and guided only by our own free will. In *Demons*, the engineer Kirillov decides to kill himself to become a martyr for the nihilistic cause, not out of fear, as he says, but on the contrary to kill fear, to show that there is nothing to fear, not even death. His personal sacrifice, he believes, will rid humanity of fear and will eventually allow us to become gods (D, 116). Humanity will reach perfect happiness, and time will stop. We will have reached the end of history. For that we only need to understand that everything is good, even the bad. In other words, there is no real difference between what we consider good and what we consider bad. Everything is good means that nothing is better or worse than anything else. It means that nothing really matters. To teach this is to end the world (possibly because history is best conceived as a constant struggle to bring about the good and to fend off the bad: with no difference between good and evil there is nothing left to fight for, or to fight over). The world will then be saved, but not by 'the God-man' (i.e. Jesus Christ), as Christian religion has it, but by 'the man-god' (D, 238), which is to say by our own liberated selves. After all, if there is no God, then *we* are God, or at least we can be if we don't shy away from the implications of God's non-existence (D, 617). If God existed, then *his* will would reign supreme, but since he does not, *ours* does. Kirillov believes it to be his duty to proclaim self-will, one practical expression of which is murder, but whose highest expression is suicide, or more precisely suicide for no particular reason other than to assert one's will. God is a human invention, and Kirillov, for one, refuses to invent him. 'I kill myself to show my insubordination and my new fearsome freedom' (D, 619).

Kirillov's ideas do not make much sense and reveal an underlying despair, similar to that later experienced and more coherently expressed by Ivan Karamazov. Kirillov wants to believe, but finds himself unable to. He is scared. Scared not only of death but also of a world in which there is nothing left to fear and nothing left to hope for. The godless world is a world that has lost its moral compass, one in which it ultimately makes no difference whether we live or die, or how we live and die. Kirillov tries valiantly to see the positive side of this, but he does not seem to fully believe his own rather feverish assertions. When pushed (by the devilish Pyotr Verkhovensky) to take his life as he had said he would, he hesitates and at first cannot bring himself to do it. Clearly, life is precious, even to him. When he eventually does do it, his deed comes across not as a heroic sacrifice and triumph over nature, but as pitiful and useless. Just another life wasted in the pursuit of an inherently destructive, life-negating idea: the idea that nothing matters. And yet, what is the alternative? Kirillov claims that God is necessary, and therefore *must* exist, knowing at the same time that he does not and *cannot* exist

(D, 615). To live with this contradiction he finds impossible. God is necessary because only through God can death be overcome. God, for Kirillov as well as for Dostoyevsky, is the resurrector, the one who makes sure that nothing we do gets forgotten, that the good get rewarded and evil punished, that no loss is final. Human immortality is linked to the existence of God, and without human immortality nothing makes sense, and it does not matter what we do or do not do because it will all disappear without a trace anyway. Therefore God must exist. His existence is a *moral* necessity. On the other hand, we have no convincing empirical evidence for God's existence; much of what happens in this world speaks positively against the existence of (an all-powerful and benevolent) God, and everything we know about nature suggests that when we die we really are gone for good and will not come back. Even Jesus Christ, we must assume, died properly and for good, his corpse rotting in the ground like everybody else's. God's existence may be morally necessary, but it is also a scientific and perhaps even logical impossibility.

Kirillov tries to persuade himself that God is not needed, and we can in fact live much better without God. He wants to see the death of God as an opportunity for human self-empowerment. Dostoyevsky, on the other hand, tries to persuade us that Kirillov is wrong, which is why, in *The Brothers Karamazov*, Kirillov's optimistic nihilism is advocated by the devil himself who appears to Ivan Karamazov in a dream: 'Once mankind has renounced God,' he suggests to Ivan,

> then the entire old world view will fall of itself ..., and, above all, the entire former morality, and everything will be new. People will come together in order to take from life all that it can give, but, of course, for happiness and joy in this world only. Man will be exalted with the spirit of divine, titanic pride, and the man-god will appear. Man, his will and his science no longer limited, conquering nature every hour, will thereby every hour experience such lofty delight as will replace for him all his former hopes of heavenly delight. (BK, 649)

The devil, of course, is the father of lies. The attempt to put nihilism in the service of utopian socialism does not work. Ivan's devil – an amiable and well-mannered, if a little tatty gentleman – makes it sound as if the reinvention of humanity was a community project, but in a godless and thus essentially lawless world there can be no real community. People will come together, the devil says, but in truth they will drift further apart, become completely detached from each other. In that new – allegedly totally rational – world it is every man for himself and *après moi le déluge*. Each of us will continue to be concerned about their own happiness, but no longer about anybody else's. Why would we? Humanity, as a morally relevant category, will then have ceased to exist. The devil knows this, of course, which is why he advises Ivan not to wait until everyone is ready for universal happiness in this world (which, he casually admits, may never happen anyway) but to immediately draw the appropriate practical consequences from his theoretical understanding of the true (viz. godless and very mortal) nature of the world. Since God and immortality do not exist, 'the new man is allowed to become a man-god, though it be he alone in the whole world, and of course, in this new rank, to jump lightheartedly over any former moral obstacle of the former slave-man, if need be. There is no law for God!' (BK, 649).

Note: *God*, not god*s*. There cannot be a society of gods. If I am to be God, then you can never be more than just another obstacle in my eyes. There may be many worlds, but in each of them there is only room for one god. Rational egoism equates to a practical solipsism. The man-god is not going to replace the slave-man because without slave-men he cannot be a man-god. A god without slaves that do his bidding or that he can force his will upon is not a god. There will be equality, but that equality will be for the masses only. As the social theorist Shigalyev in *Demons* explains, in the ideal society of the future the vast majority of people will simply have to obey. Their equality will thus be ensured, 'everything reduced to a common denominator' (D, 418). They won't be free, of course, but that is no problem because they wouldn't know what to do with their freedom anyway. Freedom is for the few, not the many. But to those few, everything is permitted. Or is it?

Of lice and men

In *Crime and Punishment*, the main protagonist Rodion Raskolnikov overhears a dialogue between a student and a young officer. The student is justifying, as a theoretical possibility, the killing and robbing of an old pawnbroker and moneylender that Raskolnikov knows and has done business with. Young people like him, the student argues, could do so much good with the money that old woman has. They could use it to benefit humanity. The old woman, on the other hand, does not need it and certainly does not do any good with it. Yes, it would be a crime to kill and rob her, but then again not really much of a crime given that her life does not matter anyway, or not more than that 'of a louse, a cockroach, and not even that much, because the old crone is harmful' (CP, 65). People like her do not really deserve to be alive. To think otherwise is a mere prejudice. So why not be rational about it and correct the course of nature? Surely, 'thousands of good deeds make up for one tiny little crime' (CP, 65), so killing her is 'simple arithmetic'.

Raskolnikov finds the student's utilitarian reasoning so convincing that he decides to take him by his word and put the theory to the test. So he goes and kills the pawnbroker (as well as her simple, kindly sister who gets in the way), takes her money and runs. All this happens in the first part of the book. The remaining five parts deal with the aftermath of the crime. So what happens next? The first thing Raskolnikov notices is that his relation to his environment, and especially to other people, has changed drastically. He suddenly feels cut off from the rest of the world. 'One new, insurmountable sensation was gaining possession of him almost minute by minute: it was a certain boundless, almost physical loathing for everything he met or saw around him, an obstinate, spiteful, hate-filled loathing. All the people he met were repulsive to him – their faces, their walk, their movements were repulsive' (CP, 110). Clearly, his crime has created a rift between himself and the world, which has now become a strange, unwelcoming, loathsome place. The awareness of that rift is not exactly a moral feeling. It is certainly not remorse, and it won't be for a long time. He does not *think* he did anything wrong. At first the only real worry he has is that he might get caught. He is keen to get rid of the money he has stolen because it might be used as evidence against him. It does not occur to him that getting hold of the old woman's money was supposed to be the end to which the murder was only the means. Yet suddenly the money seems no longer needed, which indicates that the real reason for the murder must have been something else. The police inspector Porfiry Petrovich who investigates the murder and who suspects and tries to outsmart Raskolnikov finds the answer in an article that the former student wrote a while ago. According to that article, certain persons exist 'who not only can but are fully entitled to commit all sorts of crimes and excesses and to whom the law supposedly does not apply' (CP, 258). Such 'extraordinary' people have the right to 'step over certain obstacles', provided that is necessary to accomplish their goals (which are 'sometimes perhaps salutary for the whole of mankind') (CP, 259). If Newton, for instance, could not have made his discoveries without killing a hundred people, he should have done it (but just those). Great men tend to be criminals. They have to be because they have more important things to care about than the morality of their actions. It is in fact a law of nature that there are two classes of people: those who have to obey and who are mostly there for reproductive purposes, and 'people proper', such as Napoleon. People proper are those who are willing to transgress the law to bring about the new and who can do so with impunity. They move the world by calling 'for the destruction of the present in the name of the better' (CP, 261). To them (and to them only) 'everything is permitted' (CP, 274).

There is, however, one problem with this theory, which Porfiry is quick to point out: How does one know to which category one belongs? Surely it is possible that one only *thinks* that one is extraordinary without actually *being* extraordinary. Great men are rare; what is not rare is people who have persuaded themselves they are great. For Raskolnikov this is indeed a problem. As he later confesses to Sonya (a young prostitute whom he befriends and who later accompanies him to Siberia), he had doubts himself, which is exactly why he resolved to kill the old woman. He wanted to know what he is, wanted to know whether he, too, is a louse 'like all the rest' (CP, 419) or a 'person proper'. He was hoping that by committing murder and just taking what he wanted and needed, he would prove to himself that he is not like all the rest, that he is indeed exceptional, that to him everything is permitted. 'I just wanted to dare, Sonya, that's the whole reason' (CP, 418). Yet strangely enough, even though he did dare to commit the crime, he feels that he has failed the test. In his own estimation, he did not succeed in 'stepping over'. He is still unapologetic, insisting that he 'only killed a louse, Sonya, a useless, nasty, pernicious louse' (CP, 416), but is now willing to concede that he himself might be a louse too. Why? Because unlike the truly great person, he mulled over the question whether he had the right to kill. He was not sure, and that lack of certainty has clearly shown that he did not have what it takes. If you can ask whether a human being is a louse, then for you at least a human is not a louse. Humans are only lice for those to whom it never occurs to even raise the question (CP, 419). Yet Raskolnikov has still got it wrong. When he insists that he only killed a louse, and Sonya points out the absurdity of calling a human being a louse, he responds, 'looking at her strangely': 'Not a louse, I know it myself' (CP, 416). There is a part of him that knows that his theoretical assumptions are simply false and, moreover, that they are *obviously* false: in spite of what Raskolnikov keeps telling himself, neither he nor the old woman whom he killed is a louse. The truth is that *no* human being is a louse.

Raskolnikov also knows that the utilitarian reasoning that he (just like Ivan's devil) uses to make the alleged right of the extraordinary person to do whatever they deem necessary to achieve their ends more palatable to ordinary sensibilities is a mere facade, a smoke screen. The truth is that he couldn't care less about universal happiness. His motivation for the robbery is much more selfish or much more personal: 'Life is given to me only once, and never will be again – I don't want to sit waiting for universal happiness. I want to live myself; otherwise it's better not to live at all' (CP, 274). Ultimately, all he wants is to satisfy his own 'flesh and lust' (CP, 275). Paradoxically, the fact that despite all his theorizing and delusions of grandeur what really drives him is his thirst for life is the one thing that somewhat redeems him in Dostoyevsky's eyes. It gives rise to the hope that not all is lost yet. Raskolnikov's thirst for life makes him human. In fact, he is perfectly *right* to want life for himself. The problem is that he does not really know *how* to live and what living really means. He is also making the wrong assumptions. Since life is given to him only once, he reasons, he needs to get as much out of it as he possibly can. This suggests that the situation would be very different if life were given to him not only once, if the end of *this* life were not the end of his *whole* life. That he wants life for himself is understandable, even good. His actions, and hence his misfortune, spring not from his love for life but from the fact that he does 'not believe in a future life' (CP, 289).

This belief, or rather lack of belief, connects him to the entirely unscrupulous arch-nihilist Pyotr Verkhovensky in *Demons*, for whom the occasional murder is nothing to sweat about. It is simply a means to an end, which not to use would be decidedly irrational: 'How can a developed murderer not murder, if he needs money!' (D, 420). The same nonchalance is shown by Alyosha Karamazov's fellow seminarian Ratikin in *The Brothers Karamazov*. He has no doubt, neither in his mind nor in his heart, that 'everything is permitted to the intelligent man' (BK, 589). Verkhovensky and Ratikin, who have no thirst for life but only for destruction, are the devils in Dostoyevsky's world. They have nothing that might eventually redeem them. They are lost for good. Raskolnikov, on the other hand, is not. Nor is Alyosha's impulsive brother Dmitry, who despite being innocent of his father's murder is quite capable of killing someone out of rage or jealousy. Fortunately for him, although he thinks that Ratikin makes a lot of sense, he is not much of a thinker and pretty much immune to theoretical constructs. He just loves life a little too much or too impetuously for his own good. The third brother Karamazov, Ivan, is much more susceptible to the lure of nihilism, but he, too, loves life. He accepts, theoretically, that there is no God and no virtue, and that, in consequence, everything is permitted. Nihilism has reason on its side. But there is more to Ivan than just reason, as he finds out to his own detriment when his father is killed by Smerdyakov. Clearly, the old Karamazov is just another useless and harmful presence, like the pawnbroker in *Crime and Punishment*, another louse who sits on his money. To rob and kill him would therefore be rationally justified. That is what Ivan believes, or professes to believe, but when Smerdyakov acts on this theory and batters the old Karamazov to death, Ivan instinctively reacts with shock and dismay and is eventually destroyed by an overwhelming feeling of guilt, knowing he had let this happen and may even have encouraged it. Ivan can see no convincing reason to love life and to take the usual moral constraints seriously, but to his confusion he finds that he does so anyway. This alone lifts him high above the Verkhovenskys and Ratikins, the pure rationalists, those who really believe, not only with their rational minds, but with their heart and soul, that nothing matters. They have thought themselves out of our shared world. In contrast, both Ivan and Raskolnikov know or come to realize that life is precious. Raskolnikov remembers having read somewhere[1]

about a man condemned to death saying or thinking, an hour before his death, that if he had to live somewhere high up on a Cliffside, on a ledge so narrow that there was room only for his two feet – and with the abyss, the ocean, eternal darkness, eternal solitude, eternal storm all around him – and had to stay like that, on a square foot of space, an entire lifetime, a thousand years, an eternity – it would be better to live so than to die right now! Only to live, to live, to live! To live, no matter how – only to live! (CP, 158)

Ivan, too, explicitly acknowledges his own love of life:

Though I do not believe in the order of things, still the sticky little leaves that come out in the spring are dear to me, the blue sky is dear to me, some people are dear to me, whom one loves sometimes ... without even knowing why; some human deeds are dear to me, which one has perhaps long ceased believing in, but still honors with one's heart, out of old habit. (BK, 230)

It is not rational, but one does it nonetheless. Out of habit. You love those things with your guts, not with your mind, not with logic. Ivan wants to listen to his reason which tells him that nothing matters. But his heart or his guts tell him otherwise. The question is which trumps which? Which is the source of truth? It is pretty clear that, when it comes to the last questions, Dostoyevsky favours guts over reason. As long as you love life you are not completely lost. It is in fact the best starting point on the road to a meaningful life, which is precisely a life in which we are not lice to each other, but human beings, or persons proper.

Two times two makes five

Dostoyevsky was convinced that the love of life, and indeed life itself, was threatened by the prevalent philosophy of his day that had swept to Russia from the West in the wake of the Enlightenment: an unholy mix of atheism and utilitarianism, materialism and scientism, rational egoism and determinism that, when widely adopted and taken for granted, makes nihilists out of all of us. In *Notes from Underground* he has his Underground Man launch a furious attack on precisely that philosophy:

Once it's proved to you ... that you descended from an ape, there's no use making a wry face, just take it for what it is. Once it's proved to you that, essentially speaking, one little drop of your own fat should be dearer to you than a hundred thousand of your fellow men, and that in this result all so-called virtues and obligations and other ravings and prejudices will finally be resolved, go ahead and accept it, there's nothing to be done, because two times two is – mathematics. Try objecting to that. (NU, 14)

It is difficult to object because it all seems so eminently sensible. This kind of philosophy also promises a certain liberation, which makes it even more attractive. It makes life easier because it takes responsibility for our actions and our being away from us, so that we are no longer answerable for what we do and are. The Underground Man, however, refuses to accept that. He chooses to rebel against the spirit of the age, insisting that this new way of thinking and the resulting practical orientation rests on and promulgates a serious misunderstanding of what really matters in life. Human profit, he insists, is more than just 'prosperity, wealth, freedom, peace, and so on and so forth' (NU, 21). There

may well exist something that is dearer for almost every man than his very best profit, or (so as not to violate logic) that there is this one most profitable profit ..., which is chiefer and more profitable than all other profits, and for which man is ready, if need be, to go against all laws, that is, against reason, honor, peace, prosperity – in short, against all these beautiful and useful things – only so as to attain this primary, most profitable profit which is dearer to him than anything else. (NU, 22)

That which is missing from the equation, that most profitable thing, the Underground Man calls 'wanting'. It is far superior to our reasoning because it reaches deep down into our being and defines what we are, whereas reason touches only the surface. Reason

is a fine thing, that is unquestionable, but reason is only reason and satisfies only man's reasoning capacity, while wanting is a manifestation of the whole of life – that is, the whole of human life, including reason and various little itches. And though our life in this manifestation often turns out to be a bit of trash, still it is life and not just the extraction of a square root. (NU, 27)

The Underground Man demands and defends our right to wish for ourselves what we want, be it smart or not. Call it a right to be stupid. To have this right, to be allowed to make one's own mistakes and to live one's life as one sees fit, *that* is the most profitable thing: 'It may be more profitable than all other profits even in the case when it is obviously harmful and contradicts the most sensible conclusion of our reason concerning profits – because in any event it preserves for us the chiefest and dearest thing, that is, our personality and our individuality' (NU, 28). Because the impulse, that will to life and life of the will, is so strong in us, it will always find ways to express itself. Human nature refuses to be completely rationalized, even if that means foregoing perfect happiness. Ultimately we want more than happiness anyway. If there is nothing more in our lives than that, we will try to break out and ruin things, just for the hell of it. We are not made for socialist utopias.

> Shower him with all earthly blessings, drown him in happiness completely, over his head, so that only bubbles pop up on the surface of happiness, as on water; give him such economic satisfaction that he no longer has anything left to do at all except sleep, eat gingerbread, and worry about the noncessation of world history – and it is here, just here, that he, this man ... will do something nasty. He will even risk his gingerbread, and wish on purpose for the most pernicious nonsense, the most noneconomical meaninglessness, ... with the sole purpose of confirming to himself ... that human beings are still human beings and not piano keys. (NU, 29)

That is in fact what the whole human enterprise consists in: the self-assertion of the human as a human. The goal is less important than the process of getting there:

> Perhaps the whole goal mankind strives for on earth consists just in this ceaselessness of the process of achievement alone, that is to say, in life itself, and not essentially in the goal, which, of course is bound to be nothing other than two times two is four – that is, a formula; and two times two is four is no longer life, gentlemen, but the beginning of death. (NU, 32)

Human beings are 'comically arranged': we like achieving, but not having achieved. Two times two is four may be an excellent thing, but 'two times two is five is sometimes also a most charming little thing' (NU, 32). Well-being is not the only thing we need and love. We also, occasionally, need to suffer, because suffering is doubt, negation, destruction and chaos, and as such 'the sole cause of consciousness'. Perfection is not for us, nor is it desirable. The Crystal Palace, that glass-and-steel monstrosity of a building erected in London to house the Great Exhibition of 1851, the emblem of the industrial revolution, meant to be 'forever indestructible', is (for the Underground Man as well as for Dostoyevsky himself) a symbol of a diseased age and a false philosophy. It is something to be afraid of. For the Underground Man it is still only a chicken coop. Because there is more in life and to life than commercial gain and the comforts that come with it, perhaps a crystal palace of a different kind. The real-world Crystal Palace is a symbol of spiritual death. We have grown so unaccustomed to life that 'at times we feel a sort of loathing for real "living life", and therefore cannot bear to be reminded of it' (NU, 118). We get confused with nobody telling us what to do. We no longer know 'what to love and what to hate, what to respect and what to despise' (NU, 119), ashamed of our humanity, our bodies, our passions. We are stillborn, and like it so.

The gist of the Underground Man's tirade against the commercialization and rationalization, and resulting suffocation, of life is echoed, in *Crime and Punishment*, by Raskolnikov's much more sympathetic, loyal and compassionate friend Razumikhin, who accuses the utopian socialists of his day of ignoring nature and of disliking

the *living* process of life, ... the *living soul*! The living soul will demand life, the living soul won't listen to mechanics, the living soul is suspicious, the living soul is retrograde! While here, though there may be a whiff of carrion, and it may all be made out of rubber – still it's not alive, still it has no will, still it's slavish, it won't rebel! And it turns out in the end that they've reduced everything to mere brickwork and the layout of corridors and room in a phalanstery! The phalanstery may be all ready, but your nature isn't ready for the phalanstery, it wants life, it hasn't completed the life process yet, it's too soon for the cemetery! You can't overlap nature with logic alone! Logic will presuppose three cases, when there are a million of them! Cut away the whole million, and reduce everything to the one question of comfort! (CP, 257)

Yet as much as we crave for life, we are also afraid of it. It is, after all, easier, less risky, not to live. The question is what we want more: security or freedom. Or more importantly, what we *need* more. This question is at the heart of the Grand Inquisitor's soliloquy in *The Brothers Karamazov*. Addressing an attentive, but silent Christ, the Grand Inquisitor tries to convince him (and himself) that Christ's offer of freedom to the people has always been and will always be meaningless. People do not want freedom, he claims. They want to be fed. Since you cannot have both, freedom and bread, people will in the end always choose bread and welcome slavery as a price well worth paying. And if mere existence is not enough for them, then give them a purpose, something to live for. Tell them what is good and what is evil. Give them miracle, mystery and authority (BK, 255); that is all they need. Christ's mistake is that he thirsts for a love that is free. Yet what people truly want is someone who leads them like sheep. And that is exactly what the Catholic Church is giving them, which is to everyone's advantage: 'With us everyone will be happy, and they will no longer rebel or destroy each other, as in your freedom, everywhere. Oh, we shall convince them that they will only become free when they resign their freedom to us, and submit to us' (BK, 258). Although this is all done in the name of Christ, the Grand Inquisitor knows very well that the church has a long time ago turned its back on Christ and his vision of a community united in love for life and for each other: they have instead aligned with the devil (who, as we know from Ivan's dream, is nothing if not a very sensible, level-headed, two-plus-two-makes-four type of gentleman).

Corpses everywhere

What Dostoyevsky's Christ wants (and exemplifies) is a love freely given, an unselfish love, a love that expects no reward, a concrete and personal love for everything and everyone alive, or in a word a very uneconomical kind of love. The Grand Inquisitor denies that humans are capable of such love. His doubts are shared by several others of Dostoyevsky's characters. In *The Idiot*, Grushenka wonders whether one can 'love everyone, all people, all one's neighbors', but she already knows the answer: 'Of course not, and it is even unnatural. In an abstract love for mankind, one almost always loves oneself' (I, 454). Ivan Karamazov has similar concerns: 'I never could understand how it's possible to love one's neighbors. In my opinion, it is precisely one's neighbors that one cannot possibly love' (BK, 236). We may be capable of loving people in the abstract, but as soon as we get to know them individually, love usually disappears very quickly. Love is in fact only possible from a distance. Christ's love is therefore not for people. It is impossible for us to love like that because we are closed to each other: none of us can possibly understand what and how much the other suffers.

When the Grand Inquisitor makes this point, Christ hears him out, patiently, silently. He does not object, but it is clear he does not agree with the Grand Inquisitor. Nor does Dostoyevsky. Such love may be difficult to achieve for us, but that does not necessarily mean it is impossible. Traces of such love can, after all, be found in most of us. And no one ever said it was easy. Raskolnikov, in *Crime and Punishment*, seems to get there in the end, but it takes him a long time and lot of suffering. Both Sonya and the police inspector Porfiry urge him to redeem himself by confessing and willingly accepting punishment for his crime. They know that redemption requires suffering (CP, 420). They advise him to find faith, suffer, give himself to life, stop reasoning (CP, 460). Raskolnikov resists. Almost right to the very end of the novel he tries to hold on to the belief that he only killed a louse and committed no crime. Why should he suffer, he asks. He may have shed blood, but blood is shed every day in torrents. It is spilled 'like champagne' (CP, 518). In the grand scheme of things it does not matter. Even in Siberia his suffering and punishment appears needless and meaningless to him, and he still shows no sign of repentance (CP, 543). Sonya, meanwhile, is kind and caring to everyone, acknowledging their suffering and suffering with them, and all prisoners love her. Only after Raskolnikov falls ill and in a kind of feverish delirium has a dream in which humanity goes completely mad and enters a path of self-destruction, he is suddenly – 'as if something lifted him and flung him down at her feet' (CP, 549) – overcome by love for Sonya, and it is that newly discovered love that now promises 'the dawn of a renewed future, of a complete resurrection into a new life' (CP, 549).

If it seems to us that nothing matters, it is because we have forgotten how to love. We think too much, and live and love too little. Because we are unable to understand each other, we spend our lives in intense loneliness. When we actually connect, we do so only for a moment, then quickly drift away again. In Dostoyevsky's stories, love is constantly sought, but never quite found, and when it is found it is not kept. There is no happily ever after. Love remains fragile, doubtful, in flux. Romantic relations between the sexes are full of misunderstandings, marred by mistrust. Betrayals are normal. Symptomatic is the Underground Man who cannot relate to the prostitute Liza, pushes her away, humiliates her, incapable of loving her. 'I was no longer able to love, because, I repeat, for me to love meant to tyrannize and to preponderize morally' (NU, 115). Love is routinely misconstrued as a struggle, born in hate, aiming at subjugation of the other who, once subjugated, is gone forever. The Underground Man is scared of real love, scared of life, and he strongly suggests that these days we all are. We all live underground.

One of Dostoyevsky's short stories, 'A Gentle Creature' (also known as 'The Meek One') (1876), is about a man's inability to relate to his wife. He is forty-one, she is sixteen. She marries him because she has no other options, and he knows it. In contrast with what the story's title suggests, she is not meek, but rather independent, having her own ideas, her own 'wanting'. She is also trusting, ready to love him, open, passionate too. He, however, is essentially a bully (who, it is hinted, has been bullied himself and now takes revenge on the world). He shuts her down, blocks her attempts to relate, demands 'total respect', wants her to be submissive and obedient, relishing the thought of her humiliation, relishing his power over her. He discourages talk, prefers silence. She tries to break through the walls he erects, but he enjoys his power too much. After a while she gives up trying, distances herself from him. Eventually she jumps out of the window, killing herself, just after he finally, and too late, opened up to her. Another suicide, another wasted life. Or more precisely two wasted lives, for the husband too is as good as dead or might just as well be. 'Oh, nature!' he laments in conclusion of his narrative,

People on earth are alone, that is the calamity of it! 'Is anyone alive on the plain?' shouts the old Russian hero, and no one responds. They say the sun animates the universe. The sun will rise and look at it – is it not a corpse? Everything is dead and corpses are everywhere. Only people exist and around them is silence – that is what the earth is! (GC, 103)

The unnamed man's despair is a reflection of an empty, meaningless world. Or perhaps it is the other way around. The world might look different if people loved one another, but the problem is to find a way to do so. One must somehow rediscover the ability to love. Without love nothing means anything.

In an earlier story, 'White Nights' (1848), the young narrator had been 'living in Petersburg for eight years and had barely managed to make a single acquaintance' (WN, 3). He meets a woman, Nastenka, falls madly in love with her. Suddenly there is some contact to another human being, or the illusion of such contact, and with it comes the terror of its passing, of the loneliness to come, 'that musty, pointless existence' (WN, 25). Life passes quickly, he muses. One day we will be old and ask ourselves what we have done with our lives. Dreams fade. One should live, not dream about living. 'Look', he tells Nastenka, 'how cold the world is becoming. The years will pass, and after them will come grim loneliness, and old age, quaking on its stick, and after them misery and despair. ... Will it not be miserable to be left alone, utterly alone, and have nothing even to regret – nothing, not a single thing ...' (WN, 27). But the young man hopes in vain that Nastenka will put an end to his loneliness and help him live. She runs off with another. When he gets home, he looks around, and everything looks old, even his room:

The walls and floor had faded, everything had grown dingy; there were more cobwebs than ever. I don't know why, but when I glanced out of the window, it seemed that the house opposite had also grown decrepit and dingy, the stucco on the columns peeling and dropping off, the cornices darkened and cracked, the dark-ochre walls patchy and mottled. ... Either a darting ray of sunshine had suddenly vanished behind a rain-cloud and rendered everything dull before my eyes, or perhaps the entire perspective of my future had flashed before me, so miserable and uninviting, and I saw myself just as I was now, fifteen years on, growing old, in the same room, alone. (WN, 56)

This theme is taken up again in the late story 'The Dream of a Ridiculous Man' (1877). The once again unnamed narrator describes how he has lately begun to feel that nothing matters. 'All of a sudden, I realized that it would not matter to me whether the world existed or whether there was nothing at all anywhere' (DRM, 108). In the wake of this feeling, other people have become almost invisible to him. Not even his own life now has any importance for him. So he decides to go home and shoot himself. On the way there, however, he meets a desperate, terrified little girl on the streets, crying for her mummy. He ignores her, even though she pleads with him to help her, then chases her away. When he gets home he remembers the girl and puts off killing himself. He notices that even though he is still indifferent, he feels some kind of pain, almost like a bodily pain, thinking of her. He realizes that he must be pitying her after all, almost in spite of himself, realizing that he feels shame for not helping her, without being able to understand how that is possible. How 'can it be that awareness of my imminent absolute extinction and the consequence that nothing will exist has not had the slightest influence either on my feeling of pity for the little girl, or my shame at a mean-spirited action?' (DRM, 112). His spontaneous emotional reaction strikes him as odd because it seems to him that the girl won't even exist when he is dead.[2]

> I will shoot myself and the world will cease to exist, at least for me. Not to mention that perhaps nothing will exist for anyone after me, and the whole world, as soon as my consciousness is extinguished, will pass away like a phantom, as an attribute of my consciousness, and will abolish itself, since perhaps all this world and all these people – are but my own self. (DRM, 113)

The Ridiculous Man then falls asleep and dreams. In his dream, he shoots himself – not in the head, as he had planned, but in the heart. He is buried. A mysterious creature appears and takes him right into space and then to a twin earth in a parallel world populated by happy people, as they must have been before the fall: sinless, beautiful, full of love. It is a paradise. 'They desired nothing and were serene, they did not strive for a knowledge of life, as we do, because for them life was complete in itself' (DRM, 119). Yet clearly they are in possession of a higher knowledge: how to live without science. And they all love each other. 'It was a kind of mutual love affair, complete and universal' (DRM, 120), which is exactly the kind of thing we all secretly long for. The Ridiculous Man is happy. After a while, however, he unwittingly corrupts them with his talk or perhaps his mere presence. 'They learned how to lie, and grew to love lying and perceive its beauty' (DRM, 123). Lechery, jealousy and cruelty follow; then come grief, suffering, science, hypocrisy, rationalization and institutionalized religion. They start to believe (falsely, it is implied) that 'knowledge is superior to emotion, cognition of life superior to life' (DRM, 124). When the Ridiculous Man tells them that this is all his fault and demands that he be crucified as a punishment for his crime, they don't believe him and eventually banish him. The dream ends.

When the Ridiculous Man wakes up, he finds that he no longer wants to shoot himself. He is not unhappy. On the contrary. Suddenly he is hungry for life. He wants to preach the truth: 'That people can be beautiful and happy, without losing their ability to live on earth' (DRM, 127). Evil, he knows now, is not the normal condition of man. We *can* be different. 'The chief thing is to love others as oneself' (DRM, 128). The story ends fittingly with a declaration of his resolve to go and help the little girl he had met earlier. The Ridiculous Man has begun to live.

So many beautiful things

What the Ridiculous Man has learnt from his dream is a new, healthier attitude towards life that we find most clearly articulated in the teachings of the Elder Zosima in *The Brothers Karamazov*. The period of human isolation must end, Zosima urges. 'For everyone now strives most of all to separate his person, wishing to experience the fullness of life within himself, and yet what comes of all his efforts is not the fullness of life but full suicide ' (BK, 303). We hide from each other, push each other away, all to stay safe. But this is unnatural (and actually not safe at all). It deprives us of a full enjoyment of life: 'Look at the divine gifts around us: the clear sky, the fresh air, the tender grass, the birds, nature is beautiful and sinless, and we, we alone, are godless and foolish, and do not understand that life is paradise' (BK, 299). Paradise is in fact hidden inside us; we just need to access it. We need to be humble and understand that everyone is guilty before everyone else:

> Brothers, do not be afraid of men's sin, love man also in his sin, for this likeness of God's love is the height of love on earth. Love all of God's creation, both the whole of it and every grain of sand. Love animals, love plants, love each thing. If you love each thing, you will perceive the mystery of God in things. (BK, 319)

An inner change is required, a practical acknowledgement of the brotherhood of all men. We will then regain the Kingdom of Heaven, for what we have now is actually a form of hell. Hell, for Zosima (and Dostoyevsky), is 'the suffering of being no longer able to love' (BK, 322). Yet such a spiritual revolution will take time. This is why the world needs holy fools to set an example (BK, 304).

Alyosha Karamazov is such a holy fool. Prince Myshkin, in *The Idiot*, is another. Myshkin is an idiot in the eyes of society because he does not care about what is commonly thought to be profitable, nor does he care very much about himself. He, too, is a ridiculous man, someone who is so good that you cannot help laughing about him. For Dostoyevsky, however, he is, for this very reason, 'a positively beautiful man' (I, xv). Myshkin tries to live up to the ideal that the Grand Inquisitor attributes to Christ. Love, for him, is essentially universal compassion (which explains Dostoyevsky's frequent allusions to the importance of suffering), and compassion 'is the chief and perhaps the only law of being for all mankind' (I, 230). It alone gives meaning and understanding to our lives. Like Zosima, the prince believes that everyone is able to be happy:

> You know, I don't understand how it's possible to pass by a tree and not be happy to see it. To talk with a man and not be happy that you love him! … There are so many things at every step that are so beautiful, that even the most confused person finds beautiful. Look at a child, look at God's sunrise, look at the grass growing, look into the eyes that are looking at you and love you.' (I, 553)

Of course people do not always appear loveworthy. Sometimes they do terrible things. That is what makes it so difficult to love them in the first place. But precisely for that reason love, qua compassion, is so urgently needed. It is a key to the hidden goodness in people, the core of innocence that, as Dostoyevsky himself learnt during the years that he spent imprisoned in a Siberian labour camp,[3] can often be found even in the worst criminals. Grushenka, the love interest of both Dmitri Karamazov and his father Fyodor, understands this very well, despite being slightly confused about it: 'Everyone in the world is good, every one of them. The world is a good place. We may be bad, but the world is a good place. We're bad and good, both bad and good' (BK, 440). Dmitri Karamazov makes the same point later in the book, after having a nightmare about a desolate world, full of starving people. There are, he says, little children and big children, for even the grown-ups are like children. We are all dependent, vulnerable, afraid and hungry for love. 'All people are "wee ones"' (BK, 591).

Alyosha Karamazov, being the holy fool that he is, is hoping that one day the world will be such that all will love one another (BK, 31). In order for this to become possible, some of us have to make a start by practising active, completely selfless love. Such love is not love for humankind in general (which is a mere abstraction) but love for individual people. It is easy to love humanity, Alyosha knows, but difficult to consistently love individual people (BK, 57). In fact, these two kinds of love often stand in the way of each other: the more we love humanity, the less we love individual people. Active love is 'a harsh and fearful thing' (BK, 58). It is not flashy, not quick. It requires patience. What it does not require is prior religious faith. Alyosha believes in the immortality of the soul, but it is not such belief that motivates and grounds active love. Rather, it is the other way around: when we practice active love we will soon find it impossible not to believe in God and immortality. Active love erases all religious doubt, Alyosha claims. 'This has been tested. It is certain' (BK, 56). But is it really?

Spiders in all the corners

Dostoyevsky's proof of the existence of God (and by extension, human immortality) relies on the authority of our experience of the love we feel for the world in general and for our fellow beings in particular (as well as guilt and remorse, which are, however, mere reflections of that love). The reasoning is deceptively simple: if God does not exist, then nothing matters. But things *do* matter (to us). Therefore God must exist. Dostoyevsky knows, however, that from a rational point of view nothing is ever certain. The fact remains that we don't really *know* what will happen to us after death and whether there really is a divine force in the universe that cares and works towards the good. For all we know, death will be the end of us and all our aspirations. Or perhaps there will be an afterlife, but one that is very different from the way we like to imagine it, like the one that the enigmatic Svidrigailov, in *Crime and Punishment*, comes up with: 'We keep imagining eternity as an idea that cannot be grasped, something vast, vast! But why must it be vast? Instead of all that, imagine suddenly that there will be one little room there, something like a village bathhouse, covered with soot, with spiders in all the corners, and that's the whole of eternity' (CP, 289). When Raskolinov objects that he must surely be able to imagine something more *just* than that, Svidrigailov replies, even more alarmingly, that perhaps such an eternity *is* just for creatures such as us.

It is also possible that as a matter of fact the universe is *not* just. Looking at all the terrible things that are frequently happening in the world, we certainly have little reason to believe in a just world order. Dostoyevsky is keenly aware of the many injustices that life holds in store for us and, to his eternal credit, makes no attempt to sweep this rather inconvenient fact under the rug. His 'positively beautiful man', Prince Myshkin, the hope of humankind, ends up in an asylum for the mentally insane, unresponsive and apparently deranged. And although Alyosha Karamazov survives in *The Brothers Karamazov* unharmed, he may well have suffered an inglorious end in the sequel that Dostoyevsky had planned before his death. Apparently he told the publisher and journalist Aleksei Suvorin that in that sequel Alyosha would become an anarchist and kill the Tsar (Frank, 917–8). Be that as it may, it is clear that life, for Dostoyevsky, is seldom fair. The apparent arbitrariness of death contributes to this unfairness. In *The Idiot*, the young nihilist Ippolit Terentyev is dying from consumption. He knows he has got at best only weeks to live, and he is full of envy for those who will outlive him. It is not worth living only for a few weeks, he feels, so why start anything? And he wonders why others do not make more of the vast amount of time allocated to them. It is their fault if they don't know how to live. 'If he's alive, everything is in his power!' (I, 393). Health is all you need, he now thinks. 'The point

is in life, in life alone – in discovering it, constantly and eternally'
(I, 394). This is certainly a sentiment that Dostoyevsky would agree
with. Ippolit also realizes the opportunities for active love that life
provides and the rewards that such love promises:

> In sowing your seed, in sowing your 'charity', your good deed in
> whatever form it takes, you give away part of your person and
> receive into yourself part of another's; you mutually commune
> in each other; a little more attention, and you will be rewarded
> with knowledge, with the most unexpected discoveries. ... On
> the other hand, all your thoughts, all the seeds you have sown,
> which you may have already forgotten, will take on flesh and
> grow, what was received from you will be passed on to someone
> else. (I, 404–5)

And yet, the prospect of his imminent death overshadows everything.
It is powerful enough to deprive life of all meaning. When Ippolit
sees, for the first time, a copy of the younger Holbein's painting
Dead Christ, he is as shocked as Dostoyevsky himself was when he
saw the original in the Basel Museum in 1867.[4] The painting opens
Ippolit's eyes and mind to how terrible a thing death really is, and
makes him wonder how it can possibly be overcome if not even
Jesus Christ could overcome it. 'Nature appears to the viewer of
this painting in the shape of some enormous, implacable, and dumb
beast, or, to put it more correctly ..., in the shape of some huge
machine of the most modern construction, which has senselessly
seized, crushed, and swallowed up, blankly and unfeelingly, a great
and priceless being' (I, 408). In the wake of this experience, he now
pictures the all-powerful being that supposedly rules the world as
'some huge and repulsive tarantula' (I, 409).

But the challenge to the belief in a meaningful order of the
universe does not end here. Now that the death sentence has been
pronounced, Ippolit wants to get it over with. Why wait for the
end? Even if God is not a tarantula, even if there is somehow,
somewhere, a good reason for all of this, the injustice of having to
die when everything else lives on does not go away. So why should
he not be angry, why is he expected to love that which kills him?

> Why is my humility needed here? Isn't it possible simply to eat
> me, without demanding that I praise that which has eaten me?

Can it be that someone there will indeed be offended that I don't want to wait for two weeks? I don't believe it; and it would be much more likely to suppose that my insignificant life, the life of an atom, was simply needed for the fulfilment of some universal harmony as a whole, for some contrast, and so on and so forth. So be it! (I, 414)

The problem is that even if everything has indeed been carefully arranged by some higher power and everything that happens is necessary for some good, the fact that we have no understanding of that arrangement and those goods is sufficient grounds to reject it. If we do not understand it, and indeed *cannot* understand it because it simply transcends human understanding, how can we be asked to answer for not understanding and therefore not accepting it? Perhaps, reasons Ippolit, there is a future life and providence, but if it is impossible to understand, then he does not want this life. Under the circumstance, suicide seems the only action left for him to exercise his own free will. 'If it had been in my power not to be born, I probably would not have accepted existence on such derisive conditions. But I still have the power to die, though I'm giving back what's already numbered' (I, 414).

Ippolit's rebellion against the existing world order is taken up even more powerfully by Ivan Karamazov. Ivan is happy to concede to the believer that perhaps God exists, perhaps immortality exists, perhaps God is wise and good and perhaps there is eternal harmony. For it is not God that he does not accept, but the world he supposedly has created. Even if it all ends well, all the suffering in the world is still real and it will have *been* real whatever the end will look like. Ivan lists all the horrible things that people do to each other, even to children, also to animals and generally the helpless, the defenceless, the vulnerable. All evidence suggests that humans just *love* to torture children (BK, 241). Man has created the devil in his own image and likeness (BK, 239). And for what? What is it good for, this freedom to do evil? Perhaps it is good for something, but whatever that may be, the price is in any case too high if it requires the suffering of children: 'If everyone must suffer, in order to buy eternal harmony with their suffering, pray tell me what have the children got to do with it?' (BK, 244). A higher harmony and universal forgiveness that is bought with a child's suffering is simply obnoxious. Even if evil will be punished, that is not enough. Redemption is not possible under the circumstances: 'What do I care if they are avenged, what do I care if the tormentors are in hell, what can hell set right here, if these ones have already been tormented?' (BK, 445). Because Ivan is not willing to pay the price for admission (to the Kingdom of Heaven), he returns his ticket. Alyosha tries to argue with Ivan, but he knows that it is not possible. Ivan's argument is simply too powerful. In the end even Alyosha has to agree that if eternal peace and happiness could be bought with the suffering of 'one tiny creature', this would have to be rejected (BK, 245).[5]

CHAPTER FIVE

The inevitable end of everything
Leo Tolstoy (1828–1910)

How to live?

By all accounts, Tolstoy's life was not a particularly happy one. That it was not, had nothing or little to do with the circumstances of his life. He was born into Russian nobility, and although he lost his parents early on, he and his siblings were raised by an aunt in an apparently loving and sheltered environment. Once grown up, he enjoyed from his inherited wealth and income a lavish lifestyle (indulging in a lot of drinking, gambling and whoring in his twenties and early thirties). He lived a long and healthy life. He found a good, loving wife who bore him thirteen children (a few of which died in infancy, but that was normal at the time), assisted him with his work and loyally stayed with him until his death (which cannot have been easy). As a novelist he was immensely successful, and as a political, social and religious reformer he was, towards the end of his life, known and respected the world over. People adored him so much that he was virtually untouchable by the authorities. When he died, at eighty-two, he was mourned by millions. Tolstoy had it all. But happy he was not. It seems that all his life he had been desperately looking for something that he never found. He was haunted by the persistent feeling that everything he did, all his achievements and successes, ultimately did not matter much, if anything at all. That nothing he did was really good enough. That *he* was not good enough. That he was betting on the wrong horse. That something essential was missing. The problem, which kept him occupied throughout his long life, was to figure out what exactly it was that was missing, in the hope of then being able to correct his way of living accordingly.

Already as a young man, Tolstoy was looking for an aim, a purpose in life, but he also knew that you cannot just *give* yourself an aim. You need to find one, one that is *worth* pursuing. It cannot be just any aim; it needs to be the *right* one. Unfortunately for Tolstoy, such an aim proved rather difficult to find. The young Tolstoy was worried about his immortal soul, and resolved to develop all his faculties to perfection. He wanted to become better. Yet he did not quite know what becoming better would consist in, nor was he very good at following his own precepts. So he drifted about rather aimlessly, quitting his university studies prematurely without a degree and spending much of his time seeking sexual gratification and doing his best to gamble his wealth away. Such a life may have been empty and shallow, but then again, he lacked a good reason to seek a different life. After all, what more *was* there to life? Well, it turned out that he could write rather well, but when he did and gained recognition for it, although his life certainly became outwardly more respectable, at least intellectually (which means that it was easier for him to see himself as doing something important and worth-while), he eventually came to realize that fundamentally nothing had changed and that he was still no closer to living a life that really mattered. In a way he was even worse off than before, because not only did he still not know the 'answer to the most basic question of life – what is good and what is evil'; he even, for a time, failed to notice that the answer was still missing (C, 10). The life of a successful novelist may be more rewarding and more respectable than the life of a rich idler, but in the end it is equally pointless, not the least because it will also, no matter what, end in death.

The dragon of death, waiting to tear us to pieces

For Tolstoy, the reality and inevitability of death threatens to make life and all that comes with it utterly pointless. It also makes it particularly urgent to find an answer to the question how to live. When Pierre Bezukhov, in *War and Peace* (1869), echoes Tolstoy's own preoccupation with life's meaning and purpose, he immediately connects the question to his own mortality:

> 'What's bad and what's good? What should we love and what should we hate? What is life for, and what am I? What is life? What is death? What kind of force is it that directs everything?' he kept asking himself. And there were no answers to any of those questions, except one illogical response that didn't answer any of them. And that response was: 'You're going to die and you'll either come to know everything or stop asking.' But dying was horrible too. ... 'Death, the end of everything, and it must come today or tomorrow, either way it's a split second on the scale of eternity.' (WP, 375)

Death, when it comes, may provide the answer to the big questions of life, but if it does (which is by no means certain), then it will be too late. Too late to change anything about the way we live. We need an answer now, to give direction to our life. That answer, however, death cannot give us, whatever it may turn out to be. Death is the end of everything, in the sense that death ends our existence, but what makes it so horrible is that it may also be the end of life in the sense of being its sole purpose. Perhaps we do not just live and then die; we may actually live *in order to* die. Perhaps that is all there is to it. In any case, the fact that we have to die someday cannot but make us wonder why we bother with living in the first place. Since it will all be over very soon, it would not make much difference if it were over already. Life is so short that it could just as well not be at all. Death is the ultimate reality, and life, being forever in its dark shadow, is only a 'stupid and evil joke' (C, 20). 'Today or tomorrow', writes Tolstoy in *A Confession* (1882),

> sickness and death will come ... to those dear to me, and to myself, and nothing will remain other than the stench and the worms. Sooner or later my deeds, whatever they may have been, will be forgotten and will no longer exist. What is all the fuss about then? How can a person carry on living and fail to perceive this? That is what is so astonishing! It is only possible to go on living while you are intoxicated with life, once sober it

is impossible not to see that it is all a mere trick, and a stupid trick! (C, 21)

Life, for the mature Tolstoy, is the great deceiver. Death is the truth that life with its attractions tries to hide from us. But if we look hard enough, we will realize that it is all a sham. In truth, our situation is, according to Tolstoy, not much different from that described in a certain Eastern fable: a traveller on the steppes, trying to escape from a wild beast, hides in an empty well, only to discover that at the bottom of the well there is a dragon with his jaws wide open waiting to devour him.[1] He cannot get out because the beast[2] is waiting for him. So he hangs on to a branch that grows from the well's wall, fully aware that he cannot hang on to it forever and that eventually he will have to let go. What makes this outcome even more certain is that two mice – one white, one black – are already gnawing away at the branch, so that sooner or later the branch will no longer hold his weight, break and let him fall into the dragon's wide open jaw. The traveller cannot do anything about it. He can only, helplessly, watch it happen. The only solace he has is provided by two drops of honey on the branch, which he can lick. They are sweet and nourishing, and for a while he forgets all about the beast and the dragon, and just enjoys the taste of the honey. However, in the end he must admit to himself that those two drops of honey, sweet as they are, don't change anything about the hopelessness of his situation, and they cease to make him feel better. 'In the same way', Tolstoy explains, 'I am clinging to the tree of life, knowing full well that the dragon of death inevitably awaits me, ready to tear me to pieces. ... Those two drops of honey, which more than all else has diverted my eyes from the cruel truth, my love for my family and for my writing, which I called art – I no longer found sweet' (C, 22).

Although death, and the horror of death, is already very much present in his first great novel, *War and Peace*, it was only after he had finished and published it that he fully realized how devastating it actually is, or should be, that we all have to die. In 1869, in his fortieth year, he fell into a deep depression. The fact that he studied Schopenhauer that summer may have contributed to it.[3] That death was bad and inexplicable he had known all along. But death was only bad because it ended life, and life was precious. Contemplating death threw the preciousness of life into stark relief. Mostly, it heightened our appreciation of life, which is not altogether a bad thing. Now, however, Tolstoy felt very strongly that the prospect of inevitable death actually made it impossible to live: that the nothingness to come reduced everything else to nothingness as well, so that there was no good reason to postpone death and the arrival of nothingness. 'To deceive oneself is pointless. All is vanity. Happy is he who was never born. Death is better than life; one must free oneself from it' (C, 43). Suicide is the only logical conclusion if there is no point to anything. For a while, Tolstoy seems to have seriously considered taking his own life. Clear traces (or memories) of this pessimistic outlook can still be found in Tolstoy's second great novel, *Anna Karenina* (1878) (whose title character Anna, as we all know, kills herself towards the end of the novel, although it is not entirely clear why). When Konstantin Levin, who, like Pierre Bezukhov in *War and Peace* (and Dmitri Nekhlyudov in *Resurrection*), functions as Tolstoy's alter ego (and who is actually the main character in *Anna Karenina*), is waiting for his brother Nikolai to die, his thoughts are naturally drawn towards death, its nature and its significance. His conclusion is bleak indeed:

> Death, the inevitable end of everything, presented itself to him for the first time with irresistible force. And this death, which here, in his beloved brother, moaning in his sleep and calling by habit, without distinction, now on God, now on the devil, was not at all as far off as it had seemed to him before. It was in him, too – he felt it. If not now, then tomorrow, if not tomorrow, then in thirty years – did it make any difference? And what this inevitable death was, he not only did not know, he not only had never thought of it, but he could not and dared not think of it. ... But the more he strained to think, the clearer it became to him that ... he had actually forgotten ... one small circumstance – that death would come and everything would end, that it was not worth starting anything and that nothing could possibly be done about it. Yes, it was terrible, but it was so. (AK, 348)

Apparently, the time of death makes no difference. It is the *fact* of death that matters: the fact that it *will* come, no matter what. Because of this, nothing is even worth starting. Why start what must end, why bring into existence what must perish? Levin is also struck by the contrast between his brother's present state – his frail, wasted, collapsing body – and the way he remembers him when they were both still young: so full of strength and joy, so full of life. All gone now, forever. That is what time does to us. (The little white and the little black mouse gnawing away at our life.) Levin finds the contemplation of this contrast between what was and what is (and per implication, between what is and what will be) almost unbearable. His brother was young and strong only a short while ago, and now he is dying. Levin is still healthy and strong, but he, too, will be dying one day, and it won't be long. We can only live, he concludes, by pushing all thoughts of death away, by pretending, against our better knowledge, that things will last (AK, 350). A link is also established between the inevitability of death and a feeling of cosmic insignificance, from which the pointlessness of our lives is seen to follow. Thus Levin tells his friend Stepan Oblonsky: 'I value my thought and work terribly, but in essence – think about it – this whole world of ours is just a bit of mildew that grew over a tiny planet. And we think we can have something great – thoughts, deeds! They're all grains of sand.' When his friend replies that this is 'as old as the hills', trying to brush it off as banal, Levin insists: 'Old, yes, but you know, once you understand it clearly, everything somehow becomes insignificant. Once you understand that you'll die today or tomorrow and there'll be nothing left, everything becomes so insignificant.' To avoid this, we spend our lives trying to distract ourselves from the knowledge of death (AK, 375–6). And we are generally quite good at that.

What helps us to remain largely unaffected by the knowledge of the inevitable end of everything is the difference between acknowledging a truth in the abstract and acknowledging the same truth in the concrete. That there is a world of difference between the two, Tolstoy brilliantly shows in what may well be the most memorable of his many shorter stories, *The Death of Ivan Ilych* (1886). We all know that we are going to die. Because we know, or at least are willing to accept, that *everyone* dies, from which it logically follows that we are going to die, too. But when we accept this, then we regard ourselves as nothing more than a particular instance of a general rule that we have no rational reason to contest. If all men are mortal, that particular man that I happen to be is mortal too. I know that Michael Hauskeller is mortal, just as I know that, say, the president of the United States is mortal. But that *I* am mortal is an altogether different proposition, one that for most of the time I refuse to entertain. Ivan Ilych, in Tolstoy's story, learns it the hard way (as we all must in the end). He is dying, and, after initially refusing to acknowledge that he is, he eventually accepts it as a fact. However, he does not understand how this is possible, and does not accept it in the sense of being okay with it, on the contrary. He suffers immensely, simply because he knows that he is going to die now, and even more so because nobody else, including his family, seems to realize the immensity of what is happening, the moral outrage that his death constitutes. Thus he longs for a pity that he does not get, because for everyone else his death is far less significant than for him: for them it is not, after all, as it is for him, the end of everything. While he wants to be petted and comforted like a sick child, everyone else just wants to get on with their life. This, of course, only heightens his despair: 'He wept on account of his helplessness, his terrible loneliness, the cruelty of man, the cruelty of God, and the absence of God' (DII, 162). He is helpless because he cannot do anything about it. He is lonely, *terribly* lonely, because only he himself dies while the world carries on without even a glitch. Man is cruel because nobody seems to care or understand, at least not to the degree that the occasion would require or deserve. God is cruel because he lets it happen, and God is absent because he is not there to provide solace. Ivan Ilych has been left all alone with the dragon, which very soon now, since the branch he clings to is about to break, will tear him apart.

Looking for a way out

Tolstoy may have contemplated suicide, but in the end he did not kill himself, despite reaching the conclusion that neither his family nor his art was reason enough to go on living. Perhaps he was, like Ivan Ilych, too afraid of death. But he also increasingly came to believe that perhaps it was not life as such that was pointless, but rather a particular *kind* of life, a particular mode of living. Perhaps a meaningful existence could be found by changing his life instead of ending it. But how?

While Ivan Ilych is waiting for death to come, he also looks back onto his life and finds it wanting. He used to live well and pleasantly and at first wishes all this back, but then realizes that this is not enough. The pleasures of a comfortable life suddenly seem trivial and indeed often outright nasty, and in any case worthless. Perhaps there was some good in childhood, he thinks, but less and less so in adult life, so that his life has been very much like a stone falling downwards with increasing speed. He has, in other words, been dying all along, or his soul has.

> 'Then what does it mean? Why? It can't be that life is so senseless and horrible. But if it really has been so horrible and senseless, why must I die and die in agony? There is something wrong!' 'Maybe I did not live as I ought to have done,' it suddenly occurred to him. 'But how could that be, when I did everything properly?' he replied, and immediately dismissed from his mind this, the sole solution of all the riddles of life and death, as something quite impossible. (DII, 163)

Initially Ivan refuses to accept that he did not live his life as he should have, but eventually he acknowledges the emptiness of his previous life and comes to accept it as the only possible explanation to the puzzle of why he now has to die the way he does. However, it remains unclear how exactly he should have lived his life. One can know or believe that one's life has been wasted without having any clear idea what one should have done in order to not waste it. Yet it also remains unclear in what way accepting the fact that he got it all wrong and that he should have lived his life differently solves 'all the riddles of life and death'. If the inevitability of death makes our lives pointless, then why should we expect that our lives would become less pointless if we lived them in the right way?

In *A Confession*, Tolstoy lists four ways in which we commonly try to avoid confronting our mortality, namely, ignorance, epicureanism, suicide and weakness. Some never think much about death and how unbearable it makes life. They don't even notice the dragon waiting for them. Others understand this, but decide to make the best of it and enjoy life as best they can while it lasts. They see the dragon, but focus on the honey. Some accept the implications and take their own lives. They see no point in waiting for the branch to break, and simply let go. Some understand and accept, but are too weak to draw any practical conclusions from it. They just hang on, unable to face the dragon just yet. Tolstoy, however, rejects all of these ways to deal with the reality of death. Instead he persuades himself that his reasoning must have been wrong. That life is in fact *not* pointless at all, or at least not *all* life, even though reason clearly demonstrates that it is. Indeed, it is quite obvious (he reasons) that reason must be wrong, since millions of people happily live their lives without fear and without ever contemplating suicide and thus apparently do find their lives worth living. Since they live and keep living, they must have a reason to do so, must know something that eludes the thinker, the philosopher. They must know something about the meaning of life, or must have found a way to make it meaningful. To those people, therefore, we need to turn our attention if we want to understand what makes life worth living, and it is their way of living their lives we need to imitate if we want to live a meaningful life ourselves.

This argument is of course rather curious and on its own not very convincing. Tolstoy himself has, after all, just given us three ways to explain why people go on living despite being in a situation that is truly desperate: they could be ignorant, epicurean or weak. Also, those people are also going to die, no matter what. Whatever they may be thinking or doing, none of it makes the dragon go away. So once again, if it is death that threatens or undermines meaning, then their life cannot be more meaningful than Tolstoy's own. What makes Tolstoy think that at least some of them know something that he knows not, is the fact that they don't seem to *fear* death even when they are directly confronted with it. The dragon keeps waiting for them, but it does not seem to worry them. They look the dragon squarely in the eye. And the only way they can do that is by knowing something about the dragon, about what the dragon is, that we don't know, namely, that the dragon is not what it appears to be and that there is in fact nothing to be feared.

When, in *Anna Karenina*, Levin's brother Nikolai is dying, Levin is struck by the contrast between his own unease and uncertainty regarding how to behave in the face of death, and the self-assurance and grace with which the women in the house deal with it, just doing what is necessary without making any fuss about it and without any awkwardness on their side. It occurs to him that despite being clearly more intelligent and far more knowledgeable than his wife and his housekeeper, he does not really understand death at all, while they do.

> The proof that they knew firmly what death was, lay in their knowing, without a moment's doubt, how to act with dying people and not being afraid of them. While Levin and others,

though they could say a lot about death, obviously did not know, because they were afraid of death and certainly had no idea what needed to be done when people were dying. (AK, 496)

Similarly, in *The Death of Ivan Ilych*, it is the peasant servant Gerasim who selflessly and matter-of-factly (and indeed almost cheerfully) looks after the dying Ilych, doing everything in his power to make his last days as comfortable as possible. He is the only one who fully accepts the fact that his master is dying and who is okay with it, making no attempt to conceal it and showing no signs of fear. He understands. In both cases fear of death is taken to be a sure sign of a lack of understanding, either because it is assumed that we do not fear what we understand, or because it is assumed that death is nothing to be feared. The latter is more likely since it is also emphasized (in *Anna Karenina*) that the wife's and the housekeeper's knowledge is not 'instinctive, animal, unreasoning', but conscious, showing true understanding, because they also tend to the dying Nikolai's soul (making sure that he takes communion and becomes anointed) (AK, 497), which would suggest that what they know is that death is in fact and despite appearances *not* the end of everything.

Indeed, there are various passages in Tolstoy's literary work that suggest some kind of revelation happening at the moment of death or shortly before. While waiting for his brother Nikolai's death, Levin observes that for the dying man 'something was becoming increasingly clearer which for him remained as dark as ever' (AK, 501). What that something is, however, remains, for now, unsaid. Anna Karenina, too, has a moment of clarity and understanding before she dies: 'And the candle by the light of which she had been reading that book filled with anxieties, deceptions, grief and evil, flared up brighter than ever, lit up for her all that had once been in darkness, sputtered, grew dim, and went out for ever' (AK, 768). While there is no suggestion here that Anna's (or for that matter Nikolai's) death is not final, Tolstoy sheds the remaining uncertainty in *The Death of Ivan Ilych*: when the end of Ivan Ilych's life and suffering finally draws close, he finds to his surprise that death is not what he thought it to be: '"And death ... where is it?" He sought his former accustomed fear of death and did not find it. "Where is it? What death?" There was no fear because there was no death. In place of death there was light' (DII, 171). The dragon has finally disappeared, or rather it has turned out to be a mere illusion.[4]

THE INEVITABLE END OF EVERYTHING

Yet of course we cannot really *know* that death is not real or not what it seems to be, at least not in the way we normally know things. Nobody knows for sure what is going to happen to us after our death, simply because none of us has ever *been* dead. We have no evidence one way or another. So if there is knowledge here, then it must be a peculiar kind of knowledge, one that is not based in reason or experience (but which is nonetheless not irrational in the sense of being opposed to reason). Tolstoy calls this peculiar knowledge: *faith*.

Faith

Faith is a knowledge that goes beyond the finite. It creates a connection between the finite and the infinite (or the immanent and the transcendent). Not only does this peculiar knowledge allow us (or some people) to accept and cope with death, but it also gives us a reason not to seek death in the first place. It gives us a reason to stay alive. Without faith, Tolstoy claims, we cannot live. 'Faith is a knowledge of the meaning of human life, the consequence of which is that man does not kill himself but lives. Faith is the force of life. If a man lives, then he must believe in something. If he did not believe that there was something he must live for he would not live' (C, 58). However, those who have faith in this sense are not the ones who are commonly thought to have faith. Looking at the supposedly faithful, the devout believers and representatives of the Orthodox Church, Tolstoy does not find what he is looking for. Those believers deny reason and embrace irrationality. They believe in all kinds of mumbo jumbo. Most importantly, they still seem to live in fear. In order to understand what true faith looks like, we need to turn our attention, according to Tolstoy, to the common working people and how they live their lives, how they accept both death and life without complaint. 'It was the activities of the labouring people, those who produce life, that presented itself to me as the only true way' (C, 66). Not only do they live and continue to live as individuals; they also *produce* life, making sure that life goes on beyond their own individual existence. As their example shows, it is not life as such that is meaningless, but only Tolstoy's life, or the particular kind (or kinds) of life that he has lived, the life of a rich landowner, of a member of the aristocracy, of an artist engaging in feats of the imagination without producing anything of real value. Perhaps, in order to find meaning in life, we just need to find a different way of living our lives, one that is less reflective and more (for lack of a better word) *immersed*, less detached and more trusting. We must stop hoping that science or philosophy may be able to provide an answer to the most fundamental questions, 'What am I? And where am I? And why am I here?' (AK, 792), and whether there is 'any meaning in my life that will not be annihilated by the inevitability of death which awaits me' (C, 26). Science usually just ignores those questions, and philosophy, although it tries, gives no real answer, but only engages in endless reformulations of the question. Philosophy is ultimately useless because the best we can hope to get out of it is that it leads us back to what we have always known, and at worst it destroys the meaning that we are looking for by its means. Like children, we 'take apart the watch, pull out the string and make a toy of it, and are then surprised when the watch stops working' (C, 60).

This is why Tolstoy's hero Konstantin Levin, in *Anna Karenina*, only finds meaning in life once he has stopped trying to take apart the watch of life, that is, once he has discarded not only all intellectual ambitions and pretensions but also the rationalist, scientific world view that tends to come with it and that presents the world in a light that makes it impossible to find any meaning in it. 'Without knowing what I am and why I'm here, it is impossible for me to live. And I cannot know that, therefore I cannot live. ... In infinite time, in the infinity of matter, in infinite space, a bubble-organism separates itself, and that bubble holds out for a while and then bursts, and that bubble is – me' (AK, 788). As long as we regard ourselves in this way, as long as we believe ourselves to be nothing more than such a bubble, life cannot but appear pointless. But as Levin comes to realize, this is an 'untruth' (resulting from science and reasoning) and just 'the cruel mockery of some evil power', from which we imagine that only death can deliver us, which makes suicide an attractive option (AK, 789). Far from revealing the meaning of life, reason only serves to conceal it. 'When Levin thought about what he was and what he lived for, he found no answer and fell into despair; but when he stopped asking himself about it, he seemed to know what he was and what he lived for, because he acted and lived firmly and definitely' (AK, 789). Life was meaningless only when he thought about it, but meaningful when he did not think about it. 'Reasoning led him into doubt and kept him from seeing what he should and should not do. Yet when he did not think, but lived, he constantly felt in his soul the presence of an infallible judge who decided which of two possible actions was better and which was worse' (AK, 791).

The ability and willingness to listen to this inner, supposedly infallible, judge is the centrepiece of the kind of faith that Tolstoy is talking about. It is decidedly not a faith that consists in following the lead of others and in assuming that they, for example the authorities of the church, know best. On the contrary, Tolstoyan faith requires freeing oneself from the ruling opinions, from dogma and ritual and established rules of what one must and must not do, which for the most part only serve to distort and conceal that inner voice, which Tolstoy identifies with the voice of God articulating the true needs of the human soul. (This view eventually got Tolstoy excommunicated, a decree which still stands, more than a hundred years later.) It is this recognition that ends Levin's struggle with the apparent pointlessness of life in the face of unavoidable death (AK, 793). His solution: to live not to satisfy our needs (which is the reasonable thing to do), but to live for … something else, something beyond reason. We may call that something God or, which is the same, the soul or 'the Good'. Reason tells us to look after our belly, to always put our own individual interests first. In contrast, living for the truth, or for God, or for the Good, is (from this perspective) decidedly unreasonable. But we all know (Tolstoy asserts), deep inside us, that this is what we should in fact live for (AK, 795). For it is only by living for the good that we can give meaning to our life. We then realize that it is not life that is bad, but our thinking about it. Life is good when it is lived according to what Tolstoy calls spiritual truth. And we are all aware of that truth. We *know* what to live for. If we didn't we would not even try to be good, to help others, to be considerate, to care for other things than just the furthering of our own personal interests. Without knowing this spiritual truth we would live 'beastly' lives. But most of us don't, or at least not all the time. Or if we do, at least we know that this is not how we should live.

The reason why Tolstoy (rather unrealistically) believes this ideal life exemplified in the working classes, especially the Russian peasant, is that he sees them as working not only for their own existence, but for that of everyone. In contrast to most of the members of Tolstoy's own class, whose idle life he abhors, peasants do not live their life as parasites. Perhaps even more important is that they live a *simple* life. Simplicity, for Tolstoy, is good. It translates into purity, into freedom from the unnecessary and unessential. So what exactly is the meaning that working people give to life?

> Every person comes into the world through the will of God. And God created man in such a way that each of us can either destroy his soul or save it. Man's purpose in life is to save his soul; in order to save his soul he must live according to God. In order to live according to God one must renounce all the comforts of life, work, be humble, suffer and be merciful. (C, 78)

The fragility of meaning

Work and be humble, bear the suffering that life deals out, treat others with love and compassion: that is the secret of a good and meaningful life. All of Tolstoy's great literary heroes, Pierre in *War and Peace*, Levin in *Anna Karenina* and Nekhlyudov in *Resurrection*, end up trying to approach this ideal, although not all of them equally successful, or quite in the same way. The ideal itself only emerges and develops gradually in Tolstoy's work. In *War and Peace* all the elements are already there, the sobering experience of death, the vacuity of certain types of life, the idealization of the peasant, the sense that there must be more to life than just the satisfaction of our desires, the yearning for some kind of transcendence, the belief in the transforming power of love. But how this might all add up to create a reliably meaningful life is not clearly understood yet. Uncertainty prevails. The characters are already looking for a more meaningful life, but, like their author, they are still struggling to find it. Thus Prince Andrey exclaims, 'What happiness and peace of mind would be mine if I only could say now, "Lord have mercy upon me! ..." But who would I be talking to? ... No, nothing is certain, nothing but the nothingness of all that we can understand, and the splendour of something we can't understand, but we know to be infinitely important!' (WP, 313).

Yet death already has an important role to play. It points people in the right direction. We learn that the prospect or possibility of imminent death can actually help us to get our priorities right, that it can be the starting point of a spiritual conversion by reminding us that what we have been trained to think is important, worth pursuing or worth admiring, does not really matter much at all. This is what happens to Prince Andrey when, after being severely injured in a battle, he meets a disappointingly banal Napoleon:

> Everything in the world seemed pointless and trivial beside the solemn and serious line of thinking induced in him by weakness from loss of blood, great pain and a brush with death. Looking Napoleon straight in the eye, Prince Andrey mused on the insignificance of greatness, on the insignificance of human life, the meaning of which no one could understand, and most of all the insignificance of death, which no living person could make sense of or explain. (WP, 312)

And later, before the battle that he knows might (and indeed eventually will) cost him his life, Andrey feels that his whole life has been just a magic lantern show, projecting false images onto the wall of his soul:

> Here they are, these crudely daubed figures that used to seem so magnificent and mysterious. Honour and glory, philanthropy, love of a woman, love of Fatherland – how grand these pictures used to seem, filled with such deep meanings! And now it all looks so simple, colourless and crude in the cold light of the morning I can feel coming upon me. (WP, 854)

Andrey understands that, in the face of our mortality, none of this is very important. However, he fails to understand *what* is important or even whether there *is* anything important in the first place. Unfortunately, Andrey dies before he can find out. It is too late for him to turn his life around. To him, life has appeared, and indeed been, meaningless right to the very end, even though he has been a good man, brave and loyal. In this respect, his friend Pierre Bezukhov seems much luckier. After his long imprisonment and eventual rescue from the French, he appears to have finally found what he had been looking for all his life:

> The one thing that had tormented him in earlier days, the constant search for a purpose in life, had ceased to exist. ... And

it was the lack of any purpose that gave him the complete and joyous sense of freedom underlying his present happiness. He could seek no purpose now, because now he had faith – not faith in principles, words or ideas, but faith in a living God of feeling and experience. In days gone by he had sought Him by setting purposes for himself. That search for a purpose had really been a seeking after God, and suddenly during his captivity he had come to know, not through words or arguments, but from direct personal experience, something that his old nurse had told him long ago: God is here, here with us now, here and everywhere. In those earlier days he had been unable to see the great, the unfathomable and the infinite in anything. ... Now he had learnt to see the great, the eternal and the infinite in everything, and ... he ... now took pleasure in observing the ever-changing, infinitely great and unfathomable life that surrounded him. And the more closely he watched, the more he felt himself to be happy and at peace. The terrible question that had destroyed all this carefully structured thinking in the bad old days – the question Why? – no longer existed. His soul now had a ready-made, straightforward answer to the question Why? – because God is, and without God not one hair of a man's head shall fall. (WP, 1230–1)

Pierre has discovered, or rediscovered, his 'faith in a living God of feeling and experience', prompted by his recent liberation: the fact that he has made it through a harrowing experience that he may just as well have not survived. From Tolstoy's perspective, this is the right God. However, there is no guarantee that Pierre's faith will not disappear again in the wake of negative experiences still to come. This has, after all, happened before. After witnessing an execution, Pierre felt that 'all his faith had been undermined, faith in the good order of the universe, in the souls of men, in his own soul, even in God' (WP, 1074). Such faith, it seems, comes and goes. It is also a faith that does not really demand much. Instead of going through all the trouble of trying to figure out what is right and how best to live our life, it is much easier and less demanding to trust that everything will work out for the best because God will make sure that it does. We don't really need to do or change anything. In *War and Peace*, Tolstoy emphatically embraces a deterministic historical outlook (which he later seems to abandon). We may have no idea why things are happening the way they do, but we can be sure that everything happens for a reason. There is a purpose to everything even though we may never be able to understand that purpose in human terms:

> Only by renouncing any claim to knowledge of an immediate, intelligible purpose, and acknowledging the ultimate aim to be beyond our comprehension, shall we see any coherence or expediency in the lives of historical persons. The reason behind the effect that they produce, which does not accord with the general run of human capabilities, will then be revealed to us, and we shall have no further need for words like chance or genius. ... And not only shall we be able to dispense with chance as an explanation of the sequence of trivial events that made those men what they were, it will be clear to us that all these trivialities were inevitable. (WP, 1263)

For the Tolstoy of *War and Peace*, free will does not exist (WP, 1342, 1355, 1358). A strong sense of fate pervades the whole story, so that ultimately none of the characters are responsible for their actions. They are simply playing their part, acting out a script written for them by somebody else, a supreme agent who is arguably the only one who really knows what is going on, why they are doing what they are doing and how it will all end.

Tolstoy suggests that there is meaning to be found in such a view of the universe, but he must have had his doubts. In *Anna Karenina*, things have changed. People make their own choices. They could have acted differently. They could have lived another, better life if they had tried hard enough. They have options. God will not make sure that things work out for the best. We need to do that. Anna Karenina makes the wrong choices. She leaves her husband and child to live with her lover. She suffers the consequences. The most obvious one is that she is shunned by her peers, but it is not the worst, not by far. Tolstoy does not care about the approval of society. Much worse, in Tolstoy's view, is that Anna, through her actions, corrupts and ultimately destroys her soul, that which is good in her. She loves, but it is the wrong kind of love, a pleasure-seeking love that is inherently and irredeemably selfish. It is a hungry, destructive force, which quickly transforms into hatred when its hunger remains unsatisfied. Anna kills herself not because she has lost her place in society, out of jealousy, or because she is no longer sure that she is loved, but because she has lost her way so completely that everything disgusts her, including her own existence. That life has become meaningless to her is an understatement. The whole world emanates anti-meaning.[5] 'I don't know these streets at all. Some sort of hills, and houses, houses …. And in the houses people, people …. So many, no end of them, and they all hate each other' (AK, 763). 'Aren't we all thrown into the world only in order to hate each other and so to torment ourselves and others' (AK, 764). And on seeing a couple on the train, 'Anna saw clearly how sick they were of each other and how they hated each other. And it was impossible not to hate such pathetically ugly people' (AK, 766). It seems to her that she is 'unable to think up a situation in which life would not be suffering, that we're all created in order to suffer, and that we all know it and keep thinking up ways of deceiving ourselves' (AK, 766). Suicide provides the only possible escape. 'Why not put out the candle, if there's nothing more to look at, if it's vile to look at it all?' (AK, 766–7). Or so it appears to her. Only after she has jumped in front of the train that is bound to kill her in a split second, she experiences horror at what she is doing. But it is too late for her, too.

Yet *Anna Karenina* does not end with Anna's death (after a wasted life defined by wrong choices), but with Levin's spiritual conversion and salvation and the assertion that a meaningful life is possible after all. Levin changes his life, or at any rate his attitude to life. He may continue to make mistakes, but this no longer matters because he now knows what is good and bad, right and wrong: 'My life now, my whole life, regardless of all that may happen to me, every minute of it, is not only not meaningless, as it was before, but has the unquestionable meaning of the good which it is in my power to put into it' (AK, 817). With these lines, full of confidence and hope, the book ends.

Two kinds of love

There is, however, no guarantee that Levin will continue to feel that way. Meaning is fragile. It is prone to change and might disappear at any time. Perhaps Levin is deceiving himself, as he did before when he was freshly married and everything seemed good and full of meaning for a while (AK, 505). *That* did not last, even though he continued to love his wife. Tolstoy must have experienced something similar with his own marriage, though in retrospect it seems to him that the meaning he thought he found then was not real and in effect a distraction: 'On my return I married. The new circumstances of happy family life completely distracted me from any search for the overall meaning of life' (C, 15). Once again, Pierre, in *War and Peace*, is luckier. Thinking of his beloved Natasha, it no longer appears necessary to him to find an answer to the question 'Why? What is it all about?'

> He had only to think of her as he had last seen her, and all his doubts melted away, not because she had any answers to the questions that had been haunting him, but because her image transported him instantly into another realm of sweetness, light and active spirituality, where there was no question of being in the right or in the wrong, a region of beauty and love well worth living for. (WP, 735)

And he still feels this way 500 pages later, when he has finally secured Natasha's love: 'The whole meaning of life, for him and the whole world, seemed to be contained in his love and the possibility of being loved in return' (WP, 1253). His love to one woman even opens him up to a more inclusive love, the love of people in general: 'With his heart overflowing with love he loved people for no reason at all, and then had no trouble discovering many a sound reason that made them worth loving' (WP, 1244). This, now, is love as it should be, the kind of love that the late Tolstoy ends up recommending: a selfless, altruistic love, the Christian *agape*, the practice of which is the key to a truly meaningful life. Here, however, there is still a hint of scepticism, a slight irony. Pierre finds reasons that make people worth loving because he is in a loving mood, just as Anna, in her final hours, finds reasons that make people worth hating because she is in a hateful mood. Again, we may wonder if the feeling will last, and for how long, especially since it is so entangled with the erotic, ultimately sex-based love Pierre feels for Natasha.

Tolstoy himself had, for most of his life, very strong sexual urges, which he frequently acted upon without worrying too much about the consequences. But he tended to feel bad about it, deeply ashamed and disgusted by his erotic adventures, his own neediness and especially the sexual act itself. And so he became increasingly convinced that sex, as well as all love that springs from sexual attraction and aims at or includes sexual intercourse, was, if not the root of *all* evil, certainly the root of much of it. While in *War and Peace* romantic (erotic) love, like that between Pierre and Natasha, still appears to be an acceptable and viable route to happiness, *Anna Karenina* already denounces such love as a kind of disease. It is 'like scarlet fever, one has to go through it', one character jokingly remarks, and another replies that one should try to find an artificial inoculation against love, 'as with smallpox' (AK, 138).

In his remarkable and rather disturbing late story 'The Kreutzer Sonata' (1889), Tolstoy goes even further and suggests that sex is utterly disgusting and corruptive, even in marriage, even when used exclusively for the purpose of reproduction. To save our souls (our integrity as moral beings) we need to abstain from it, even if that will lead to the extinction of humanity (which may not be such a bad thing, all things considered). Tolstoy here betrays an almost Swiftian disgust for humanity as a whole (not unlike the hatred that clouds Anna Karenina's perception in the hours leading up to her suicide). 'The Kreutzer Sonata' is about the radical lessons that a man has learnt from his failed marriage: a marriage that ended with him murdering his wife in a jealous rage after discovering that she had been sleeping with another man. The lessons learnt are: Love and marriage are a sham. Love is an illusion, and marriage just serves to conceal the shamefulness of the sexual act that it legitimizes: 'In theory love is something ideal and exalted, but in practice it is something abominable, swinish, which it is horrid and shameful to mention or remember' (KS, 273). That is why marriage partners often hate each other (viz. as partners in crime). Women are being used as a mere means of enjoyment and are thus lowered to the level of a thing. That children result from the act does not make it any better. 'Children are a torment, and nothing else' (KS, 281). They just serve as an excuse for a swinish life. The truth is that all sexual intercourse is 'horrid, shameful, and painful' (KS, 267). In order to be fully human, we need to 'cease to be swine' (KS, 268), even if that means that the human race would cease to exist. As things stand, we have no good reason to exist anyway. We may have if we loved everyone as they deserve, but physical love hinders us from doing that. This is the main reason it must go: because it prevents humanity from realizing the ideal of 'goodness attained by continence and purity' (K, 269), which would unite humanity. If we have achieved that, then we have achieved our goal, and fulfilled our destiny. We are then no longer needed.

In *Resurrection*, his last novel, published in 1899, this hostility against the body and physical love is still dominant. Each of us has two beings in them, Tolstoy explains: a spiritual one that seeks happiness for all and an animal one that seeks only its own happiness (R, 54). They fight each other, but it is usually our animal nature that wins. We are normally not even aware of that, because our animalism tends to 'hide under a cloak of poetry and aesthetic feeling' (R, 316). We then call it romantic love. In reality, however, this love is a loathsome thing, 'repugnant and offensive to human dignity' (R, 386).

However, there is a different love, a better one, and this love is what we should strive for. *Resurrection* tells the story of a wealthy aristocrat, Count Nekhlyudov, who in his youth betrayed a woman (by first seducing her and making her pregnant, and then abandoning her). This betrayal ruined her life. She ends up a prostitute. When she is falsely accused of a murder, Nekhlyudov is one of the jurors. He realizes what he has done, which leads to an awakening or reawakening of his spiritual self. 'He prayed, asking God to help him, to enter into him and cleanse him; and what he was praying for had happened already: the God within him had awakened his consciousness. He felt himself one with Him, and therefore felt not only the freedom, fullness and joy of life, but all the power of righteousness' (R, 106). This is the beginning of his 'resurrection', the implication being that his soul was dead and is now coming to life again. Something has happened, a disruption has taken place, and he cannot turn back. From this moment on, he becomes more and more aware of the suffering around him, and of the all the injustices that are being committed, especially by the state. He sees what is wrong with the world, and begins to do something about it. He starts fighting injustice. He gives all his possessions away. He stops wanting things for himself. He helps and lives for others instead. He is, in fact, on his way to become a Russian revolutionary.

It is peculiar that Nekhlyudov is the first of Tolstoy's heroes who does not spend most of his life looking for meaning, for a reason to live. Yet he is the one who comes closest to finding it, simply by listening to his inner voice and letting it guide his actions. The good one. The one that tells us what is right and wrong, good and bad. Tolstoy is now convinced that we all have this voice in us. We just need to listen to it. Some do, and some don't. Those who don't, listen instead to the voices of others. Nekhlyudov follows the woman he has wronged to Siberia. She is forced to walk there with hundreds of other prisoners. One day, when those prisoners, all in a miserable shape, ragged and worn out, are once again on their march, a fine equipage is forced to stop to let them pass. In it are a wealthy man, his wife and their two children, a boy and a girl. Both children witness the same spectacle, but they perceive and interpret it in very different ways:

> Neither the father nor the mother gave the girl and boy any explanation of what they had seen, so that the children had themselves to find out the meaning of this curious sight. The girl, taking the expression of her father's and mother's faces into consideration, solved the problem by assuming that these people were quite another kind of men and women than her father and mother and their acquaintances, that they were bad people, and that they had therefore to be treated in the manner they were being treated. Therefore the girl felt nothing but fear, and was glad when she could no longer see those people. But the boy with the long, thin neck, who looked at the procession of prisoners without taking his eyes off them, solved the question differently. He still knew, firmly and without any doubt, for he had it from God,[6] that these people were just the same kind of people as he was, and like all other people, and therefore someone had done those people some wrong, something that ought not to have been done, and he was sorry for them, and felt no horror either of those who were shaved and chained or those who had shaved and chained them. (345–6)

For the old Tolstoy, the key to a meaningful life, a life worth living, is universal love. It is empathy, compassion and forgiveness, a lived, practical recognition of the brotherhood of man (and sisterhood of women). Death, however, still seems to pose an unsolved problem. When one of the prisoners that Nekhlyudov has befriended dies, towards the very end of the novel, the old existential question arises again with undiminished force: '"Why had he suffered? Why had he lived? Does he now understand?" Nekhlyudov thought, and there seemed to be no answer, seemed to be nothing but death, and he felt faint' (R, 460).

CHAPTER SIX

The joy of living dangerously
Friedrich Nietzsche (1844–1900)

The death of God

Towards the end of the nineteenth century the dominant world view in Western Europe was materialist and humanist. Many scientists no longer believed that they needed God to explain how the world worked. All that was needed were the laws of nature: physics, chemistry, biology and indeed human society. Educated people may still have paid lip service to the Christian religion, but to many of them religion no longer mattered much, if it mattered at all. For all practical intents and purposes God no longer existed in their lives. This did not happen overnight, but slowly, gradually, over the course of the previous two centuries. Because the change occurred slowly, it was hardly noticed. People had stopped believing in God without quite realizing it.

It was the German philosopher Friedrich Nietzsche who put an end to this complacency by demanding that we be honest to ourselves, acknowledge the fact that we live in a godless universe and face the consequences of this new reality. God is dead, he declared, brutally, in *The Gay Science* (1882), and we have killed him (II, 127). We have killed him by no longer believing in his existence. Whether that was a conscious decision or not, it is definitely our own doing and we finally need to own up to it. The disappearance of God from our lives is, after all, not a trivial matter. It cannot simply be ignored, because it changes everything. The world has now become a different place entirely: without God there is no certainty, no clarity and no guarantees about anything. With our belief in God we have also lost our trust in the world. We don't know what is going on anymore. We have lost all direction, all sense of purpose. We no longer know why we are here and where we are going. We no longer stand firmly on the ground, but find ourselves in free fall. Nothing is in the right place anymore, because we have learnt that there are no right places for things (or, for that matter, wrong places). We wander 'through an infinite nothingness'; we are surrounded by empty space. The world has become colder and darker. There is more and more night (II, 127). In other words, by killing God we have created quite a mess for ourselves.

Those who understood the significance of what had happened were prone to think that, after the loss of God and of all the security that our belief in him gave us, there is nothing left for us to do than to despair. A godless universe is a horrible thing, and the only proper reaction to it is to fall into a great depression, to decry everything as empty, indifferent and past (II, 388). For those who feel that way there is nothing left to live for, and indeed nothing left to die for. The secularization of Western societies has created a race of people who find themselves unable to live, but also 'too tired to die', so what they do is carry on living, but as if in tombs (II, 389). That is understandable, perhaps. After all, 'if you gaze long into an abyss, the abyss will also gaze into you' (II, 636). However, it does not have to be like that. There are other, healthier and more forward-looking ways to respond to the godlessness of the universe than by embracing nihilism. We can shake off our sadness and feel the loss of God not as a new darkness that has come over the world but on the contrary as an opening that has left the world brighter than it was before, as if a dark cloud had dispersed that used to hang over our lives. The death of God signals the ending of something, but every ending is also a beginning, and this particular ending may actually be beneficial to us. The death of God, far from making life meaningless, can be understood as the dawn of a new day, as something liberating, bringing with it a new lightness, full of opportunity and expectation: 'Finally the horizon appears clear again, even if it is not bright, finally our ships are free to sail again, to face any danger; every adventure of knowing is permitted again, the sea, *our* sea, lies open again, perhaps there never was a sea so open' (II, 206).

So even though we may have killed God, by doing so we have actually done ourselves and those who come after us a great service. Perhaps the world is not as valuable as we thought it was, but that doesn't mean it is now any *less* valuable, only that it is not valuable in quite the same way (II, 211). From the death of God new values emerge, which need to replace the old ones, values that are not malformed and tainted by religious beliefs and the worship of an entirely fictional Unity that is complete, unmoving, and eternal (II, 344): new values that are less hostile to humanity, less hostile to life; values that do not reflect the false conviction that death is an evil, but a full appreciation of the fact that without death there is no life, that the emergence of the new requires the perishing of the old, that in order to create we must also destroy (II, 345). The death of God has given us the chance to reinvent ourselves, to truly come to life as a higher form of human. God's death can be our resurrection (II, 522), but only if we prove ourselves worthy of the great deed, which the killing of God no doubt is, by becoming gods ourselves (II, 127), which is to say, free spirits who no longer need to be told what to do in order to do it and who no longer desire certainty; souls who don't need a safety net, who only require possibilities, delighting in their freedom and their power of self-determination; free, cheerful souls who know how to dance, no matter what life brings them, even at the edge of an abyss (II, 213).

The last human and the superhuman

Nietzsche unfurls this new anti-pessimistic, anti-nihilistic free-soul philosophy of life in his most unusual and most enigmatic work, *Thus Spoke Zarathustra* (1883–5). Speaking to us in the guise of the Persian prophet Zarathustra, he acknowledges the uncanniness and apparent meaninglessness of human existence, only to insist that this meaninglessness is largely owed to our own decadent attitude towards life. What we call life is in fact a long, slow suicide (II, 314). Some of us may still have 'a little chaos' in us, which is necessary to 'give birth to a dancing star' (II, 284) – which Nietzsche thinks is a very desirable thing to do – but it won't be long before that has passed too and the 'last humans' will reign supreme. The last humans will no longer be capable of giving birth to stars. They are the most despicable of all humans because they have forgotten how to despise themselves (II, 284). This is not what humans should be like, nor is it necessarily what we have always been. Nietzsche suggests that there may well have been periods in the history of humanity in which we were different, ages more heroic and more passionate than ours, when the giving birth to stars was still possible. But these times are gone. We don't even understand the words anymore that remind us of the possibility of such ages and modes of life. '"What is love? What is creation? What is longing? What is star?" – thus asks the last human and blinks. Then Earth has become small, and on it bounces the last human, who makes everything small. His lineage is ineradicable like the flea beetle; the last human lives longest. "We have found happiness" speak the last humans and blink' (II, 284). Nietzsche strongly implies that the last human's happiness is not worth having. It lacks depth. It lacks greatness. The last humans all want the same, and what they want does not amount to much. They also all want to *be* the same, and those who feel differently have little choice but to commit themselves to a lunatic asylum (II, 284).[1]

This is how things will be if nothing changes. This is how things almost are already. Yet they don't *have* to be that way. A change of direction is still possible. What we need in order to avoid the miserable, all-too-happy life of the last humans is someone who can shake things up and show us the way, someone like Zarathustra, someone like Nietzsche. Zarathustra's role is to help Nietzsche teach us the meaning of our existence. That meaning, Zarathustra reveals, is 'the superhuman' (II, 287). The superhuman is the meaning of our existence in the sense that we are meant to be more than what we commonly manage to be. There is a potential in human existence that we have not yet realized, or have forgotten how to realize. The superhuman is what we could be if we changed the way we look at the world and at ourselves. That is our destiny. It is that what we are here for and what is meant to happen: 'The superhuman is the meaning of the earth' (II, 280). We are currently in the middle of a trajectory that leads from the animal we once were to the superhuman we may one day be. Nietzsche calls this intermediary state the 'great noon' (II, 340). For the superhuman to become real, we need to positively welcome what must come next, namely, humanity's evening and night, leading up to the arrival of a new dawn. For the superhuman to become real, the human in us must be overcome. The human in us is everything in us that has no true value – which is most of what we think is valuable. Just as, today, we laugh at monkeys and are embarrassed by them, we should learn (or relearn) to laugh at ourselves. The human must become a joke and an embarrassment to the superhuman (II, 279), or more precisely the human should become a joke and an embarrassment to the human, that is, to us, because if that happens we are already en route to becoming superhuman. We need to learn to despise everything that is commonly held dear: reason, and virtue, and most of all our so-called happiness, because none of this is of any importance or value (II, 280). Our purpose is to pave the way towards our own overcoming. 'Man is a rope tied between animal and superhuman – a rope over an abyss' (II, 281). Man is a bridge, a transition, an ending, not an end in itself. Our task, our historic mission, is to sacrifice ourselves to the earth and to 'build a house for the superhuman', which is to say, make all necessary preparations for the superhuman's arrival (II, 282). In teaching the superhuman, Zarathustra teaches a new pride and a new resolve: to 'no longer bury one's head in the sand of heavenly things, but to bear it freely, an earth-head, which gives meaning to the earth' (II, 298).

For a long time we tried to satisfy ourselves with heavenly things, tried to construct a meaning for our existence out of the belief in a non-existent God. That seemed to work for a while, but since the whole construction was based on a lie, it had to give way eventually. We finally have to acknowledge that we cannot create God. However, what we *can* create is the superhuman (II, 344). God's death and our acceptance of it have not doomed us to cosmic insignificance. On the contrary, they have restored hope to humanity, finally enabling us to pursue our own destiny: 'All gods are dead; now we want the superhuman to live' (II, 340).

Beyond good and evil

It is easy to misunderstand the idea of the superhuman. These days we may be tempted to interpret the superhuman as a version of the radically enhanced human or posthuman that transhumanists and others wish to see emerge from certain technological interventions into our nature. Nietzsche did indeed toy with eugenic ideas, even envisaging a future 'party of life', whose task it would be to take care of the upbreeding of humanity and the 'pitiless extermination of all degenerates and parasites' (II, 1111). This is certainly disturbing. However, on the whole, Nietzsche's conception of the superhuman appears to be attitudinal rather than biological. His superhuman does not have any superhuman abilities, like super-strength, vastly improved cognitive abilities or a much longer life span. What distinguishes the superhuman from the human is mostly the way they understand life and themselves, as well as their moral outlook. Superhuman is what we will become if we manage to discard the whole set of (Christian) values that most of us have been trained to unquestioningly adhere to and that, in Nietzsche's view, mostly serves to hold us back and prevent us from living life to the full. It is the successful 'transvaluation of all values' that makes the superhuman (II, 1152). Accordingly, it is problematic to understand the superhuman as a *better* kind of human or an embodiment of the human ideal because the superhuman is not even *good* in the usual sense of the word. The superhuman is not half saint, half genius. As Nietzsche gleefully points out, the ruthless, power-hungry Cesare Borgia was in fact more superhuman than Wagner's holy fool, the chaste and compassionate Parsifal (II, 1101), whom Nietzsche detested.

Nietzsche takes pride in being 'the first immoralist' and the 'destroyer par excellence' (II, 1153). What he attempts to destroy is what he sees as our collective illusions and hypocrisies, starting with our wilful misconceptions about what kind of place this world is, and what kind of place it needs to be to allow for the living of a meaningful life. He flatly denies that there are any objective values in nature. It is valuing that creates values (II, 323), and because we are the ones who do the valuing, all values we find in nature are there only because we have previously put them there. We have 'gifted' the world with values. The world that matters to us is thus entirely a world that we have created for ourselves (II, 177). Accordingly, good and evil are not natural facts, but human creations, which also means that we bear responsibility for the kind of moral values that we live our lives by. Nothing and nobody compels us to keep the values that we happen to have inherited from our forebears. It is up to each one of us to decide, for ourselves, what should count as good and what as evil and, accordingly, how we should live our lives. Making those decisions is a lonely business. 'Terrible it is to be alone with the judge and avenger of your own law' (II, 326). It also requires a lot of courage, because there cannot be any creation without destruction. One cannot create something new without destroying things that already exist. However, destroying things is commonly regarded as evil, so we need the courage to do what is commonly regarded as evil. In truth, however, there is no higher good than the good of creation, so that what we tend to think of as evil must be understood as an integral part of the good (II, 372).[2] The world could not exist without the so-called evil, and there is indeed a lot to admire in it: 'I am blessed to see the wonders that the hot sun breeds: tigers and palms and rattlesnakes' (II, 398). Tigers and rattlesnakes are no doubt dangerous. They know no mercy. They destroy living things without pity. But they are also strong and beautiful. Despite their supposedly 'evil' nature, which is evil only from the perspective of the victim, we can still admire them for what they are. Can we not do the same with human tigers and human rattlesnakes? Can we not find them equally admirable in their fortitude and ruthlessness? What prevents us? Is it morality?

But what is morality, and where does it come from? Nietzsche attempts to answer these questions in his 'prelude to a philosophy of the future' *Beyond Good and Evil* (1886) and its more tightly focused sequel *On the Genealogy of Morality* (1887). As Nietzsche sees it, morality is an invention of the weak designed to help them gain some control over the strong. The root of morality is fear and resentment. The ordinary human senses the danger that the extraordinary, exceptional human poses to them and begrudges them their natural superiority. They then react by doing all they can to instil a belief in the strong that there are certain things they ought not to do, that they need to curtail their will and be considerate of everyone else, that other people's good, and especially that of the weak, should be as important to them as their own. Because it is the human as a herd animal that defines what virtue is, the exceptional being that refuses to live by the rules of the herd is branded as evil (II, 1155). The superhuman looks like a devil in the eyes of those who declare themselves good (thus idealizing their own shortcomings), because it is in relation to them that the superhuman is superhuman in the first place (II, 1156).

Precisely because we herd animals are in fact *not* better than those we fear, we create morality as an elaborate ruse that not only serves to protect us from the strong but also allows us to think of ourselves as superior. We use morality to brush up our mediocrity (II, 218), to make us appear nobler (in our own eyes as well as those of others) than we are. What we like to think of as our moral superiority is often just a sign of laziness and complacency. After all, pledging and demanding allegiance to a shared, valid-for-all, morality makes life a lot easier. To subject oneself and others to the so-called 'good' is a temptation, because the 'good' promises a more comfortable and less dangerous existence. However, it also poses a danger itself, perhaps even the greatest of all dangers, because living one's life in compliance with the demands of morality constitutes a degeneration: it may well make life easier, but it also makes it smaller and lower (II, 768). In fact, it is the very purpose of morality to make sure that we stay low, namely, tame, predictable and manageable, true to the first imperative of herd-fearfulness: that someday there be nothing left to fear. Getting closer to that goal is what we call 'progress' (II, 659). Meanwhile, under the pretence of making us better, morality succeeds in sucking the life blood out of us. Morality is in fact a form of vampirism (II, 1158).

The morality of pity and the value of suffering

Morality's function is to tame us (or tame those of us who are still wild, who still have some chaos and spunk in them). Once we have been tamed, we no longer have to be feared. Yet the reason we no longer have to be feared is that there is nothing left in us that still wants to become greater than we are, and that is actually the worst that can happen to us. We are then (like the last humans) content in our mediocrity and seek only comfort and a shallow happiness. What needs no longer to be feared can no longer be

admired, respected or even loved: with our fear we have lost our
awe of humanity, our hope in it, even our will to it. We have reached
a stage where the human only exhausts us: we have become tired of
the human, tired of ourselves, which is the very essence of nihilism
(II, 789). Our fear of the human has been replaced by disgust[3] and
pity, which is a perilous combination, one that feeds the will to
nothingness (II, 863), because it encourages us to think that nothing
really matters and consequently makes us stop wanting things.
The only thing that we now want is for things to end. Our pity
for each other does not redeem our disgust for humanity. On the
contrary, it reinforces it. Pity is the worst of the Christian virtues
that constitute our cherished morality. Because the 'stupidity of the
good is fathomless' (II, 434), pity makes us lie, and it stifles all free
spirits. Pity is intrusive and shameless, so that it can often be nobler
not to help (II, 503). Pity diminishes power, it reduces life. 'We
lose strength when we feel pity' (II, 1168). It multiplies suffering.
It endangers the life force.[4] For once Schopenhauer got it right,
declares Nietzsche, when he argued that pity facilitates the negation
of life. Pity is the practice of nihilism, a practice that persuades us
to nothingness, although we don't call it that. Instead, we call it the
beyond, heaven, salvation, eternal bliss and similar (II, 1168), all
of which are representations of nothingness because their function
is to turn us away from life, that is to say, from living our life here
and now and to the full. That is why the morality of pity must be
understood as 'the last disease' (II, 767).

Nietzsche concedes that there might be some value in pity if
it comes from those who are strong, but coming from the weak,
from those who suffer themselves, it is worthless (II, 753). We pity
each other mostly out of weakness, because we find other people's
suffering contagious and because we attach too much importance
to suffering in the first place, as if the worst that can happen to
people is that they suffer some degree of mental or physical pain.
Nietzsche contemptuously rejects the self-indulgence that pity
encourages, although, or perhaps precisely because, he was no
stranger to suffering himself. For much of his life Nietzsche suffered
from various kinds of maladies, including excruciating headaches,
temporary blindness and severe bouts of vertigo. Yet through all
this he kept writing, kept developing his philosophy of life, which
in his mind justified the suffering and made it not just bearable
but indeed welcome. Nietzsche refused to let his suffering defeat

him and instead decided to use it to gain additional strength and resolve from it. 'What does not kill me, makes me stronger' (II, 943), Nietzsche defiantly declares in *Twilight of Idols* (1889), the book that promises to teach us 'how to philosophise with a hammer' and that ends with the hammer itself speaking to us and telling us to 'become hard', like itself (II, 1033). Suffering makes us hard; it disciplines us. According to Nietzsche, all elevation of humankind has its root in suffering: the tension of the soul in misery which makes it stronger, inventiveness and the courage to bear a misfortune, to withstand, to pull through, to use, to overcome (II, 689). And if we are not open to at least the possibility of great pain, then we will never be able to experience the highest pleasure either (II, 45). Because we know all this, because we know the value of suffering, we cannot live without it. If we want joy, if we want knowledge, if we want greatness, then we must also want suffering, because all things are connected (II, 557). That is why if there is no real suffering to be found we invent some. We thrive on real or supposed misery (II, 74).

This is not to say that suffering can never be bad. It very often is. Yet what makes it bad is, according to Nietzsche, not the suffering itself, but the *meaninglessness* of it (II, 809). Because we cannot bear the thought that all our suffering is in vain, that it has no purpose and no good comes from it, we have invented a god and a heaven and a divine plan that allow us to make sense of our suffering. We have thought up the ascetic ideal, according to which salvation lies in an orientation towards some supposedly otherworldly reality, the renunciation of all earthly concerns and goods, a denial of the will to live, all in exchange for something supposedly better, something that we call by some grand-sounding word to disguise the fact that we don't really know what it is we are talking about and that really has no reality at all. We did this because we were unable to make sense of our existence any other way. Our human life, which is to say the life of the human animal, does, after all, not seem to have any fixed purpose in itself. No clear answer can be given to the question of what we are here for, nor to the question what our suffering is good for. That is because there are no final ends in nature, no purpose, no beyond, no transcendence, no Kantian thing in itself. The universe is not beautiful or heartless or reasonable or unreasonable. It just is. There are no laws either, but simply necessities (because laws can be violated, whereas nature cannot). Death is not opposed to life, but an integral part of it. 'What is alive is only a particular kind of what is dead, and a rare kind at that' (II, 116). There is not even truth in the traditional sense, since there is no such thing as the one, and only one, true world. There are only interpretations, which ultimately all root in our biological nature. All our ideals are in fact misinterpretations of physiological needs and desires; they are sublimations. When philosophers tell us what the value of existence is, it is in fact their body that speaks to us. They never really aim at truth at all: what they are really interested in, what their bodily existence *tells* them to be interested in, is health, future, growth and power, or in short, life (II, 12).

Sacred, healthy selfishness

We have evolved into a 'fantastic animal', one that needs to believe that it knows why it exists (II, 35). As such, we are quite willing to endure even considerable suffering as long as we understand and appreciate its purpose. The ascetic ideal has provided us with such a purpose, which is nothing less than the negation (crushing) of the will. This ideal reflects a deep-seated hatred against everything human (i.e. our animal nature and our physicality); a disgust of sensuality, but also of (human) reason; fear of happiness and beauty; the longing to escape from appearance, change, becoming, death and desire. It is expressive of a will to nothingness, an aversion to life and a rebellion against the most fundamental conditions of life (II, 900). The best that can be said about the pursuit of this ideal is that there is at least still a *will* active in all such attempts to negate the will. Unfortunately, it is also quite clearly a perverted will: a will that aims at its own destruction. Consequently, a new ideal and a new perspective on life is needed, one that does not attempt to thwart the will, but one that promotes and fosters it.

Nietzsche finds this ideal by adopting an evolutionary perspective. Everything that we are and do serves the continuation and development of humanity. If it didn't, we would no longer be here. From that perspective everything we do is good and none of it is bad, let alone evil. It is all necessary. It all has a role to play. Those we call evil are usually the strong ones. They challenge us, which is good because it creates newness. If it weren't for evil, things would always stay as they are. Stagnation would result, which stifles life. 'What is it to live? – To live, that means to constantly shed something of oneself that wants to die. To live, that means to be cruel and implacable towards everything that is weak and old about us, and not only us' (II, 59).

Life knows no good and evil, and in the interest of life we should not trust such moral distinctions. But just because good and evil are human fabrications, it doesn't mean good and *bad* are too (II, 797). There are things that are objectively good for life and others that are objectively bad for it. Christian morality with its emphasis on pity is on the whole bad for it. Good is not what we are told it is. Initially, good is simply what increases our sense of power. Accordingly, bad is all that results from weakness and that makes us weaker. Happiness is the feeling of power growing. Pity for things that are malformed and weak is bad because it only serves to prolong the existence of those things (II, 1164). We actually know this, or at least we used to before we succumbed to the corrupting influence of Christianity. Before that, the good signified the noble: the strong, healthy and brave, those who were destined to be masters and not slaves. The bad, on the other hand, were the weak and cowardly, those who could not defend themselves. This is where notions of the higher and the lower stem from. However, all this was upended when the resentment of the weak became itself a creative force, staging a 'rebellion of the slaves' and actually effecting a first transvaluation of all values, which obliterated the morality of nobility. Noble or aristocratic morality springs from a triumphant 'Yes' to oneself, whereas slave morality says 'No' to anything that is different, anything that is not self (II, 782). The 'good' is now conceived as the opposite of the other (II, 785), and what formerly counted as good (strength and natural superiority) is now reinvented (through resentment) as the bad. The natural predator is tamed and turned into a pet (II, 787), which not only constitutes a violation of their nature, but is actually absurd because it demands from the strong that they be not strong (II, 789). And while everyone is now supposed to be nice to each other within a defined group, people still, true to the spirit of othering, tend to behave like wild animals to everyone who does not belong to that group (II, 786), which is an overcompensation resulting from a previous repression: at the heart of all natural nobility is the predator, the blonde beast, which every now and then needs to find some release and come out in the open (II, 786), which is just as well because that which we call evil is actually 'our greatest power, the hardest stone to the highest creation: man must become better *and* more evil' (II, 464).

This may all sound harsh and rather unappealing in light of the horrors that we all know tend to follow when people start thinking of themselves as superior beings to whom the usual rules of human decency and mutual consideration do not apply. Whoever wants to wage war on humanity, or a substantial part of it, can easily find a justification in Nietzsche's writings. I am not sure whether someone who concludes from his study of Nietzsche that he is well within his rights to take what he wants if he can get away with it, no matter what carnage he leaves in his wake, can actually be said to have *misunderstood* Nietzsche. But that doesn't mean that Nietzsche's critique of Christian slave morality is completely misguided. What he resents so much about the kind of morality that most of us have learned to accept rather unquestioningly is that it undermines the self (II, 1126), and there is some truth to that. What the so-called virtues actually represent is the demand that we pack our bags and leave, that we commit a kind of suicide (II, 311). It is an attempt to eliminate the individual, to make us all the same by dragging us all down to the same level of mediocrity. But people are not the same, nor should they be (II, 358). If there were no higher and lower, no struggle, no conflict, no climbing up and pushing down, we would never advance any further. We would forever be stuck where we are. Nietzsche also resents the hypocrisy and smugness of those who think of themselves as virtuous: they claim that virtue is necessary, but what they actually believe is 'that police is necessary' (II, 353). Their supposed love of justice is often enough just a desire to see people punished. Their call for justice simply masks a drive to power.

Most importantly, though, there are other virtues besides those of the crowd (II, 486). Real virtues are not shared with others. Everyone has their own virtue: there is such a thing as *my* good, *my* way of willing it (II, 302), and we should focus on that. Virtue should be understood as the most natural condition of one's own best existence, one's most beautiful fertility (II, 850). Nietzsche is full of praise for 'sacred, healthy selfishness' (II, 438), convinced that we need to love ourselves first in order to be able to accomplish things that are actually worth accomplishing. 'If you want to learn how to fly, you first need to learn to stand and walk and climb and dance: one doesn't learn how to fly through flying' (II, 442). Accordingly, we should not be ashamed of ourselves, as Christian morality with its condemnation of supposedly sinful behaviour asks us to be, thus turning us all into 'virtuous monsters and scarecrows' (II, 114). This shame goes hand in hand with the pessimistic world view: we are disgusted by life as we are disgusted by ourselves (II, 808).[5] Instead, we should embrace 'noble selfishness' (II, 52). This would also be more honest, less hypocritical. Selflessness is, after all, mostly praised because the selflessness of others benefits us: we want others to be selfless because we are not. Freedom consists in no longer being ashamed of oneself (II, 160). Instead of fearing ourselves and expecting ourselves to act ignominiously, we should fly without shame and concern, like a free-born bird (II, 173).

In sum, Nietzsche rejects all moralities that demand the curtailing of the self, that tell us not to do this and not to do that. He rejects all negative virtues whose essence is negation and instead favours moralities that encourage us to do things well and the way only *we* can do them (II, 179). The whole point is that we allow ourselves to live our life without doing violence to what we are, which, not unreasonably, Nietzsche believes, makes us ill.

All good things laugh: Against the spirit of heaviness

We should bear in mind here that an unwillingness to do violence to one's self does not automatically translate into a propensity to do violence to others. On the contrary, it is precisely our forced and unhealthy attempt to stifle the expression of our self that can foster a desire in us to inflict suffering on others. Because we suffer from doing violence to ourselves, we enjoy making others suffer, which provides some relief from our own suffering (II, 1181).

Admittedly, Nietzsche sometimes talks as if the superhuman that he envisages is pretty much a ruthless killer, but what marks the superhuman more than anything else is not his potential ruthlessness but his ability not to take things too seriously, which entails being utterly unconcerned about what other people think or want (and especially what they want him to do), but also not being overly concerned with himself.

In the first of the speeches of Zarathustra we are told about the three transformations of the spirit. The first transformation turns the spirit into a camel, which is willing to bear even the heaviest burdens to prove and exercise its strength. The camel must then transform into a lion, who seeks freedom, wanting to be the master of his own desert. In order to gain it, the lion confronts the great dragon, which is called 'Thou shalt' and which insists that there are no other values than the ones that are inscribed in his skin and that no new values can ever be created. The lion defeats the dragon claiming his right to new values, the right to ignore the dragon's 'Thou shalt' and to affirm himself by saying 'I will' instead. But that is not enough yet, because it is one thing to tear apart existing values and assert one's freedom and quite another to create new values. For that, a third transformation is needed, which is the transformation of the lion into a child (II, 294). The child represents a 'holy Yes' to life and to oneself, an unashamed anxiety-free affirmation of one's own being. 'Innocence and forgetting is the child, a new beginning, a game, a wheel rolling on its own, a first movement, a holy Yes' (II, 294). There is no violence and no bloodlust in this image, only the joy of discovering the world anew, to experiment with it, to find out what is possible, to exercise one's natural powers. There is no ill will, just the calm, trusting and joyful welcoming of the adventure that is life. This child is the true Nietzschean superhuman.

Perhaps more than anything else, Nietzsche wants to restore a certain lightness of being that we have lost somewhere along the way. We need to learn how to *dance* when we approach our goals: dance with light feet over the mud as if it were ice (II, 530). What makes all things fall, he says, is the 'spirit of heaviness', and it is that spirit that we need to kill. The devil is a very serious person, and that is not how we should aspire to be. Real gods, on the other hand, know how to laugh and to dance. A god like this would actually be worth believing in. It would be a god that perhaps even Nietzsche himself would be happy to believe in (II, 307). Like this god, we should be cheerful, in acknowledgement of the fact that the world is full of possibilities and full of perfect little things. We should surround ourselves with those things and learn to laugh about ourselves (II, 528), because 'all good things laugh' (II, 529). Nietzsche even suggests ranking philosophers not in accordance with the quality of their writings but in accordance with the quality of their laughter. The best ones are those that laugh best, those that are capable of 'golden laughter' (II, 753).

We tend to see life as a tragedy, and looking at life this way has not been altogether bad for us because it has at least encouraged us to attach some value to life. However, it is still misguided. What we have to realize is that life is in fact a comedy, something to laugh about, something that can only be properly captured by a 'gay science', which encourages us to explore life with a certain amused detachment (II, 34). Art can help us do that because it distances us from ourselves. As an aesthetic phenomenon the world is still bearable, and art helps us turn not only the world but also ourselves into an aesthetic phenomenon. It teaches us to look at ourselves from afar and above, to laugh and cry *about* us, to discover the hero and the fool that is hiding in our passion for knowledge, especially the fool. We need art 'so we don't lose that freedom over things' (II, 113), which also allows us to stand (or more precisely to float and play) above morality (II, 114). Life, which is essentially will to power (II, 578), should be lived joyfully, as a learning experiment and not as a duty, a fate or a fraud (II, 187). We don't need the kingdom of heaven to find meaning in life. All we want and need is the 'kingdom of earth' (II, 550), which is a kingdom well worth living in (II, 552).

To live well in that kingdom we need to abandon the spirit of heaviness and instead adopt a playful, aesthetic attitude to life. That requires among other things a keen appreciation of the many ways in which things appear to us: colours and sounds, smells and tastes and our whole bodily existence.[6] We don't want to, and don't need to, dig too deep to find the essence of things, to see what lies beyond. We don't want to tear apart the veil of appearance. Not all things have to be seen and studied naked; to insist on that would be improper. Nature may well be hiding for a reason. To live well requires the celebration of surfaces, the worship of appearances. If the Greeks were superficial, Nietzsche writes, it was their very depth that made them so (II, 15). They understood that there are no essences, that ultimately *everything* is appearance and that true happiness can only be found there. 'All humans of depth find their bliss in being like flying fish, playing on the uppermost crests of the waves; what they appreciate most in all things is that they have a surface: their skinliness' (II, 157). Appearance is not just a dead mask, which we are free to put on and take off. Appearance is 'agency and life itself' (II, 73). It may well be a dream, but what does that matter? What matters is that this world of appearances matters *to us*, which it obviously does. If it is a dream, then it is one that we all dream together, and in doing so we make sure that the dream continues. If it is a fiction, we are all busy writing it and immersed in reading it. To insist on knowing *the* truth is generally misguided. Truth is not even always more useful than non-truth (II, 207), and error could in fact be one of the conditions of life (II, 124), in which case the unconditional will to truth could easily turn out to be a principle that is destructive and hostile to life, 'a concealed will to death' (II, 208), another form of nihilism. Instead of thinking about the world in terms of true and false, we should simply distinguish between different 'grades of appearance' or lighter and darker shades of it (II, 600). The truth is that there is no one truth about the world, which is in fact open to an infinite number of different interpretations – which is just as well because 'an essentially mechanical world would be an essentially meaningless world!' (II, 249). A meaning*ful* world on the other hand is essentially non-mechanical: changing constantly, unpredictable, accidental and chaotic.

Death and eternal recurrence

It is also a world in which things die, we included, which Nietzsche suggests is something we should welcome rather than deplore. Death is, after all, a condition of all real progress, which is progress to more power. It is a sacrifice in the service of a greater good, and the more is sacrificed the more is achieved (II, 819).[7] All happiness on earth results from struggle (II, 26), from war. 'War is the father of all good things' (II, 99), and 'war and courage have done more great things than charity' (II, 312). Death is a consequence of that war we call life. It cannot be avoided, nor should it be. A long life is not desirable (II, 313), not as such. It all depends on the way a life is lived, which is vastly more important than how long it lasts. Accordingly, 'many die too late, and some die too early'. What matters is that we 'die at the right time' (II, 333). Yet in order to be able to do that we also need to *live* at the right time. If we don't know how to do *that*, it would have been better if we had never been born in the first place. Everyone is concerned about dying, but dying is not the problem. The problem is that we don't know yet how to properly *celebrate* death. We ought to die as victors, surrounded by people who are full of hope and promises (II, 334). If that is not possible, then the second best way to die is to die fighting. Praised be the quick death (II, 335). A bad death is one that creeps in like a thief to overpower us. A good death is a free death, which comes because we want it. We need to know when it is time to go, and then go willingly, without clinging to life. We need to become 'holy naysayers' when the time to say yes is over (II, 335). Death is good because it is a condition of life. There is no growth without death. Life is self-transcendence (II, 371).

If we can accept death gracefully and without resentment, we can accept everything else as well. The secret to living one's life well is to stop fighting against that which is presumed ugly and to instead start seeing the beauty in it, to stop making accusations and complaints against life and instead to start saying yes to everything that happens in it (II, 161). Nietzsche calls this *amor fati*, the love of one's fate. Loving our fate enables us to recognize that everything that happens to us is actually good for us in some way, be it something as trivial as bad weather or something more serious, such as the loss of a friend, an illness, a slander, a betrayal or any other thing. Whatever it is, we can be sure that it was needed for something, that it has some use and that it means something specifically for *our* life (II, 162). Because everything is necessary, we should learn to not just resign ourselves to it, or to accept it (II, 1098), but positively *love* everything about it, no matter how strange it might be (II, 1110). We would then put into practice the Dionysian philosophy that Nietzsche started developing already in his first book, *The Birth of Tragedy from the Spirit of Music* (1872), which requires the consistent affirmation of passing and destruction, of contradiction and war, a disavowal of being, in favour of a life of radical becoming (II, 1111).

That affirmation is what Nietzsche's famed doctrine of eternal recurrence, which he introduces in *The Gay Science* and which takes centre stage in *Thus Spoke Zarathustra*, is all about. Everything that can happen, he argues there, must have happened already. Everything that is happening now, this very moment, has happened before and will happen again, recurring eternally (II, 409):

> Everything goes, everything comes back; eternally rolls the wheel of being. Everything dies, everything blooms again, eternally runs the year of being. Everything breaks, everything is joined

anew; eternally builds itself the same house of being. Everything parts, everything comes together again; eternally faithful to itself is the ring of being. In every Now being begins; around every Here rolls the sphere of There. The centre is everywhere. Bent is the path of eternity. (II, 463)

That is a fascinating, bewildering idea, if we take it literally. However, it is not quite clear whether we should. Perhaps Nietzsche really believed that time is circular and that everything will come back exactly like it was before and has happened endless times before, in an endless cycle of life. He probably did not, because he must have noticed that it jars with his philosophy of radical becoming. Nietzsche takes the idea of eternal recurrence from Schopenhauer. As we saw in the first chapter, for Schopenhauer time is not real, it is just one of the lenses through which things appear to us. The really real, which for Schopenhauer is the will, does not change. But since we look at things through the lens of time, what in reality remains unchanged appears to repeat itself.[8] But Nietzsche's version of eternal recurrence also denies the reality of time, because what makes time real is that things *pass*, and that once they are past they will *remain* past; they will never come back. If they do come back, as the doctrine of eternal recurrence seems to suggest, then they are not really past, or if they are in some sense, they are also and just as much future, since what once was will be again.

Yet even if the doctrine is not quite credible as a metaphysical assertion about the nature of time, it still fulfils an important practical function by providing us with a paradigm by which to measure the quality or well-livedness of our lives. It functions as a thought experiment. As Nietzsche writes in *The Gay Science*,

What if some day or night a demon were to steal after you and say to you: 'This life, as you live it now and have lived it, you will have to live again, and do so countless times, and there won't be anything new, but every pain and every pleasure and every thought and every sigh and all that is inexpressibly small and big in your life must come again to you, and all in the same succession and sequence – and also this spider and this moonlight between the trees, and also this moment and I myself. The eternal hourglass of existence is turned over and over again – and you with it, you speck of dust.' (II, 202)

What would we say if that really happened to us? Would we recoil in horror at the prospect or would we rejoice over this eternal affirmation of our life and say yes, let's do it all over again? In order to do that, we would have to be able to say unreservedly yes to ourselves and to life. For Nietzsche this is where our salvation lies. Those who want it all back are the most joyful, most alive, most world-affirming people imaginable (II, 617). Our will always rages against time, which constantly and permanently removes a growing number of things from our grasp. Yet time is defeated once the 'it was' is transformed into a 'this is how *I* wanted it' (II, 394). To actually make that transformation, in our minds, in our attitude towards life, takes courage, but if we find that courage, the courage to say 'That was life? Let's do it again!', then we can defeat even death itself (II, 408).

CHAPTER SEVEN

The dramatic richness of the concrete world
William James (1842–1910)

Making a difference

'There can *be* no difference anywhere that doesn't *make* a difference elsewhere' (P, 50), writes William James in his book *Pragmatism* (1907). 'Pragmatism' is the name that James gives to a particular philosophical attitude of orientation and method of inquiry that is more interested in fruits than in roots, more in consequences than in first principles. It operates on the assumption that in order to understand what a claim means we need to understand what the practical *effects* of it being true or false would be. If it makes, in practical terms, no difference to us whether or not a certain proposition is true, then that proposition is, for all intents and purposes, meaningless. If we, for instance, debate the question whether there is such a thing as free will, then we have good reason to do so only if something depends on there being or not being free will. How we answer that question needs to have an effect on how we *act*, or at least on what we can expect to *happen* to us in the future. We need to ask ourselves: Does it really make a difference whether our will is 'free' or causally determined? Does it really matter whether we could have done something other than we actually did (if that is what we mean by 'free' here)? If we find that it makes no noticeable difference one way or the other, then 'free will' is a meaningless notion, and we can stop arguing about it. If it does, then it has meaning to the extent that it does, and *what* it means is exactly the difference that it makes.[1]

James recommends that we use the pragmatic method to resolve contentious metaphysical issues, such as whether the world is one or many, in its essence material or spiritual, the product of design or chance. We will then see whether it makes a difference, and if it does, what that difference consists in. James does not say so explicitly, but it is clear that questions about meaning in life can and should be subjected to the same test. When we ask whether life in general, or a particular individual life, is meaningful or meaningless, we need to first clarify what difference it makes whether or not life has a meaning. We need to ask what the practical cash-value of 'meaningfulness' is, which requires identifying its place in the stream of experience. For James, what is not experienced in some way by someone is not real. It is not real because what is never experienced in any way by us cannot make any difference to us. It could just as well not exist. Experience, however, is tied to action. It changes our behaviour, and if it does not seem to do that, then we have not really experienced anything at all. So in what way is a life that is meaningful pragmatically different from one that is not? How does it affect our experience and behaviour?

Clearly, 'meaning' *does* make a difference to us. We want our lives to be meaningful and we deplore a life that seems to be not. But what exactly do we mean when we call a life meaningless? If someone believes their life to be meaningful, then we can expect them, at the very least, to experience their life as worth continuing and, accordingly, to go on living. If someone takes their own life (without any good reason),[2] it is safe to say that they no longer experience their life as worth living. That their life was meaningless (in their own perception, which is ultimately all that counts) is then proven by their self-inflicted death. However, from the fact that someone does *not* kill themselves it does not necessarily follow that they experience their life as worth living. They may simply be too weak-minded or too much afraid of death to act on their experience of pointlessness. But if there is a positive drive to go on, if life is really *wanted* (rather than just tolerated), then it is obviously experienced as still worth living and, accordingly, as meaningful (or, as James prefers to call it, as significant and important). 'Wherever a process of life communicates an eagerness to him who lives it', writes James in 'On a Certain Blindness in Human Beings' (1898),

> there the life becomes genuinely significant. Sometimes the eagerness is more knit up with the motor activities, sometimes with the perceptions, sometimes with the imagination, sometimes with reflective thought. But, wherever it is found, there is the zest, the tingle, the excitement of reality; and there is 'importance' in the only real and positive sense in which importance ever anywhere can be. (TT, 234)

This, then, is what the pragmatic method reveals the distinction between a meaningful and a meaningless life primarily to consist in: a life is meaningful if the one who lives it experiences a certain eagerness – 'the zest, the tingle, the excitement of reality' – a certain enjoyment of life that urges him on towards the future. In contrast, a meaningless life is one that lacks such eagerness. I am inclined to say that what we mean when we think of our life as meaningful is that we have a reason to go on living, and as meaningless if we have no such reason. However, this does not quite capture what James is saying here. To say that we have a reason to live puts too much emphasis on the self-conscious, reflective, conceptualizing mind. We don't need *reasons* to live to have a life worth living.[3] All we need is an intense *interest* in some aspect of life, whatever it may be, and the *pleasure* that accompanies, or results from, the pursuit of those interests. James approvingly cites Robert Louis Stevenson to make his point: 'To miss the joy is to miss all.'

The rapture of bones under hedges

Susan Wolf has argued that in order for our lives to be meaningful two things need to come together: there needs to be *love* (i.e. an active engagement with something we love) and there needs to be *objective value* (i.e. that what we love doing also *deserves* our love and attention).[4] If either of these two ingredients is missing from a life, then it is not meaningful. Meaning 'arises from loving objects worthy of love and engaging with them in a positive way' (Wolf 2010, 8). James, I imagine, would have disagreed with Wolf, on solid pragmatist grounds. Yes, he would have said, love is important for meaning, and love is real (it has a place in our experience), but all we can mean when we call certain activities or ways of life *objectively valuable* is that *we* find them so, that *we* find them worth doing and having for their own sake, that *we* (perhaps) love them. Pragmatically speaking, the only way we can find out what is worth loving and what is not is by looking around to see what kind of things are actually being loved.[5] And we need to be very careful not to judge other people and creatures by our own standards. In fact, we should always assume that 'the truer side is the side that feels more, and not the side that feels less' (TT, 231). So if you find interest in, and love doing, something that I couldn't care less for, then I should not conclude that what you are doing is not really worth doing, but rather that you have access to aspects of reality that are (unfortunately) closed to me. Reality is a multilayered and multifaceted thing, and our grasp of it can only ever be partial. We actually understand very little about the nature of the universe.

> I believe rather that we stand in much the same relation to the whole of the universe as our canine and feline pets do to the whole of human life. They inhabit our drawing-rooms and libraries. They take part in scenes of whose significance they have no inkling. They are merely tangent to curves of history the beginnings and ends and forms of which pass wholly beyond our ken. So we are tangent to the wider life of things.' (P, 300)

In fact, those canine and feline pets that inhabit our drawing rooms and libraries are part of that wider life of things and may well be privy to aspects of reality that are concealed from us. The blindness that James speaks of in his essay 'On a Certain Blindness in Human Beings' is the common inability to understand and appreciate what is important for others and generally all beings that are different from us. We are usually so absorbed with the demands and opportunities of our own life that we are prone to look down on other ways of living and other ways of experiencing the world. This misleads us into thinking that we could 'presume to decide in an absolute way on the value of other persons' conditions or ideals' (TT, 230). In reality, all lives that are found worth living by those who live them *are* worth living. This includes the lives of animals (which are often excluded from the academic discussion on meaningfulness – as if the life of an animal couldn't possibly be meaningful). We may not appreciate what makes life significant to, say, a dog, but that only shows our own limitations. A dog may be blind to 'the delights of literature and art', but we are equally blind to 'the rapture of bones under hedges, or smells of trees and lamp-posts' (TT, 230), which, for the dog, are very significant indeed. The life of a dog does not have less significance than ours: it is simply significant in a different way. And that which makes life significant for the dog makes his life worth living.

James does, however, seem to suggest a way in which life can become even *more* significant for us, namely, if we manage to open ourselves up to the 'teeming and dramatic richness of the concrete world' (WB, 69). As practical creatures we are usually blind to 'the vast world of inner life' that surrounds us (TT, 241), to all that joy (and pain) that can be found everywhere where life is, the rapture of bones under hedges and a myriad of other things. We may find some significance, some meaning, in our own busy little lives, but those who are able to look further, to take in, and to take part in, the significance that life has for others, reality becomes even more exciting and worth being part of. Poets like Shelley and Wordsworth have described the peculiar exaltation that can suddenly come over us when we leave our practical interests behind, give 'foolishness a place ahead of power' (TT, 247), and open our eyes and heart to the life of non-human natural things that is everywhere around us (TT, 242).

We may then be overcome by a 'mystic sense of hidden meaning' (TT, 242). The poet Walt Whitman (whose sexually frank *Leaves of Grass* had scandalized America some decades before) has proven particularly responsive to this mystic sense of a communion with and participation in all life. He sees divinity everywhere, and he is, in James's view, right to do so because 'this world never did anywhere or at any time contain more of essential divinity, or of eternal meaning, than is embodied in the fields of vision over which [the ordinary Brooklynite or New Yorker's] eyes so carelessly pass. There is life, and there, a step away, is death. There is the only kind of beauty there ever was' (TT, 252–3). In other words, it is all *here* and there for the taking. For the pragmatist, even transcendence must be immanent if it is to mean anything. Even what points beyond that which we can experience must, in order to be real, have a place in our experience, the infinite in the finite, the divine or sacred in the profane. 'To be rapt with satisfied attention, like Whitman, to the mere spectacle of the world's presence, is one way, and the most fundamental way, of confessing one's sense of its unfathomable significance and importance' (TT, 258–9). That significance is 'unfathomable' because although we can feel that life is serious and not just a game, that it matters and deserves our interest and attention, we don't quite understand *why* it matters and in what way it does. We *feel* the significance (*if* we feel it) and live accordingly. And that is all we can say for sure. The rest is speculation, a mere maybe.

How we can learn to access this deeper significance, James does not know. There is, he says, no recipe. We either feel it or not, or we may feel it at certain times, but not at others, or only very occasionally feel it. Some of us experience an abrupt change, a conversion, prompted perhaps by certain events in our life, and our blindness is gone. This conversion does not have to be a conversion to a particular religious faith. Conversions can take on different forms, some of which James later describes in his *Varieties of Religious Experience* (1902). What they have in common is that they bring about happiness and a changed, more open and responsive attitude towards life, one that unlocks significance. As a matter of fact, significance can be found everywhere and anywhere, not only in the extraordinary but also in those aspects of life that are so ordinary that we seldom pay much attention to them. In 'On a Certain Blindness in Human Beings' James recalls Tolstoy's Pierre Bezukhov,[6] who only starts fully appreciating the delights of the elementary functions of life when he is taken prisoner by the French and deprived of the luxury and comfort that he was used to: 'The happiness of eating when he was hungry, of drinking when he was thirsty, of sleeping when he was sleepy, and of talking when he felt the desire to exchange some words' (TT, 255). The destitution forced upon him makes him realize how rich life is already on a basic level, how wonderful, even in seemingly dire circumstances, and for the first time he is truly happy. But others may very well experience such a situation very differently, without any noticeable change in their outlook. 'The occasion and the experience, then, are nothing,' comments James. 'It all depends on the capacity of the soul to be grasped, to have its life-currents absorbed by what is given' (TT, 257). And if we are lucky enough to find that capacity in us, then we no longer have to wonder whether our lives are truly meaningful. 'Life is always worth living, if one have such responsive sensibilities' (TT, 257).

James emphasizes the importance of the 'fundamental static goods of life', which Whitman celebrated and to which we ordinary human beings are too often largely unreceptive, to the good 'of seeing, smelling, tasting, sleeping, and daring and doing with one's body' (TT, 258). It is not the thinking about it that makes life good. That our life 'means' something to us, is largely due to the 'intense interest that life can assume when brought down to the non-thinking level, the level of pure sensorial perception' (TT, 259). It is in the senses that meaningfulness has its natural or first home. Meaning is thus thoroughly democratized in James's philosophy. We don't have to be political activists, medical researchers or human rights lawyers to live a meaningful life. We certainly don't have to be saints. We don't really have to do anything special at all. We just have to be there and enjoy our being there, forget our determination to get things done, loosen up and take it all in. 'The holidays of life are its most vitally significant portions, because they are, or at least should be, covered with just this kind of magically irresponsible spell' (TT, 263).

Since life is actually 'soaked and shot-through ... with values and meaning' (TT, 264), we don't have to go far to find it. However, most of those meanings are only fully there for others, and not for us, which is why we should never pronounce on the 'meaninglessness of forms of existence other than our own; and it commands us to tolerate, respect, and indulge those whom we see harmlessly interested and happy in their own ways, however unintelligible these may be to us. Hands off; neither the whole of truth nor the whole of good is revealed to any single observer' (TT, 264).

The healthy-minded and the sick souls

Whether and to what extent I am able to appreciate the basic goods of life depends largely on what kind of person I am. If I am the wrong kind of person, then I will find it difficult to access all the sources of meaning that might be available to me if I were, say, more open and responsive. Ultimately, it is all a question of temperament. Everyone, writes James in his first lecture on *Pragmatism*, has their own personal philosophy, a particular way of understanding the world, which determines how they look at it. By 'philosophy' James here means 'our more or less dumb sense of what life honestly and deeply means' (P, 4). Meaning is thus inscribed in our perception. The world, and what happens in it, always means *something* to us. (And if it means nothing, if it has no positive significance in the sense discussed in the previous section, then *this* is what it means to us.) The world is, in any case, subject to a particular, personal interpretation, so that it looks and especially feels different to each one of us. There is, then, no such thing as *the* world, as far as our experience is concerned. The world is always very much *my* world (and *your* world, and *his* and *her* world, a multitude of overlapping eaches, and nothing that unites them all, a multiverse rather than a universe). This is pragmatically important because the way we feel about the world determines how we act in it. It also determines how we *think* about it, that is, what strikes us as a plausible account of the world's ultimate character. James suggests that, accordingly, the history of philosophy be best understood as essentially a clash of different temperaments, the ideal types of which he calls the 'tender-minded' and the 'tough-minded'. The tender-minded like principles and are likely to adopt a rationalistic (idealistic) outlook, whereas the tough-minded like facts and lean towards empiricism (P, 12). The tender-minded also tend to be optimists, the tough-minded pessimists.[7] Philosophical disputes, therefore, are not about objective facts, James tells us, about what is (objectively) true and what is not.[8] There is no clear right or wrong here. The two opposing temperaments simply focus on different, but equally real, aspects of the world. Each is sensitive to certain truths and blind to others. The two perspectives thus complement each other.

In *The Varieties of Religious Experience*, James introduces a similar, though not quite identical distinction between two different (philosophical and religious) temperaments: the 'healthy-minded' and the 'sick souls'. The healthy-minded focus on the good and do their best to ignore or downplay evil. They trust that everything is good or at least that it will work out for the best in the end. Things are right as they are, or will be made right in due time by some power greater than us. Often that kind of attitude really makes things good, or at least better, because it prompts us to act differently, and our actions may actually change the world, may change what is the case. (Truth, for the pragmatist, is not fixed once and for all; it is always in the making.) The religious feeling is here, like science, a genuine key 'for unlocking the world's treasure-house' (VRE, 116). There is in fact more than one key that may fit the lock. The world is, after all, complex, with perhaps 'many interpenetrating spheres of reality' (VRE, 116). The healthy-minded have no problem finding meaning and significance in the world. They naturally find the world a joyful place, and life, without doubt and without question, worth living. The healthy-minded are at home in the world. Walt Whitman, celebrating life in all its forms, was the champion of healthy-mindedness.

The sick soul, on the other hand, focusses on the bad, which is not exactly conducive to a good life. Sick souls are those who are plagued with doubt about the meaningfulness of their lives, who search for something significant, but have trouble finding it, and who do *not* feel at home. Tolstoy, in James's assessment, was such a sick soul. There is a genuine sadness in the sick soul: that the world is not as it should be (not as *good* as it should be). The state of the sick soul is serious, solemn. Some pessimists like Schopenhauer or Nietzsche[9] do not always fit that bill. 'They lack the purgatorial note which religious sadness gives forth.' Consequently, their sallies 'remind one, half the time, of the sick shriekings of two dying rats' (VRE, 42). For James's taste they are apparently not dignified or 'solemn' enough in their lamentations about how bad a place the world is.

It is hard to deny, though, that the bad really exists: there is plenty of suffering and death *will* get us in the end (VRE, 132). To the extent that the healthy-minded tend to ignore those facts of life, the sick souls have a better grasp of reality. There is, says James,

no doubt that healthy-mindedness is inadequate as a philosophical doctrine, because the evil facts which it refuses positively to account for are a genuine portion of reality, and they may after all be the best key to life's significance, and possibly the only openers of our eyes to the deepest levels of truth. The normal process of life contains moments as bad as any of those which insane melancholy is filled with, moments in which radical evil gets its innings and takes its solid turn. The lunatic's visions of horror are all drawn from the material of daily fact. Our civilization is founded on the shambles, and every individual existence goes out in a lonely spasm of helpless agony. (VRE, 152)

James does not explain what he means when he says that evil facts 'may after all be the best key to life's significance'. We will get back to this question later. The main point that James is making here is that the suffering in this world counts, that there is a lot of it, that this suffering is as real as it gets and that it cannot and should not be rationalized away. The real world is a messy place, full of 'sweat and dirt' (P, 72). Sick souls know that. They do not shy away from acknowledging the reality of evil, which is exactly what makes it so hard for them to live. If there is nothing else than that, it seems to them, then life is not really worth living. The fact that there are also some perks to life provides no consolation. If anything, it makes the situation even worse:

> For naturalism, fed on recent cosmological speculations, mankind is in a position similar to that of a set of people living on a frozen lake, surrounded by cliffs over which there is no escape, yet knowing that little by little the ice is melting, and the inevitable day drawing near when the last film of it will disappear, and to be drowned ignominiously will be the human creature's portion. The merrier the skating, the warmer and more sparkling the sun by day, and the ruddier the bonfires at night, the more poignant the sadness with which one must take in the meaning of the total situation. (VRE, 133)

The problem for the people in James's fable is that they *know* the ice will melt. They know they are going to die. Here James acknowledges the reality of death and how the awareness of its inevitability can overshadow a person's life (as it did for Tolstoy), resulting in the sadness of the sick soul who wonders what the point of it all is, and why we should bother living at all. Luckily, sick souls can recover from their sickness (as Tolstoy also did, at least partially). Those who do recover, James calls the 'twice-born', in contrast to the healthy-minded who never worry about the state of the world and only need to be born once to be happy (VRE, 155).[10]

From midnight to daylight

How such a recovery is possible James indicates in an essay written and published some years earlier, in 1895: 'Is Life Worth Living?'

The essay starts off with a joke: whether life is worth living, it used to be said, depends entirely on the liver. Even though the pun, originally, is not James's, it perfectly captures his suggestion that whether we find our lives meaningful or not largely depends on our temperament (which in turn may well root in our physiology[11]). However, James is quick to point out that the question is no laughing matter. It results from a sadness that we all, in our 'deepest heart', feel when we turn our attention away from 'the surface-glamour of existence' and towards the 'profounder bass-note of life' (WB, 32). Few of us manage to be and stay healthy-minded all the time. We may all be like Walt Whitman occasionally, finding happiness and significance in the mere presence of the world, but such moods tend to pass. It is then that the question whether life is worth living suddenly arises.

> If moods like this could be made permanent, and constitutions like these universal, there would never be any occasion for such discourses as the present one. No philosopher would seek to prove articulately that life is worth living, for the fact that it absolutely is so would vouch for itself, and the problem disappear in the vanishing of the question rather than in the coming of anything like a reply. (WB, 34)

Unfortunately, the optimistic mood is rarely permanent, and the healthy-minded constitution far from universal. Every now and then most of us become aware of 'the ultimate cruelty of the universe' (PU, 89), and when we do, we may well wonder whether we should not end the whole misery here and now. As James points out, the great number of suicides strongly suggests that life may in fact not be worth living.[12] Many of those who take their own life may do so because their life is going badly. Others may do it out of a 'sudden frenzied impulse' (WB, 38). But there are also those who are quite sane and are not driven to their decision by the particular circumstances of their life. Those are the victims of a peculiar kind of life weariness or *tedium vitae*, which seems to befall only those who are 'devoted, for good or ill, to the reflective life' and who spend their time 'grubbing in the abstract roots of things'. *Tedium vitae* is usually a result of 'too much questioning and too little active responsibility' (WB, 39). Those who are overcome by it see the world through a particularly dark lens, adopting what James calls the 'midnight view' of things or the 'nightmare view of life' (WB, 39/40), which contrasts sharply with the 'daylight view of things' of the healthy-minded.[13]

The midnight view presents the world as a miserable place. We try to make sense of it all and find we cannot. There is no intelligible unity. 'Beauty and hideousness, love and cruelty, life and death keep house together in indissoluble partnership; and there gradually steals over us, instead of the old warm notion of a man-loving Deity, that of an awful power that neither hates nor loves, but rolls all things together meaninglessly to a common doom' (WB, 41–2). For the nightmare view of life, the universe is an uncanny and sinister 'moral multiverse' (WB, 43). And then there is death, not only our own personal death, but eventually, the death of everything we know and value (Tolstoy's 'inevitable end of everything'), which is what modern science tells us we must expect: that all 'elements of preciousness' that our life contains and uncovers will be gone one day. 'This utter final wreck and tragedy is of the essence of scientific materialism' (P, 105).

This nightmare view of life has its organic sources (individual temperament and mood), and it is nourished and supported by the dominant scientific world view, but its deeper root is a desire and need, a 'craving of the heart', for some kind of spiritual order that provides atonement and reconciliation and puts us in 'communion with the total soul of things' (WB, 40). This creates a problem because when the midnight view comes over us we feel that the world is not as it should be, as it needs to be, that we cannot and do not want to live in such a world. It just does not give us the communion that we crave. Consequently, we wish that the world were different, and if there really is a god who has created this world and who has put us in it, then that god is not the kind of god we want and need. We so wish that the way it seems to be may not be the last word, that there is something more and better out there that is currently still hidden from us, but we cannot see it, and so we despair. That is why James sees this kind of pessimistic view of life as 'essentially a religious disease' (WB, 39). It results from a religious demand remaining unanswered. There is a tension, a discord. It is exactly the kind of discord that Albert Camus shall later call 'the absurd': the experience of a clash between what we need (to be able to perceive our lives as meaningful and worth living) and what the universe grants us. James suggests that there are at least two ways out of this, two ways to overcome the midnight view of life. One is to lower our expectations and to no longer ask that the universe be what we want it to be and what it stubbornly refuses to be. We accept that there is no god and nothing that ultimately matters, no hidden, transcendent meaning, and that what we call evil is not a fatal flaw in the fabric of the world but simply an obstacle to be overcome, something finite, to be dealt with as pragmatically and efficiently as possible. The other option is to find an interpretation of the world that meets our heart's demands, and then put our faith in it.

In many cases dropping our demands may prove to be quite sufficient to once again see life as worth living. Freed of the 'burden of metaphysical and infinite responsibility' (WB, 46), we may very well rediscover the springs of vitality, simple curiosity perhaps (to see what will happen next) or our general love of things which we can now pursue without having to worry about anything beyond that. And even if those forces fail us, there are deeper forces still that may keep our interest in living alive: 'For where the loving and admiring impulses are dead, the hating and fighting impulses will respond to fit appeals' (WB, 47).[14] We often assume that the world must be good for our life to appear worth living to us. So if we realize it is not, we despair of life. In fact, however, the world does not have to be good at all. On the contrary, it is often enough the very existence of some evil that makes us go on, because at least it gives us something to fight against and an opportunity to prove ourselves. Evil is evil, but the fact that there is evil is not. In fact, its existence makes life more interesting and in a way more worth living because it provides us with an excellent reason to go on living. 'Need and struggle are what excite and inspire us.' They give our lives a 'keener zest' (WB, 47). We are all familiar with the peculiar kind of cheerfulness that comes with and from fighting ills. So there is nothing wrong with having to fight, as long as there is a chance to win the fight. 'Life is worth living, no matter what it bring, if only such combats may be carried to successful terminations and one's heel set on the tyrant's throat' (WB, 49).[15] I don't think what James means here is that we necessarily have to *win* our battles to make our lives meaningful. All we need is a *chance*, a 'maybe'.

Finally, if this does not work either (so that we neither find enough love nor enough hate in us to carry on), we may also find a reason to continue our life in our sense of *honour*, by recognizing the fact that others have suffered and given their lives so that we could live (especially the millions of animals that we routinely use and kill to sustain ourselves). The sacrifices made by others for our benefit puts an obligation on us not only to make the best of our life and to appreciate it, but even 'to take some suffering upon ourselves, to do some self-denying service with our lives, in return for all those lives upon which ours are built' (WB, 50).

The right to believe

Curiosity, pugnacity and honour – these are the *natural* resources that we can draw upon if we decide to stifle our religious impulses and our desire for a more welcoming, kinder and generally more satisfying universe than the one we seem to have got. But what if none of this works? Sick souls may, after all, be so sick that they do not have much love for anything anymore, nor do they believe that there is anything left worth fighting for or feel an obligation to honour a sacrifice that may well seem utterly pointless to them. In that case there is only one other option left, and that is religious faith in the widest possible sense, not in any particular dogmatic religion, but simply the belief, and more importantly the *trust*, that there is, despite all appearances to the contrary, a higher, spiritual order that, somehow, makes it all good or at least acts as a force towards the good. We cannot know for sure that there is such an order, or what its exact nature and influence is, but equally we cannot know for sure that there is no such order. The universe is, after all, a very big place, and we actually know very little about it (like the aforementioned cats and dogs in our drawing rooms and libraries who understand very little about the human life they take part in), so that there is plenty of room for such faith. 'Faith means belief in something concerning which doubt is still theoretically possible' (WB, 90). Faith is always needed, even in science. 'The only escape from faith is mental nullity' (WB, 93). As scientists we need, for instance, to believe in the uniformity of nature and the stability of laws (WB, 91), but we have no proof for it. We must put our faith in it, and we do, because we cannot do science without it. Religious faith simply fulfils a different need. However, pragmatically speaking it is a much better option than the alternative, scientific materialism, which has ultimate practical results that we must be dismayed about because it crushes all hopes we may have for permanent significance. Materialism also requires faith, or the negative equivalent of faith, a certain kind of distrust. The materialist believes that there is *nothing but* this, so why should we not believe that there is *more* than this, some higher order, something that helps and sustains and preserves and perhaps even cares? The notion of God, writes James in *Pragmatism*, has practical superiority because it 'guarantees an ideal order that shall be permanently preserved' (P, 106). If there is a God, then 'tragedy is only provisional and partial, and shipwreck and dissolution not the absolutely final things. This need of an eternal moral order is one of the deepest needs of our breast' (P, 106–7). Its practical value is that it allows for *hope*. And if trusting that there is more to the world than what has so far been revealed to us can make us find our life worth living again, then, James insists, we have every right to do so, and indeed should do so, because if we don't, we may actually *prevent* the existence, or the coming into existence, of that which we don't believe in. Beliefs have consequences, and so does the absence of a belief. Beliefs translate into actions, and what we don't do affects the course of events just as much as what we do. In that respect inaction is just like action.

Moreover, faith is needed to achieve things. Even scientific discoveries are often the result of one individual's persistent belief that something is real and has to be there, even though there is no proof of that. We have, after all, a greater chance of finding something if we look for it, and we are unlikely to find it if we don't think there's something to be found in the first place. Generally speaking, in most areas of life success depends on the energy of the act, which in turn depends on the faith that we shall not fail, which in turn depends on the faith that we are right (WB, 100). If we expect to fail we actually make it much more likely that we will indeed fail. Understanding this is particularly important when it comes to how to live our lives. Moral and religious questions always, by their very nature, concern things that we don't know, but we have to decide one way or another. Here we cannot stay neutral and cannot afford to doubt and hesitate. We *must* take sides.

> If I refuse to stop a murder because I am in doubt whether it be not justifiable homicide, I am virtually abetting the crime. If I refuse to bale (!) out a boat because I am in doubt whether my

efforts will keep her afloat, I am really helping to sink her. If in the mountain precipice I doubt my right to risk a leap, I actively connive at my destruction.

Moral optimism is appropriate not because the world is already, in and by itself, a moral world but because without my optimism it is unlikely that it ever will be, so if I want the world to be a moral one, then I should act as if it were. 'Scepticism in moral matters is an active ally of immorality' (WB, 109). Our belief, our trust, our faith in the reality of the good is needed to make it real. We believe what we desire and thereby create a new truth. Belief fosters energy, and energy gets things done (though not necessarily in our own lifetime). Things matter if we believe they matter. What the universe is in itself is irrelevant. The universe is nothing in itself. It is whatever we can turn it into, an open project.

Accordingly, James recommends that, to fend off the midnight view of life, we act as if what we do now had indeed a significance that transcends reality as we know it. If that is what we need in order to find our life worth living, then we should act as if we were 'certain that our bravery and patience with it were terminating and eventuating and bearing fruit somewhere in an unseen spiritual world' (WB, 57). That we cannot be *certain* that it ever will bear such fruit should not deter us. If we always waited until we were certain about the outcome or the objective worth of an action before we do anything, we would never do anything at all. 'Not a victory is gained, not a deed of faithfulness or courage is done, except upon a maybe; not a service, not a sally of generosity, not a scientific exploration or experiment or text-book, that may not be a mistake. It is only by risking our persons from one hour to another that we live at all' (WB, 59).

To have faith means taking a risk, but by taking it we can overcome the pessimism of the sick soul, which clearly speaks in its favour. However, this does not (or should not) lead us back to the optimism of the healthy-minded. The outlook that James recommends we adopt is neither pessimistic nor optimistic, but what he calls *melioristic*. While pessimism declares the salvation of the world for *impossible* and optimism declares the salvation of the world for *necessary*, meliorism merely trusts that the salvation of the world is *possible* (P, 285). It encourages us to vote with our actions for this better place that we wish the world to be because

THE DRAMATIC RICHNESS OF THE CONCRETE WORLD

it may well be the case that our act of faith will 'create the world's salvation so far as it makes room for itself, so far as it leaps into the gap' (P, 287). In that sense our actions are 'the workshop of being' (P, 288).

If this is right, then if life does not seem worth living to us, we can always make it so by believing it is and then acting accordingly. Therefore, it really does very much depend on the liver whether our life is worth living or not. 'You make one or the other of two possible universes true by your trust or mistrust, – both universes having been only maybes, in this particular, before you contributed your act' (WB, 59). By committing suicide and thus declaring life to be not worth living, we just confirm the midnight view of things: we prove it right by making the universe an even bleaker place than it was before our self-destructive act. Similarly, by refusing to give in to such a bleak view of the universe we have already made the universe a little brighter, a little better to live in. Some faiths verify themselves. 'Be not afraid of life. Believe that life is worth living, and your belief will help create the fact' (WB, 62). Naturally, whether our faith will *ultimately* prove justified or not, nobody can say for sure. But we know that in order to matter at all, the fight we fight must be a *real* fight with real losses and real gains, and the least we can say right now is that it definitely *feels* real (WB, 61). That way our faith has its roots not only in our religious needs but also in our experience of reality.

The atrocious harmlessness of things

We fight because we feel that it matters, that there are things (really) worth fighting for. But equally, we feel that things are real, that we and what *we* do matters, because the world is not yet as it should be and perhaps never will be without our efforts. We feel that things are real because there still is something to fight against and to fight for. Life would be intolerable and utterly *in*significant if everything were already perfect, all hopes fulfilled, all enemies vanquished, all achievements in the bank. 'A few summers ago', reports James in his last great essay on the topic 'What Makes a Life Significant?' (1898), 'I spent a happy week at the famous Assembly Grounds on the borders of the Chautauqua Lake' (TT, 268). Apparently

Chautauqua had everything one could possibly wish for. It was 'equipped with means for satisfying all the necessary lower and most of the superfluous higher wants of man' (TT, 269). Everything there was as perfect as it can be:

> You have no zymotic diseases, no poverty, no drunkenness, no crime, no police. You have culture, you have kindness, you have cheapness, you have equality, you have the best fruits of what mankind has fought and bled and striven for under the name of civilization for centuries. You have, in short, a foretaste of what human society might be, were it all in the light, with no suffering and no dark corners.

It was, in short, a 'middle-class paradise, without a sin, without a victim, without a blot, without a tear' (TT, 269–70). James was happy there, or so it seemed to him, until he left. When he got back to the 'dark and wicked world', he felt relief rushing over him, and to his own surprise he realized that he couldn't stand so much peace and harmony, all that triteness, that 'flatness and lack of zest' (TT, 273) and that he now longed for a little bit of evil as an antidote:

> Now for something primordial and savage, even though it were as bad as an Armenian massacre to set the balance straight again. This order is too tame, this culture too second-rate, this goodness too uninspiring. This human drama without a villain or a pang; this community so refined that ice-cream soda-water is the utmost offering it can make to the brute animal in man; this city simmering in the tepid lakeside sun; this atrocious harmlessness of things, – I cannot abide with them. Let me take my chances again in the big outside worldly wilderness with all its sins and sufferings. There are the heights and depths, the precipices and the steep ideals, the gleams of the awful and the infinite; and there is more hope and help a thousand times than in this dead level and quintessence of every mediocrity. (TT, 270–1)

What a remarkable statement that is! It is almost an endorsement of evil, and at any rate a sharp rebuke of all attempts to turn our world into an earthly paradise. It is a kind of anti-utopian mini-manifesto. Even though paradises may look good on paper, the problem is that we would not and could not be happy in a paradise, in a heaven on earth. It would not satisfy human nature. (Walhalla might, though.) What we always need and always will need is 'the element of precipitousness …, of strength and strenuousness, intensity and danger' (TT, 271). We don't want the world to be entirely safe. We need the risk, the walking on the brink of an abyss, the living on the edge, need at least the 'potentiality of death'. We need to be able to think that we play a part and have a say in 'the everlasting battle of the powers of light with those of darkness'. Ultimate victory in that battle might be as destructive for life's worth as ultimate defeat. 'The moment the fruits are being merely eaten, things become ignoble' (TT, 272).

In other words, our happiness and our sense that life is worth living depends on there being opportunities for heroism. Yet we don't need to fight wars to meet this need. We just need suitable equivalents. James finds heroism, and opportunities for heroism, practically everywhere where people meet some challenge or other. 'Not in clanging fights and desperate marches only is heroism to be looked for, but on every railway bridge and fire-proof building that is going up to-day. On freight-trains, on the decks of vessels, in cattle-yards and mines, on lumber-rafts, among the firemen and policemen, the demand for courage is incessant; and the supply never falls' (TT, 274–5). For James, the industrial age is clearly an age for heroes. There are certainly echoes here of Tolstoy's adoration and elevation of the common labourer whose simple life struck Tolstoy as the most meaningful. James knows this and indeed applauds what he sees as Tolstoy's democratization of meaning, but insists that 'the deepest human life is everywhere, is eternal' (TT, 278). The key to a meaningful human life is courage, and there are many different occasions for courage (the willingness to fight for what one believes in and to overcome obstacles that stand in the way), and many different ways to display it. Meaning, or significance, can be found not only in manual labour, in the dirty boots of the peasant, but also in more intellectual and abstract pursuits. Nor should we forget that manual labour can, and often is, merely mindless drudgery and far from something that makes life worth living. But why is that? It is obviously because something is missing from it. But what exactly is that? James thinks what reduces labour to drudgery and destroys the significance that it could have is the absence of an *ideal*.

Whatever it is we do, whatever work or path of life we pursue, in order to appear significant *to an outside observer*, and thus to be 'objectively and thoroughly significant' (TT, 296), it needs to be motivated and guided by some ideal. Somebody else's action's inner meaning, James says, can be 'complete and valid for us also, only when the inner joy, courage, and endurance are joined with an ideal' (TT, 291–2). This is an interesting development in James's argument because it seems to somewhat contradict what he writes in 'On a Certain Blindness', which 'What makes a life significant?' expressly links back to. Suddenly it seems no longer enough for someone's life to be worth living that there is something in it that still engages that person's interest. The term 'significance' seems now to have acquired a new and more demanding meaning (which would probably no longer allow for the life of, say, a dog to be 'significant'). James does not spell this out, but we may perhaps reconcile the two accounts by drawing a distinction between what lives are to be *respected* and what lives are to be *admired*. No life that seems worth living to the one who lives it should be seen and treated as worthless by us. This is what respect for other ways of living and other life forms requires and entails. But to concede significance to their lives in this way does not require us to admire them or attach a *particular* and *public* importance and significance to them. For that we need the presence of ideals. Yet the 'ideals' that James is talking about can be virtually anything, so it still is a pretty democratic notion. Some, he says, may aspire to not much more than 'to keep out of the gutter'. On the other hand, even the grandest and loftiest ideals are not enough. Ideals are cheap, easy to come by. Everyone has them. To lend (objective, or at any rate public) significance to our life, we need more than just ideals. We need to be able to translate them into action, to stand up for them, to work as hard as we can towards their realization. Ideal visions must, in other words, be backed up 'with what the laborers have, the sterner stuff of manly virtue' (TT, 294). Such virtue is necessary to give reality to the ideals, just as the ideals are necessary to bring about change, to make progress possible. 'The significance of a human life for communicable and publicly recognizable purposes is thus the offspring of a marriage of two different parents, either of whom alone is barren. The ideals taken by themselves give no reality, the virtues by themselves no novelty' (TT, 294). This is still a far cry from Susan Wolf's insistence that in order to be meaningful what we love also needs to be *worthy* of love and have some kind of *objective* value. For James, the subject who experiences his or her own life is the ultimate judge, and none of us has the right to, or is even able to, pronounce judgement on other people's ideals. 'What Makes a Life Significant?' ends with a renewed plea for humility, tolerance and understanding, for letting others live their lives as they see fit and to live our own as we do. 'The solid meaning of life is always the same eternal thing, – the marriage, namely, of some unhabitual ideal, however special, with some fidelity, courage, and endurance; with some man's or woman's pains. – And, whatever or wherever life may be, there will always be the chance for that marriage to take place' (TT, 299).

CHAPTER EIGHT

The only life that is really lived
Marcel Proust (1871–1922)

On the face of it, nothing much happens in the more than 3,000 pages of Marcel Proust's most memorable creation, the stupendous, sprawling, semi-autobiographical *À la recherche du temps perdu* (initially translated as *Remembrance of Things Past* and later, more literally, as *In Search of Lost Time*), published in seven instalments between 1913 and 1927, the last three of which appearing only after Proust's death in 1922. The novel's characters talk a lot about various things, mostly about themselves and each other. The narrator, Marcel, falls in love, and out of love, repeatedly, and so do several other characters. When they are in love, they are consumed by jealousy, worried (and generally rightly so) that the object of their love might not be faithful to them, and when they are falling out of love, they quickly lapse back into complete indifference. Several characters are homosexual or bisexual (as Proust himself supposedly was). Time passes, and the narrator gets older, and everybody else does too. The Dreyfus affair comes and goes, as does the First World War. People talk about it, but the real action is taking place elsewhere. Social and political revolutions are only ever present as a backdrop to a conversation. Occasionally someone dies and is quickly forgotten. Nobody is happy, but nobody is particularly unhappy either, at least not as a result of any of life's many misfortunes. What suffering there is stems mostly from the characters' desire to possess what cannot be possessed, and an inability to love, and indeed to know, someone other than oneself. They all just sort of hang around and drift along through time, without aim or purpose, essentially alone, confined to their own private world, living a privileged social, yet monadic existence, some vaguely searching for something they don't know what, something that might give some meaning to their life, but most of them getting old and dying before they have found it (or have even started looking in earnest). With one notable exception. That exception is of course the narrator himself, Proust's alter ego, Marcel, who eventually finds his own purpose, which is the writing of the book that we are reading, and discovers what life is all about, which is the transition to a higher, more truthful, more real plane of existence – a transition that can only be achieved through the transformation of life into art.

So what exactly is *In Search of Lost Time* about? On a surface level, much of it seems to be about love-related emotions, especially jealousy, which stems from our desperate desire to not be alone and the realization that we are and always will be. (It is *not* about love, only about infatuation and appropriation. There is no room for genuine love in Proust's world. Everybody is with themselves only.) Mostly, however, it is about the apparent impossibility of holding on to the present and retrieving the past, about loss and regret, about having to deal with the fact that youth and love will inevitably pass and can never be recaptured (3: 127) and about finding a way to cope with the continuous death of everything we know, including ourselves, or in other words with the passage of time. Yet there is a silver lining. We are reminded of the contrast between mere appearance and true being, between the fleetingness and vacuity of the life we live and the existence and significance of a more steady and reliable reality underlying it, which we only occasionally, in rare and brief blissful moments, get a glimpse of, so that we know, intuitively, that it is there. What we don't know, however, is how to access it more reliably and how to live in it. The novel tries to answer this question, or at least to point us in the right direction. Ultimately, it is about the possibility of liberation and redemption, about the power of art and creativity to regain the time that has been lost, and thus defeat death itself.

The terrible deception of love

Time lost is a past that cannot be retrieved. It is also *wasted* time. It is time spent on things that have no intrinsic worth, time that would have been spent better on something else. Most of us seek pleasure, but the pursuit of pleasure is mendacious because instead of satisfying the soul it allows the soul to abandon itself (1: 404). The soul seeks something that lasts, something eternal, but all pleasures are fleeting, which is why they can and should be sacrificed to something more lasting. This includes the pleasure we derive from talking to other people, which is almost always nothing more than a 'superficial digression'. Instead of bringing us closer to truth and thus doing us a valuable service by making our lives more meaningful, it holds us back: 'We may talk for a lifetime without doing more than indefinitely repeat the vacuity of a minute, whereas the march of thought in the solitary travail of artistic creation proceeds downwards, into the depths, in the only direction that is not closed to us, along which we are free to advance ... towards a goal of truth' (1: 1003).

Wasted is also the time we spend on and with friends. Breaking with the Aristotelian tradition, which lauds friendship as one of the most important things in life, something without which life cannot be really good, Proust strongly suggests that we don't really need friendship in our lives. Not only are the pleasures of friendship of a decidedly mediocre quality; it does not have any intellectual value either (2: 420–1). In truth, friendship just distracts from duty, which for the artist is the duty to create, which they can do best if they live for themselves and don't get distracted by social relations and bonds.

The greatest waste of all, though, is the time and energy we spend on love. There are several reasons for that. First of all, when we are in love we project qualities into the one we love that they don't really possess. We think they are special, while in fact they aren't. We think it matters enormously what they do and what happens to them, while in fact it doesn't. Others who are not in love with them see this very clearly and cannot really understand what is going on with us. They think we suffer from some kind of temporary insanity, and they are right. Love distorts our view. What we see is not really there. It is our own subjective imagination that creates the one we think we love, a persona that strikes us as worthy of being loved, but which has little if anything to do with the person that is really there. Through the power of imagination, the most ordinary can assume immense value for us. Imagination alone makes what is in fact very ordinary, even contemptible, extraordinary and precious.

> Other people are, as a rule, so immaterial to us that, when we have entrusted to any one of them the power to cause so much suffering or happiness to ourselves, that person seems at once to belong to a different universe, is surrounded with poetry, makes of our lives a vast expanse, quick with sensation, on which that person and ourselves are ever more or less in contact. (1: 270)

Love, in Proust, is an infatuation, a malady. Once it passes, health and sanity are restored and we realize that there was in fact nothing special about the other person at all.

Yet we have wasted our time with those we think we love not only because they weren't really worth the attention we gave them but also because in loving them we sought to get close to them, to bridge the gap that separates the other from ourselves, which, it turns out, is not really possible. The truth is that we don't know the other, and we will never know them, no matter what we do or how much time and effort we invest in them. All we ever get to see is a mask beneath which anything can be hidden. Other people remain forever opaque to us. We only ever touch 'the sealed envelope of a person who inwardly reaches to infinity' (3: 397). The reason why we are not usually aware of this is that we do not care enough for the vast majority of people to notice (3: 537). When we love, we care, and only then, because it is suddenly so important to us, do we become fully aware that we don't really know what the other is thinking or feeling, how they really see us, not even whether they love or loathe us (2: 69). Ultimately, all human closeness is an illusion. Communication is impossible. Others don't understand us, and we don't understand them. Words pass between us as if 'through the moving curtain of a waterfall' (1: 685), distorting meaning and making what we say virtually incomprehensible to the other. If we try to make ourselves understood, we are forced to 'fashion ourself in the likeness of strangers', so that it is no longer we who are speaking, but if we don't, we remain too different from them to stand any chance of being understood. We are, therefore, 'irremediably alone' (1: 1003). That is also why when we feel connected to someone this connection is just as unreal as the constructed persona of the person that we feel connected to.

> The bonds that unite another person to ourself exist only in our mind. Memory as it grows fainter relaxes them, and notwithstanding the illusion by which we would fain be cheated and with which, out of love, friendship, politeness, deference, duty, we cheat other people, we exist alone. Man is the creature that cannot emerge from himself, that knows his fellows only in himself; when he asserts the contrary, he is lying. (3: 465)

Sometimes we invent a person in our dreams and fall in love with them, and when we awake the love is still there and we try, always in vain of course, to find in real life the man or woman that only exists in our dreams, as a figment of our imagination. The supposedly real people we love, even more so those we don't love, do not have any more reality than those of our dreams. In fact, they have less because they are less our own, and what little reality they have comes to them through our imagination. The 'terrible deception of love' is that we think we are in love with a real person, while in fact we love only 'a puppet fashioned and kept in our brain', which, moreover, is 'the only one that we shall ever possess', for our efforts to transform the real woman into that puppet are forever doomed to fail (2: 395). This, however, is not as bad as it may sound because that puppet constructed by our imagination is in fact more real than what is commonly understood as real and which, if we are honest, we don't care about all that much anyway. 'Certain philosophers assert that the outer world does not exist, and that it is in ourself that we develop our life. However that may be, love, even in its humblest beginnings, is a striking example of how little reality means to us' (3: 586).

For Proust the supposedly real world (the world of becoming, the world of time) is just a pale, imperfect reflection of a more stable and ideal world, which is the really real, just as it was for Plato. Proust, however, thought more highly of art than his spiritual ancestor. Taking his cue from Schopenhauer (and the British writer and art critic John Ruskin), he thought that, instead of removing us even further from the world of ideas and that means from truth, art brings us closer to it. That is why if we want to meet truly real people, our best chance to find them is in literature, in novels. Fictional characters are more real than the supposedly real persons out there, because they are far less opaque (1: 97). To the extent that real people are outside of ourselves, we can never reach them. All the glamour that we find in things, including people, is really just in us, in our imagination, which, however, is not mere fancy but a link to what is truly real. Other people always elude us, and can never be fully possessed. When we realize that, which sooner or later we all do, to a greater or lesser extent, we become disappointed, disillusioned (1: 99), which of course we shouldn't be because once we have realized that the so-called reality always disappoints, and only then, can we turn around and look for reality where it can actually be found. Literature – and art in general – brings things to our attention: their essence, that which makes them real. Art lets imagination roam free, which is so much richer and more satisfying than what we call the real world. They create and recreate entire worlds. We need to understand that truth is not out there, but in us. If we look for it outside ourselves, we are, once again, wasting our time.

The paradox of desire

However, none of this means that love itself is not real. What it means is simply that we tend to misunderstand its nature, which leads us to act foolishly and to pursue what is not really worth pursuing. For Proust, love is not an emotion that is awakened by a particular object or person. The love, or what constitutes it – a certain desire, a longing for beauty or perfection, perhaps for unity – is already in us, and when there is an opportunity, it finds itself an object, and when that object is gone, it is replaced by a new one. Gilberte, the narrator's first unrequited love interest, who means everything to him while he is still in love with her, is eventually forgotten and then becomes someone who means nothing to him, but his love, or what is real about his love, is still there, except that it is no longer directed towards her:

> This love of ours, in so far as it is love for one particular creature, is not perhaps a very real thing, since if the association of pleasant

or unpleasant trains of thought can attach it for a time to a woman so as to make us believe that it has been inspired by her, in a necessary sequence of effect to cause, yet when we detach ourselves, deliberately or unconsciously, from those associations, this love, as though it were indeed a spontaneous thing and sprang from ourselves alone, will revive in order to bestow itself on another woman. (1: 719)

This is of course not the way we usually think about love. We tend to think that our love has been aroused by the person we love, by their beauty, their charms, their wit or their virtue. Yet according to Proust this is an illusion. Our love does in fact not originate in other people: it originates in us, and it is there even if there happens to be nobody to love around. It is true that it only becomes fully active when a suitable object to love comes along, but the point is that the object itself is accidental. If we hadn't fallen in love with this person, we would have done so with somebody else. Love, therefore, is not an 'external reality' but a 'selfish pleasure' (1: 1022). Yet this selfish loving is still important because it allows us to discover who we are and to explore aspects of our being that would have remained concealed from us if not for the enactment of our love.

I had guessed long ago in the Champs-Elysees, and had since established to my own satisfaction, that when we are in love with a woman we simply project into her a state of our own soul, that the important thing is, therefore, not the worth of the woman but the depth of the state; and that the emotions which a young girl of no kind of distinction arouses in us can enable us to bring to the surface of our consciousness some of the most intimate parts of our being, more personal, more remote, more essential than would be reached by the pleasure that we derive from the conversation of a great man or even from the admiring contemplation of his work. (1: 924–5)

And yet, love also seems to be a way of reaching out beyond ourselves, to other people, an almost desperate attempt to cross the divide between us and everyone else, to open up and become more than just oneself. When the narrator, Marcel, sees his third love, Albertine, for the first time, she is just one in a group of young girls that arouse his interest during a summer holiday that he spends, as a young man, with his grandmother in the (semi-fictional) seaside resort Balbec on the Normandy coast. He immediately falls in love with all of them, with the whole 'little band' of girls, enchanted by their youth and beauty, their carefreeness and impertinence. He wants to know them, get close to them, have what they are having, be part of it, enrich his life with theirs:

> I knew that I should never possess this young cyclist if I did not possess also what there was in her eyes. And it was consequently her whole life that filled me with desire; a sorrowful desire because I felt that it was not to be realised, but exhilarating, because what had hitherto been my life, having ceased of a sudden to be my whole life, being no more now than a little part of the space stretching out before me, which I was burning to cover and which was composed of the lives of these girls, offered me that prolongation, that possible multiplication of oneself which is happiness. (1: 884)

The word 'possession' is key here. Love, for Proust, is a desire to possess the other, and that means to possess the world they inhabit. Those worlds are other ways of being, thinking, feeling and experiencing. There is 'not one universe, there are millions, almost as many as the number of human eyes and brains in existence' (3: 196). Marcel sees Albertine and her friends as a gateway to those universes, but he already knows, or feels, that he won't be able to make them his own. For one thing because those worlds, which are the souls of other people, must, by their very nature, remain elusive and essentially inaccessible, and for another because if we do manage to bring the other under our control, to own them (to the extent that this is possible), they no longer have what we so desired to get hold of. The paradox of desire is that we desire to have something that is only there as long as we don't have it. Love is sustained by the uncertainty of possession (3: 74). We 'love only that in which we pursue something inaccessible, we love only what we do not possess' (3: 395). Only as long as we cannot be sure of the other, do we love them. Love, then, when it is directed towards other persons, is essentially unfulfilled desire and jealousy and can never be more than that. Once we believe that the other is wholly ours (which of course they never are – which does not prevent us from falsely *believing* that they are), we lose interest and cease to desire and love them. Boredom sets in (3: 405) and we desire to move on to something new (3: 145). Happiness in love is therefore impossible (3: 424). That is why prostitutes hold little interest for Marcel: because they offer themselves to anyone willing to pay, which means that no conquest is needed. What he wants is what we all want: to overcome the indifference that we perceive in the other's eyes, to make it go away, to make them love us, to become wholly ours (3: 144). Yet once we have achieved that goal, we see the other for what they really are: nothing special and not worth exploring any further. This is why Albertine, who appeared so beautiful to Marcel when she was still free, 'a mysterious bird', loses her shine completely once she has submitted to his control, to become 'the grey captive, reduced to her dreary self' (3: 177). Only in the light of other people's desire can Marcel still, on occasion, recapture the beauty that he once saw in her. The experience of falling out of love makes him realize that it never really was Albertine that he loved: 'My love for Albertine had been but a transitory form of my devotion to girlhood. We think that we are in love with a girl, whereas we love in her, alas! only that dawn the glow of which is momentarily reflected on her face' (3: 667).

The constant dying of the self

One reason why we can never truly know other people is that our first impressions are never quite right and once we have had time to correct them, the other has already changed and is no longer the same person (1: 968). People, or people's identities, are more transitory than we think. People never are what they used to be. This is how our memory misleads us: not by presenting us with a false image of what was but by distorting our perception of the present. The problem with our memory is not that it is too weak, but that it proves too powerful to allow the present to fully register. We have in our mind a fixed image of the ones we love, so that we do not normally notice how they change, and they change all the time. Yet what we see is determined by the idea that we have formed of them some time in the past. It requires a special moment, a disruption of habit, for us to notice how the other really looks, how old they have become, how changed they are from when we first knew them, and when we do, it always comes as a shock. When his beloved grandmother is already very old, shortly before her death, Marcel, coming back to see her after a prolonged absence, suddenly sees her as she really is: 'I saw, sitting on the sofa, beneath the lamp, red-faced, heavy and common, sick, lost in thought, following the lines of a book with eyes that seemed hardly sane, a dejected old woman whom I did not know' (2: 149). It is then that he realizes that the grandmother he loves is already dead, a thing of the past. This realization, which is simply the realization that time is real, pains him. 'There is nothing more painful than the contrast between the alteration in beings and the fixity of memory' (3: 998).

In this world, time passes and things do not stay the same. We all know that. The world is in many ways very different from how it was fifty years ago. 'Thus the face of things in life changes, the centre of empires, the register of fortunes, the chart of positions, all that seemed final, are perpetually remoulded, and during his lifetime a man can witness the completest changes just where those seemed to him least possible' (3: 1027). Yet things change even more, and more persistently, than we commonly realize. We believe for instance that we can meet the same people and visit the same places again, but that, too, is an illusion. People and places are linked to times. They always are only what they mean to us, and *what* they mean to us depends on *when* they do. Consequently, 'houses, roads, avenues are as fugitive, alas, as the years' (1: 482). The reality of change is usually hidden from us, because things change slowly and imperceptibly. Yet change they do, not just every now and then, but permanently, including people. This means that our desire to recapture certain moments of our past cannot be quenched unless transferred to a new object (because the original object, a place or a person, is long gone). Proust's view of this world is Heraclitean: we can never step into the same river twice (except, as we will see shortly, when we do, which is when we step outside time).

That is one reason why the dead tend to be quickly forgotten: not only because our 'memory and our heart are not large enough to be able to remain faithful' (2: 561), but also because we, who seem to survive them, are no longer the ones who used to know them. 'It is not because other people are dead that our affection for them grows faint, it is because we ourself are dying' (3: 617). We die in fact constantly. The self is not continuous, as we tend to believe. Rather, it dies with each change and is replaced with a new self.

Love and jealousy are not continuous either. Each moment of a love is a new love (1: 423). It is indeed horrible to think of a future when we will be deprived of the ones we now love, but it is even more horrible to us to realize that there may come a time when we no longer feel that loss (and there *will* come such a time), because we know that that would be 'in a real sense the death of ourself'. The fact that this death is followed 'by resurrection but in a different ego' provides little solace because the life and the love of that ego 'are beyond the reach of those elements of the existing ego that are doomed to die' (1: 751). That is why we resist change: we want to keep things as they are because we want to continue to exist, which is of course not possible. So we keep on dying throughout our life, and so does everyone else, which makes knowing them virtually impossible: 'The other person is destroyed when we cease to see him; after which his next appearance means a fresh creation of him' (1: 1014). Naturally, this also makes people utterly unpredictable. You cannot rely on them staying the same. They can love you one day and, for all you know, hate you the next. Contrary to how we are used to think of them, people are not stable entities, but 'series of events' (3: 105). 'On each occasion a girl so little resembles what she was at the time before ..., that the stability of nature which we ascribe to her is purely fictitious and a convenience of speech' (3: 63). Albertine, muses the narrator, is one of those girls 'beneath whose envelope of flesh more hidden persons are stirring, than in ... the whole, vast, ever changing crowd' (3: 93), but in truth *everyone* is like that, as Marcel eventually comes to realize:

> It was not Albertine alone that was simply a series of moments, it was also myself. ... I was not one man only, but the steady advance hour after hour of an army in close formation, in which there appeared, according to the moment, impassioned men, indifferent men, jealous men – jealous men no two of whom were jealous of the same woman. (3: 506)

Our constant dying and resurrection as a new person is perhaps at its most conspicuous and daunting in the experience we call 'ageing'. The horrors of old age, 'that most miserable condition' (3: 1026), take centre stage in the final sections of the book when various characters that the reader was introduced to when they were still in their prime are shown in the last stages of their life, and we are invited to share the narrator's surprise at finding them not only old and frail, both mentally and physically diminished, but also dramatically changed in their behaviour and even character. The message is clear: when we are old we have little in common with the young person we once were. All that defined us at the time is long gone, and the death of that young person we used to be is as incisive and unfathomable (primarily for others, but perhaps also for ourselves) as the eventual death of the material substrate that is our body:

> In the same way that one has difficulty in realising that a dead body was alive or that he who was alive is dead to-day, it is almost as difficult, and the difficulty is the same (for the annihilation of youth, the destruction of a personality full of strength and vitality is the beginning of a void), to conceive that she who was young is old. (3: 953)

When we are old, the young person we used to be is, for all intents and purposes, dead. Similarly, when we fall out of love, both the one that we were when still in love and the one we were in love with are dead, because both the one who loved and the one who was loved no longer exist.

> And indeed when we are no longer in love with women whom we meet after many years, is there not the abyss of death between them and ourself, just as much as if they were no longer of this world, since the fact that we are no longer in love makes the people that they were or the persons that we were then as good as dead? (3: 713)

While old age may be disturbing when one thinks about what has been lost, we are not usually disturbed by the changes we have gone through (3: 664). When we are no longer in love (or more generally no longer concerned about something), we do not regret that things have changed for us and we are no longer who we used to be. The worry and the fear about change are almost always prospective, not retrospective. We wish to stay who we are, but once we have changed we don't mind being different from what and who we were. Proust suggests that we draw a lesson from this and stop worrying about death altogether. Death is simply too common in our life, and too insignificant from a post-death perspective, to merit our fears. The narrator seems to understand this. He has suffered a lot, but he has learned from his suffering. 'If the idea of death had cast a shadow over love, the memory of love had for long helped me not to fear death. I realised that death is nothing new; ever since my childhood I had been dead numbers of times' (3: 1045). What we think of as our personal death is, after all, not substantially different from the countless deaths that we have already gone through: one self (or a particular series of selves) dies and some other self takes its place. There is, therefore, nothing to fear. 'These successive deaths, so feared by the self they were to destroy, so indifferent, so sweet, were they, once they were accomplished, when he who feared them was no longer there to feel them, had made me realise how foolish it would be to fear death' (3: 1045). It is equally foolish to wish and hope for personal immortality because that would require the self to remain forever unchanged, which is pointless. 'We passionately long that there may be another life in which we shall be similar to what we are here below. But we do not pause to reflect that, even without waiting for that other life, in this life, after a few years we are unfaithful to what we have been, to what we wished to remain immortally' (2: 903). There is no value in staying who we are, which also means that there is no value in continuing to exist, for every change consists of an extinction and the coming into existence of a new being.

Stepping into the same river twice

This very much sounds as if Proust were embracing even the most radical changes, including death, and advising us to embrace them too: don't worry about dying, because once you're dead you won't mind. It smacks a lot of resignation, Epicurean-style. Yet the *Recherche* as a whole points us in a different direction. The search for lost time does not conclude in a trivialization of the loss in question. That loss is real and deserves to be taken seriously as one of the greatest threats to our ability to live a meaningful life. That we have no reason to worry about death because we are permanently dying anyway is one of several red herrings in the novel that seem to make a valid suggestion about how to live, but that most likely do not represent Proust's final word on the issue. Here is one such red herring:

> Certainly, it is more reasonable to devote one's life to women than to postage stamps or old snuff-boxes, even to pictures or statues. Only the example of other collectors should be a warning to us to make changes, to have not one woman only but several. ... Live with a woman altogether and you will soon cease to see any of the things that made you love her. (2: 375)

Collecting women may indeed be more worthwhile than collecting postage stamps, but that does not mean that it is the best we can do with our life. Here is another tongue-in-cheek suggestion:

> It is, after all, as good a way as any of solving the problem of existence to approach near enough to the things that have appeared to us from a distance to be beautiful and mysterious, to be able to satisfy ourselves that they have neither mystery nor beauty, (which) gives us a certain tranquillity with which to spend what remains of life, and also – since it enables us to regret nothing, by assuring us that we have attained to the best, and that the best is nothing out of the ordinary – with which to resign ourselves to death. (1: 1047)

For the narrator, this is clearly only one stage on life's way, as Kierkegaard would have put it: a possible solution to the problem of existence from the aesthetic point of view, but still falling woefully short of what would make life truly meaningful. A 'certain tranquillity with which to spend what remains of life' is simply not good enough. More is required.

Fortunately, amidst all the constant dying and becoming there are certain experiences in our life, or at any rate in the narrator's life, that hint at the existence of something more permanent and for this reason more truthful. There are various incidents in the novel when an object, or more precisely the sensation that it induces, evokes a sense of significance, a sense of some hidden truth beneath the surface (the colour, smell and form) of things that one doesn't quite understand. There is the sudden certainty that something important is happening, but without a clear understanding of what exactly it is. Once Marcel spots the twin steeples of a church that reflect the light of the setting sun in a disorientating way, and he is immediately struck by something, he knows not what: 'I felt that I was not penetrating to the full depth of my impression, that something more lay behind that mobility, that luminosity, something which they seemed at once to contain and to conceal' (1: 206). On another occasion he spots three trees in the distance, and the sense of mystery is renewed: 'I could see them plainly, but my mind felt that they were concealing something which it had not grasped, as when things are placed out of our reach, so that our fingers, stretched out at arm's-length, can only touch for a moment their outer surface, and can take hold of nothing' (1: 801). It is clear that there is something more beneath the outward appearance, but what? Marcel senses 'a meaning as obscure, as hard to grasp as is a distant past' (1: 801–2). It is as if they were trying to speak to him, but in a language he does not understand. 'Like ghosts they seemed to be appealing to me to take them with me, to bring them back to life' (1: 802). It is like a sudden tear in the fabric of time, which is greeted with spontaneous pleasure. These are the moments when we feel that life is worth living (3: 1040). There is a promise of true happiness there, but at the time of the incident Marcel cannot grasp it, and the carriage takes him away before he can understand what just happened, leaving him wretched.

Sometimes that feeling of a not-quite-understood significance is evoked by a sensation that vividly recalls a moment in our past, so vividly in fact that we feel as if we had been transported back in time. We are suddenly there again, reliving the moment or a whole period of our life, being once again the person we used to be at that time. Memories like these always come unbidden, and when they do, they take us out of time by merging the past with the present, annulling their difference and bringing what was dead back to life.

> I feel that there is much to be said for the Celtic belief that the souls of those whom we have lost are held captive in some inferior being, in an animal, in a plant, in some inanimate object, and so effectively lost to us until the day (which to many never comes) when we happen to pass by the tree or to obtain possession of the object which forms their prison. Then they start and tremble, they call us by our name, and as soon as we have recognised their voice the spell is broken. We have delivered them: they have overcome death and return to share our life. (1: 52)

The same holds for our own past. Our own previous selves are also souls we have lost and that remain hidden away until some accident helps us retrieve them. This is what happens in the famous scene in the first part of the book in which the taste of a Madeleine sponge cake dipped in tea throws the narrator back in time to his childhood in Combray when his aunt used to give him the same Madeleines dipped in the same tea. One moment, one sensation, connecting the present to the past, and everything comes back to him, resulting in intense pleasure and the distinct feeling that everything is good: 'And at once the vicissitudes of life had become indifferent to me, its disasters innocuous, its brevity illusory. ... I had ceased now to feel mediocre, accidental, mortal' (1: 53). It is true that things and people pass, change all the time, die, that time destroys everything. Yet what time destroys, memory retains and brings back to life:

> But when from a long-distant past nothing subsists, after the people are dead, after the things are broken and scattered, still, alone, more fragile, but with more vitality, more unsubstantial, more persistent, more faithful, the smell and taste of things remain poised a long time, like souls, ready to remind us, waiting and hoping for their moment, amid the ruins of all the rest; and bear unfaltering, in the tiny and almost impalpable drop of their essence, the vast structure of recollection. (1: 56)

Memory changes things, but can also recover the truth, the essences that the world is made of and that usually elude us when we are too busy living our shallow lives.

Memory does that by suddenly bringing back to us what we do *not* remember. It is *that* kind of memory that Proust is talking about: involuntary and previously unconscious memory. What we consciously remember is what we have a use for, but such memory is blind to the essence of things. But there is a different memory that preserves in us unchanged what we have long forgotten, what has left conscious memory because we had no direct use for it. We forget how things really were, how they looked, how they tasted, how they smelled, because none of this seems important for the life we live. However, sometimes something as trivial as the name of a place, a 'blatter of rain, the smell of an unaired room or the first crackling brushwood fire in a cold grate' (1: 720) can trigger the memory of this forgotten past and take us back there, so that 'we feel the original entity quiver and resume its form, carve itself out of the syllables now soundless dead' (2: 10) and the self that has long been dead is suddenly there again with all the accompanying emotions (1: 720).

That kind of memory (the kind that comes unbidden) plays the same role in Proust as the Socratic, maieutic method does in Plato: it does not merely bring a past event back to our attention, but leads us back directly to the reality that manifests itself both in the past and the present moment, an ideal[1] world that exists beyond and independent of its temporal instantiations. True recollection is the intuition of essences. A particular morning with its familiar smells and sounds may thus evoke all similar mornings, and that means a certain type or generalized idea of morning, which is exactly what makes it so pleasurable: 'This ideal morning filled my mind full of a permanent reality, identical with all similar mornings, and infected me with a cheerfulness which my physical ill-health did not diminish' (3: 23). Experiences like this, Proust claims, are the 'foundation-stones for the construction of a true life' (3: 267). They may be rare, because in our waking life we are almost completely cut off from that ideal world and the true life that results from our correspondence with it. We do, however, often get a glimpse of it in our dreams, when the conscious self retreats and our animal soul, which reaches deeper, is freed: 'Suddenly I was asleep, I had fallen into that deep slumber in which are opened to us a return to childhood, the recapture of past years, of lost feelings, the disincarnation, the transmigration of the soul, the evoking of the dead, the illusions of madness, retrogression to the most elementary of the natural kingdoms' (1: 910–1). What we gain here is knowledge of the great mysteries of life. This is why sleep is so important to us, not only because it is physically necessary but also because while being asleep we dream, which allows us to take a welcome leave of the rigid temporal structures that govern our waking life, thus helping us to regenerate our strength.

In this respect, Proust's novel, *In Search of Lost Time*, is very much like a dream. It, too, opens to us 'a return to childhood, the recapture of past years, of lost feelings, the disincarnation, the transmigration of the soul, the evoking of the dead, the illusions of madness, retrogression to the most elementary of the natural kingdoms'. It is no accident that the narrator never mentions any dates. We never know when something happens, or how many years lie between one event and another, or how old any of the characters are when certain things happen to them, which is disconcerting but has the effect that must have been intended: that past and present, the recent and the remote, all blend into one single, many-layered tapestry of experiences, into one eternal present. Such is the power of art.

Explorers of the unseen

The role of art in life can hardly be exaggerated. According to Proust, it is 'the only means of regaining lost time' (3: 913). Proust was forty-two when, in 1913, he published the first volume of the *Recherche*, *In Swann's Way*. Before that he had published very little. It took him a long time before he found what he clearly came to see as his life's purpose: the writing of that one book, but once he had started he couldn't stop and do anything else before it was finished. Suffering from asthma and severe allergies for most of his life, he spent his last years locked in his soundproof room, sleeping during the day and working on his masterpiece at night. When he died nine years after the publication of the first volume, he was still busy revising the final ones. In his own estimation, this is what he had lived for.

In the novel, Proust's alter ego Marcel is captivated by a number of different artists, the actress La Berma, the composer Vinteuil, the painter Elstir and the writer Bergotte (all of whom are composites of artists Proust knew and admired), but for a long time struggles to produce anything of much value himself. Despairing of his supposed inability to be an artist, which is what he desires to be, he seeks fulfilment in friendship and love, but without much success: 'Could life console me for the loss of art, was there in art a more profound reality, in which our true personality finds an expression that is not afforded it by the activities of life?' (3: 161). The answer is that life cannot console him (and should not console us) for the loss of art because there is indeed in art a more profound reality that affords our true personality an expression that the activities of life cannot afford it. There is a 'priceless element of truth hidden in the heart of everything' (1: 618), which we occasionally get a

glimpse of, but which only the artist can extract and fully bring
to the fore. It is only by becoming creators ourselves that we can
rise to a higher level of existence (1: 856). Artists are 'explorers
of the unseen' (1: 399). They have access to the divine world and
bring – in their acting, their music, their painting or their writing –
supernatural creatures down to our world, letting them shine for
a brief moment, without having a clear understanding what they
are doing and how they are doing it. They are messengers from
a world beyond ours, a better, more stable and true world, which
they explore in their artistic dreams, sharing with us what they have
discovered, thereby enhancing the value of our lives by showing
us how great that value actually is (3: 743). 'Each artist seems
thus to be the native of an unknown country, which he himself
has forgotten' (3: 262). From this unknown country they get their
inspiration. The work of art they create already pre-exists in them.
They just need to rediscover it and bring it into the open. Art brings
the truth to light; it is 'the most real thing, the most austere school
in life and the true last judgment' (3: 895). It is 'the promise and
proof that there exists something other, realisable no doubt by art,
than the nullity that I had found in all my pleasures and in love
itself' (3: 269). Art's purpose is to recapture reality, 'a reality we
run the risk of never knowing before we die but which is our real,
our true life at last revealed and illumined, the only life which is
really lived and which in one sense lives at every moment in all men
as well as in the artist' (3: 910). Yet how do we know that this is
not just all an illusion, that the apparent profundity of art is just
some kind of wishful thinking and doesn't really mean anything at
all? Marcel considers this possibility (3: 392), but ultimately rejects
it. Sufficient proof lies in the intensity of feeling to which a work
of art can rouse us. 'It is not possible that a piece of sculpture, a
piece of music which gives us an emotion which we feel to be more
exalted, more pure, more true, does not correspond to some definite
spiritual reality. It is surely symbolical of one, since it gives that
impression of profundity and truth' (3: 386).

Yet the spiritual reality that art uncovers does not consist in a
particular set of ideal forms, as Plato might have imagined them.
Proust's ultimate reality is more open and manifold, not a universe
but an infinitely rich and varied multiverse. It is a reality in which
even the most subtle nuances in the way different individuals
experience the world are eternally preserved. Vinteuil's music for

instance is said to have 'the unknown quality of a unique world which no other composer had ever made us see' (3: 386). Art communicates what can normally not be communicated, and that is, more than anything else, individuality. It makes visible 'the intimate composition of those worlds which we call individual persons and which, without the aid of art, we should never know' (3: 263). The only true voyage of discovery is seeing the universe through somebody else's, or many others', eyes. Great artists do that for us and allow us to 'fly from star to star' (3: 264). Art thus does what love and friendship and direct communication with other people cannot but fail to do: it helps us overcome our existential solitude.

> By art alone we are able to get outside ourselves, to know what another sees of this universe which for him is not ours, the landscapes of which would remain as unknown to us as those of the moon. Thanks to art, instead of seeing one world, our own, we see it multiplied and as many original artists as there are, so many worlds are at our disposal, differing more widely from each other than those which roll round the infinite and which, whether their name be Rembrandt or Vermeer, send us their unique rays many centuries after the hearth from which they emanated is extinguished. (3: 910)

Accordingly, the *Recherche* allows us to see the universe through Proust's eyes, who died almost one hundred years ago, but who becomes alive to us again through his work, which lets us experience what he has experienced, giving us an intimate knowledge of the unique world that he was.

Yet art does even more: it gives a meaning and a purpose to our sufferings. All the bad things we have experienced, all the betrayals and disappointments in our life, prompt us to discover new worlds of experience, teach us what really matters and prepare us for a higher level of existence. 'The whole art of living is to regard people who cause us suffering as, in a degree, enabling us to accept its divine form and thus to populate our daily life with divinities' (3: 913). Physical hurt is turned into spiritual knowledge. To witness our bodies grow weaker and gradually disintegrate reveals new truths about ourselves and the world (3: 920). Mental suffering does the same: 'The painful dilemmas in which love places us at every instant, instruct us, disclose to us successively the matter of which we are made' (3: 923). Artistically, the bad things we experience are actually more valuable than the good ones. From this perspective the years we have spent on trivial pursuits, on ephemeral pleasures, on sex and love and other futile attempts to get close to other people, on society and politics, have not been wasted after all, despite the unhappiness they tend to cause. The time we spend on all this is only wasted if we don't do anything with it: if we don't transform it into art. Happiness on the other hand is only valuable insofar as it prepares the ground for the unhappiness that must inevitably follow. 'Happiness serves hardly any other purpose than to make unhappiness possible' (3: 921). We need to be happy first to experience 'the precious shattering called misery' (3: 921), and only after we have experienced that are we ready to do what is needed to save us. But apart from that, the 'happy years are those that are wasted; we must wait for suffering to drive us to work. ... And, realising that suffering is the best thing life has to offer, we think of death without horror and almost as a deliverance' (3: 923).

Placed beyond time

Almost, but not quite. The whole point of art is that it allows us to go beyond a more or less graceful acceptance of what we know cannot be avoided, no matter how much we rage against the dying of the light. Instead of encouraging us to see death as a necessary evil or even, given the misery of life, as a welcome relief, it hints at the unreality of death and provides a pathway to an existence that is not affected by it. Its effect is sublimation, not resignation.

In our ordinary lives death is always close to us. Even though we don't like to dwell on it too much, we know it can strike at any time (2: 333). Sometimes death even takes a hold in us long before it actually occurs. We feel the stranger within, doing his secret work. We ask life what is going on, but life stays out of it and finally abandons us (2: 336). The reason for this is that we cannot detach ourselves from our bodies whose fate we must share. According to Proust, what we are is the mind within, which finds itself tied to a thing that is bound to perish and that drags us down with it. Because it is so fragile, so easily destructible and so short-lived, 'the body is the great menace of the mind' (3: 1043). We find ourselves at the mercy of it, which is rather unfortunate because the body is not the kind of thing that can be merciful.

> It is in moments of illness that we are compelled to recognise that we live not alone but chained to a creature of a different kingdom, whole worlds apart, who has no knowledge of us and by whom it is impossible to make ourself understood: our body. ... To ask pity of our body is like discoursing before an octopus, for which our words can have no more meaning than the sound of the tides, and with which we should be appalled to find ourself condemned to live. (2: 316)

By involving ourselves in artistic creation we gain the power needed to ignore the octopus and to rise above the frailty of our body and get a more solid and durable footing in the world of essences, which is untouched and untouchable by death and whose existence we first discovered in those moments when, prompted by some seemingly trivial sensation, we suddenly felt the past rushing back to us and merging with the present. Importantly, these moments are not moments of the past. Rather, they are moments common to *both* past *and* present and as such are 'more essential than both' (3: 887). That is why certain visions of the past would cause the narrator 'a joyous certainty sufficient without other proofs to make death indifferent to me' (3: 883). Those visions, which art seeks to emulate, bring about a 'deep sense of renewal' (3: 886), simply because the past is imposed upon the present so that the deep gulf that normally separates different times disappears, and we discover ourselves to be beings whose true existence is not really in time at all:

> The being within me which sensed this impression, sensed what it had in common in former days and now, sensed its extra-temporal character, a being which only appeared when, through the medium of the identity of present and past, it found itself in the only setting in which it could exist and enjoy the essence of things, that is, outside Time. (3: 886)

Consequently, the fear of death disappears, because death cannot touch a being that is not in time. But we need to be careful to not let that being, which is what we actually, essentially are, go to waste. To live meaningfully, we need to nurse and cultivate that inner being, to not let it wither away, to make it stronger, by providing it with the food it requires:

> That being within me can only be nourished on the essence of things and finds in them alone its subsistence and its delight. It languishes in the observation by the senses of the present sterilised by the intelligence awaiting a future constructed by the will out of fragments of the past and the present, from which it removes still more reality, keeping that only which serves the narrow human aim of utilitarian purposes. But let a sound, a scent already heard and breathed in the past be heard and breathed anew, simultaneously in the present and in the past, real without being actual, ideal without being abstract, then instantly the permanent and characteristic essence hidden in things is freed and our true being which for long seemed dead but was not so in other ways awakes and revives, thanks to this celestial nourishment. An instant liberated from the order of time has recreated in us man liberated from the same order, so that he should be conscious of it. And indeed we understand his faith in his happiness even if the mere taste of a madeleine does not logically seem to justify it; we understand that the name of death is meaningless to him, for, placed beyond Time, how can he fear the future? (3: 888).

CHAPTER NINE

Our hopeless battle against the boundaries of language
Ludwig Wittgenstein
(1889–1951)

Ludwig Wittgenstein was born in Vienna into what at the time was one of the richest families in the whole of Europe. However, he had no interest in enjoying the privileges that his family's wealth bestowed on him. Instead, he went off and first studied mechanical engineering in Berlin and then aeronautics in Manchester, where he developed not only a new propeller but also a keen interest in the foundations of mathematics. In 1911, that interest led him to Cambridge where he read philosophy with Bertrand Russell whom he quickly became friends with and who expected great things from him. Yet a degree was refused to him, and when war broke out, he joined the Austro-Hungarian army, fighting valiantly against his British friends and winning several medals for bravery over the course of the next four years. He also found time to read Tolstoy's *The Gospel in Brief* and Dostoyevsky's *The Brothers Karamazov* and was so impressed by the ideals of a simpler, purer life he found expressed in there that when he came back to Vienna after the war he disclaimed his vast inheritance, gave away everything he had, took a teacher training course and then spent the next six years as a frugally living elementary school

teacher in rural Austria. Despite his best intentions, this did not turn
out well. By all accounts, he was a committed, but all too strict and
hence unloved, teacher who expected and demanded far too much
from his pupils and did not understand the needs of the village
community. It didn't help that he also had a habit of hitting his pupils
in a misguided attempt to focus their attention. Eventually he had to
quit. The experiment had failed, and he was very much aware of it:
'I had a task, did not do it, and now the failure is wrecking my life. I
ought to have done something positive with my life, to have become
a star in the sky. Instead of which I remained stuck on earth, and now
I am gradually fading out' (Monk, 198).

Throughout his life, Wittgenstein was driven by an almost
pathological desire to do 'something positive' with it. He just
couldn't quite figure out what it was he needed to do in order to
make his life matter. After giving up his elementary school teaching
career, he worked for a few years as a gardener and helped design
his sister's ultra-modernist town house in Vienna, but that did not
bring him much satisfaction either. Finally, in 1929, he went back
to Cambridge to resume his philosophical work, first as a fellow
and later, grudgingly, as a professor of philosophy. He needed the
money, but did not enjoy teaching. If he could have afforded it,
he would have resigned 'the absurd job of a prof. of philosophy',
which he thought was 'a kind of living death' (Monk, 483).

The nature and use of philosophy

Today, Wittgenstein is known the world over as one of the most
important and influential philosophers of the twentieth century. In
a way he has become just what he wanted to be: a 'star in the sky'.
Yet during the course of his reasonably long life (he died of prostate
cancer at the age of sixty-two) he published only two books, a
seventy-five pages long treatise on the logic of language, which he
wrote during the war, called *Tractatus Logico-Philosophicus*, and a
spelling dictionary for elementary school children in Austria. The
bulk of his work was published posthumously from his extensive
notes, mostly because he was never quite happy with what he wrote
and kept revising and reordering it. But he also published so little
because he thought that, at the end of the day, philosophy, or what

is commonly taken for it, is not all that useful. His best students he tried to dissuade from pursuing a career in philosophy and instead encouraged them to do things that are more worthwhile, like learning a trade or working in factories. He did not read much philosophy himself, preferring hard-boiled crime fiction to the work of his colleagues. And what little philosophy he read, mostly from contemporaries, he tended to condemn as false and misguided, or simply as nonsense because it was an attempt to answer questions that could not be answered. In fact, he thought, it is already a mistake to even *ask* those questions.

> Most of the propositions and questions that have been written about philosophical matters are not false, but nonsensical. This is why we cannot answer questions of this kind: we can only discover their meaninglessness. Most of the questions and propositions of the philosophers stem from the fact that we don't understand the logic of language. ... And unsurprisingly, the deepest problems are actually *no* problems. (TLP, 4.003)

Philosophy, Wittgenstein insisted in the *Tractatus*, does not tell us anything new about the world. There are no philosophical truths that one could add to the body of knowledge we have. The natural sciences tell us all there is to be known about the world, everything that is the case, and philosophy is *not* a science. What philosophy can do is help clarify our thinking. This is because that process or *practice of clarification* is precisely what philosophy is (TLP, 4.112). While scientists build houses (viz. of new facts), philosophers do not even lay the foundations of those houses; they merely 'tidy up a room'. That, however, has 'immense importance' (Monk, 299). Philosophy cures the mind of its unhealthy confusions. 'The philosopher treats a question; like a disease' (PI, I.255). The practice of philosophy helps us understand what we can meaningfully talk about and, more importantly, what we can *not* meaningfully talk about. We can of course talk or chatter about a lot of things, but it is in the nature of some of them that we cannot talk *clearly* about them. We can still talk, but what we say has no clear meaning no matter how much effort and care we put into saying it: we will just utter words that do not represent anything real and that no thought corresponds to. 'Everything that can be thought at all can be thought clearly. Everything that can be said can be said clearly' (TLP, 4.116).

Accordingly, what cannot be thought or said clearly cannot be said or thought at all. If we try, we always end up spluttering nonsense. Philosophy, properly understood, is a practice of delimitation: it determines the limits of what can be said and thought, and through doing this it points us towards, or hints at, the unthinkable and unsayable (TLP, 4.114–15). Strictly speaking, the unthinkable and unsayable is not part of our world because 'the limits of my language are the limits of my world' (TLP, 5.6). Naturally I cannot describe what cannot meaningfully be talked about, but I also cannot even properly identify it by saying *this* is what I cannot talk about and, accordingly, *this* is not part of my world. I cannot even say whether that which I cannot meaningfully talk about is possible or impossible (TLP, 5.61).

Shortly after Wittgenstein makes this declaration in the *Tractatus*, however, he seems to contradict himself by giving his readers an example of (and thus talking about) something that is not part of the world and cannot be meaningfully talked about: the 'subject' that philosophers are so fond of discussing. The subject, he says, 'does not belong to the world, but is a limit of the world' (TLP, 5.632). All we can ever (meaningfully) talk about is what is *experienced* by the subject. That alone is real; that alone is part of one's world. Just as the eye cannot see itself, the subject that supposedly experiences that world remains elusive. It is nothing in itself, just an extensionless point (TLP, 5.64). That is why solipsism – the view that the subject or self is in fact *all* that exists, or at any rate all that can be *known* to exist – is in fact indistinguishable from pure realism. Wittgenstein does not say much more about this, but it is probably safe to read this as an example of how the practice of philosophy can solve certain philosophical problems, or rather, how it can show that such problems are actually only pseudo-problems. If the subject as such can never be an object of our experience, then it does not make any sense to claim that *only* the subject exists because we don't have any knowledge of the subject apart from what we can know about its *object*. We can therefore conclude that solipsism, as a doctrine, is meaningless. We can also conclude that asking questions such as 'Does the external world exist?' merely shows our own confusion and lack of understanding of what we are asking, because quite *obviously* the world exists (so that to say that I *know* the world exists sounds decidedly weird), and what we call the 'external' world is precisely that world. The subject, on the other hand, does not exist. Or more precisely, there is no reality, no identifiable fact, to which the *word* 'subject' (which no doubt does exist) corresponds, which is why the word defies our understanding: we cannot make sense of it and cannot say anything meaningful about it or rather (since we are talking about a word) we cannot say anything meaningful *with* it. One could instead also say: it has no proper *use* in our language. 'In philosophy, the question "To what purpose do we actually use this word, this sentence?" leads, time and again, to valuable insights' (TLP, 6.211).

In his preface to the *Tractatus,* Wittgenstein states that the meaning of the whole treatise (which, ironically, contains a lot of propositions that are not very clear at all) can be summarized as 'what can be said at all can be said clearly, and whereof we cannot speak thereof we must be silent.' He informs his readers that he believes he has solved all philosophical problems in his book, but he does not think that this is why his work has value. Rather, it has value as a demonstration of how little has been achieved by solving those problems. The really important problems are the ones that cannot be solved. 'We feel that even if all *possible* scientific questions have been answered, our life problems have not even been touched yet' (TLP, 6.52). Science cannot solve those problems; it is not even aware of their existence. But philosophy cannot solve them either. Indeed, it cannot even properly articulate them.

The riddle of life and its dissolution

And yet, we all feel, at least occasionally, that there *is* a problem, one that has got nothing to do with anything that science, which deals with everything that is the case in the universe, can reasonably concern itself with. We feel that something is missing from the world that ought to be there and yet cannot be there. There is, if you will, a gap in the world that we feel needs filling. We have a name for this problem that Wittgenstein himself clearly was haunted by right up to his death. We call it the question of the *meaning of life*. According to the young Wittgenstein, instead of meaning of life we could also say *God*. 'What do I know about God and the purpose of life?' he wonders in his diaries and immediately gives the answer to his own question: 'I know that this world exists. That

I stand in it like my eye in its field of vision. That something is problematic in it, what we call its meaning. That this meaning does not lie in it, but outside of it' (D, 11.6.16). The last, highly evocative pages of the *Tractatus* draw on these convictions or insights: 'All propositions have the same value', declares Wittgenstein (TLP, 6.4). Yet propositions – that which can be said clearly – are all we have. True propositions state (or 'picture') the facts that constitute our world. Those facts are just what they are. None of them is in itself more important or relevant or meaningful than any other. There are no values in a world of facts. So if there still *are* values, if some things are better than others, if there is good and bad, virtue and vice, then all this (without which life cannot have any meaning) must somehow spring from outside the world.

> The meaning of the world must lie outside of it. In the world everything is as it is, and everything happens as it happens; there is no value *in* it – and if there were, then it would have no value. If there is a value that has value, it must lie outside of all that happens and all that there is. Because all that happens and all that there is, is contingent. What makes it not-contingent cannot lie *in* the world because then it would again be contingent. (TLP, 6.41)

So clearly, for the young Wittgenstein things can only have meaning if there is a compelling reason for them to be as they are. The laws of nature do not explain anything, for there is no apparent reason for those laws to be as they are. In this world everything could in fact be different from what it is (or at least we can imagine it to be different). Also, meaning presupposes the existence of values: for the world to be meaningful, it must, somehow, *matter* what happens, not just to us (which would just be another fact of the world, that is, a 'value' that has no real value), but *in itself*. (Of course, we do not really understand what having a value 'in itself' is actually supposed to mean, but that is exactly Wittgenstein's point when he says that there are some things we cannot meaningfully talk about.)

After his return from the war, Wittgenstein struggled to find a publisher for his *Tractatus*. In an effort to interest Ludwig von Ficker to publish the book in his journal *Der Brenner*, he wrote to him: 'My work consists of two parts: of the one which is here, and of everything which I have *not* written. And precisely this second part is the important one.' Thus, he continued, the book really had much to say, even though the editor may not notice that it is said in it (Monk, 178). Quite understandably, Ficker remained unimpressed by Wittgenstein's sales pitch and declined the offer.[1] Who, after all, would want to publish a book that contains only what is *not* important?

What Wittgenstein did *not* write about in the *Tractatus*, and which is the important part, is the unsayable. However, on the last pages of the *Tractatus*, he at least starts hinting at it. What ostensibly began as an analysis of the logical structure of language now takes a decidedly mystical turn (which is probably the main reason why the book is so intriguing and has proved so enduring). Because all propositions are of equal value, there can be no ethical propositions. 'Propositions cannot express anything higher' (TLP, 6.42). Accordingly, we cannot really talk about moral issues. To say that such and such an action is morally *wrong* or that such and such a behaviour is *evil* or that one *ought* to act in such and such a way does not really say anything at all. It is, logically speaking, nonsense. Ethics, Wittgenstein says, 'is transcendental', adding without further explanation and in parenthesis: '(Ethics and aesthetics are one)' (TLP, 6.421).

One important connection between ethics and aesthetics is that we cannot explain what makes certain actions 'good' and others 'bad' any more than we can explain what makes things beautiful and ugly. It is not that the explanation given is wrong; what is wrong is that we seek and give an explanation in the first place (Monk, 305). The good and the beautiful are not reducible to or deducible from any facts in the world. Nor do they change those facts in any way. And yet, Wittgenstein adds, if morality changes anything, then it changes everything at once. Even though the facts stay what they are, the whole world becomes a different one (TLP, 6.43). The good and the bad, the happy and the unhappy, live in different worlds, even though those worlds share the same facts. It is not entirely clear what Wittgenstein means here, but later in life he became very interested in *aspect-seeing*, which may help us understand what he says in the *Tractatus*. His favourite example of aspect-seeing used to be a now famous drawing that can be perceived as either a duck or a rabbit, but not as both at the same time (cf. PI II.xi).

What is so interesting about this is that no matter whether we see it as a duck or as a rabbit, the drawing always remains the exact same drawing. The objective *facts* remain unchanged when we suddenly see a rabbit where only a second ago we saw a duck, but *something* – the aspect under which we see it – has changed. And since every line in the drawing now has a different role and significance, we can say that the *whole* has changed all at once. In a way, we now live in a different (perceptual) world. Apparently the younger Wittgenstein thought that ethics and aesthetics worked in a similar way: an appreciation of goodness in all its forms (and beauty is one of them) makes us live in a different world. Nothing has changed, and yet everything has changed, namely, for us.

Wittgenstein insists that the facts of the world do not give us the answers we seek. 'The solution to the riddle of life in space and time lies outside of space and time' (TLP, 6.4312). The facts are part of the problem, not the solution (TLP, 6.4321). But what exactly do we want to know here? What exactly *is* the problem that cannot be solved by any facts of the world? We already said that it is the problem of meaning. But then again, what exactly do we mean by *that*? We don't seem quite to understand what we are asking when we ask about the meaning of life, which should not surprise us because if there is no possible answer (that we could give in a coherent, comprehensible way) to a question, then the question itself is bound to be equally vague and unclear. 'The question to an answer that cannot be expressed cannot be expressed either' (TLP, 6.5). Does that make matters worse? Not according to Wittgenstein, because once we realize that the question we intended to ask has no clear meaning, the riddle we intended to address disappears. 'Scepticism is not irrefutable, but clearly nonsensical if it wants to doubt where no questions can be asked' (TLP, 6.51). Accordingly, our questions regarding the meaning of life are being answered precisely when we stop asking those questions. 'We know that the problem of life has been solved when the problem has disappeared. (Isn't that the reason why people who have, after having doubts for a long time, finally grasped the meaning of life, are then unable to say what this meaning consists in?)' (TLP, 6.521)

So where does that leave us? We have learnt that there are some things we cannot meaningfully talk about and that of those things 'we must be silent' (TLP, 7). With this declaration the *Tractatus* ends. Yet what we cannot talk about is still important. In fact, it is much more important than the things we *can* talk about. Fortunately we don't *have* to talk about what we cannot talk about because we won't find the meaning of life by putting words together (not even in cases where such activity amounts to writing philosophy). We find the meaning of life by *not* talking about it and by *living* a meaningful life instead.

> The way to solve the problem you see in life is to live in a way that will make what is problematic disappear. The fact that life is problematic shows that the shape of your life does not fit into life's mould. So you must change the way you live and, once your life does fit into the mould, what is problematic will disappear.

To live one's life like this is not the same as living it blindly. The problem is not ignored; rather, it is no longer felt to be a problem (Monk, 375).

An alien in the world

Unfortunately, for many people that may prove easier said than done. Wittgenstein was one of them. He thought he had solved all the problems of philosophy by showing that they are not really problems and thus dissolving them. We don't realize that standard philosophical questions such as 'What is time?' or 'What is knowledge?' or 'What is meaning?' cannot be answered, because we assume (and do not question our assumption) that there really are such things as 'time', 'knowledge' and 'meaning' and that they can be looked at and understood without taking into account the diverse and changing linguistic, pragmatic and experiential contexts in which we encounter them. We don't realize that these questions (which ask for the presumed *essence* of things) are simply the wrong questions. But if that has been shown and we finally understand that there are no philosophical problems, then philosophy is no longer needed, which as far as Wittgenstein is concerned is just as well: 'The real discovery is the one that makes me capable of stopping doing philosophy when I want to – the one that gives philosophy peace, so that it is no longer tormented by questions which bring *itself* in question' (Monk, 325).

Yet the 'problem of life' is not a philosophical problem, and judging by the way he lived his life and how he talked about it, it is quite obvious that Wittgenstein himself never stopped feeling that problem very keenly. Despite all his efforts, he was unable to think it away, as he thought away so many other problems. Living itself was difficult for him, and ending his life was never very far from his mind. Depression seems to have run in the family. Three of Wittgenstein's four brothers committed suicide. Being frequently lonely and unhappy, he must often have been close to doing the same. 'It is as though I had before me nothing more than a long stretch of living death. I cannot imagine any future for me other than a ghastly one. Friendless and joyless.' 'I cannot see how I can bear this life. I see it as a life in which every day I have to fear the evening that brings me only dull sadness' (Monk, 442). 'I feel myself to be an alien in the world. If you have no ties to either mankind or to God, then you *are* an alien' (Monk, 516). When Wittgenstein's mood was like this, the prospect of death must have had considerable appeal to him, especially since he tended to have (or at least profess) an Epicurean attitude to death. Death, he writes in the *Tractatus*, does not change the world, but ends it (TLP, 6.431). Death is not a part of life because we do not experience it (TLP, 6.4311), and those who seek temporal immortality are misguided because being immortal would not solve the riddle of life: an eternal life would be just as incomprehensible and mysterious as the one we have now (TLP, 6.4312). Death, in other words, is not the problem: life is.

Wittgenstein also struggled with his homosexual inclinations and his sexuality in general, with what he saw as his animal nature. He was antisocial to a high degree. He was frequently disgusted by people and frequently disgusted by himself. He longed for an ill-understood purity, spending his life looking for some form of spiritual elevation without ever quite being able to reach it. He went to the war in order to give his life meaning, which, unsurprisingly, did not work out.

> Yesterday I was shot at. I was scared! I was afraid of death. I now have such a desire to live. And it is difficult to give up life when one enjoys it. This is precisely what 'sin' is, the unreasoning life, a false view of life. From time to time I become an animal. Then I can think of nothing but eating, drinking and sleeping. Terrible! And then I suffer like an animal too, without the possibility of internal salvation. I am then at the mercy of my appetites and aversions. Then an authentic life is unthinkable. (Monk, 146)

An *authentic* life is what Wittgenstein craved, but for him an authentic life was also a *happy* life, and he found it very hard to be happy, except perhaps during those rare moments or at best short periods in his life when he was in love with someone and felt that his love was returned. There is little indication that the practice of philosophy ever made him happy. He was a natural thinker who did not want to be one. He could not stand the idea of living his life like an animal, unthinking and 'at the mercy' of his appetites and aversions, but it was precisely his inability to let go, to stop thinking and live his life in the moment – as animals are wont to do, that prevented him from finding the inner peace that he longed for and from being happy. 'In order to be happy one must not fear anything. And that includes death. Happy is only the one who lives not in time but in the present. For life in the present there is no death' (D, 8.7.16). 'In order to be happy, I need to live in harmony with the world'. Living in harmony with the world means doing the will of that on which one depends, or in other words, doing God's will. 'Fearing death is the best indication of a false, and that is, bad life' (D, 8.7.16). 'And thus Dostoyevsky is probably right when he says that the one who is happy fulfils the purpose of existence. Or one could also say that the one who fulfils the purpose of existence is the one who no longer needs any purpose but life itself. Because that means that he is satisfied' (D, 6.7.16).

For Wittgenstein himself, however, 'life itself' was never quite good enough. He needed a purpose. And because happiness eluded him, he knew that he did not live his life as he should. In his diaries he insists that the happy life is good, the unhappy life bad. This claim, he says, does not have to be justified. No explanation is needed because the happy life justifies itself; it is the only *right* life. The happy life is more harmonious than the unhappy life, even though once again we cannot quite say in what sense exactly it is more harmonious. There is no objective marker of the happy, harmonious life, or at least we cannot *say* what it is. If there is such a marker, it must be metaphysical, not physical (D, 30.7.16). It must transcend the realm of facts and hence the realm of what can be articulated. Yet that realization does not keep Wittgenstein from tentatively putting up a few markers for us (and himself) to follow, little hints about where we may want to look for happiness. How is happiness possible, he wonders, given the misery of this world? The answer (designed to convince himself that he is on the right path after all) is: through a life of knowledge. 'Good conscience is the happiness that the life of knowledge grants us' (D, 13.8.16). Doubts remain, however. Knowledge may not be the key to a happy life after all. Perhaps *renunciation* is, 'The only life that is happy is the one that can relinquish the comforts of the world' (D, 13.8.16). Wittgenstein certainly tried that, but apparently to no avail. Or perhaps happiness results when we adopt an aesthetic perspective on the world: 'It is precisely the beautiful that makes us happy' (D, 21.10.16). Or not. At any rate, nothing is explained here because we could just as well say that it is happiness that makes the world (appear) beautiful. As Wittgenstein pointed out in the *Tractatus*, when we are happy we live in a world that is different from the one that unhappy people live in. Happy people live in a world full of beauty, unhappy people do not. The upshot is that, as Wittgenstein knew very well because he kept talking about it, there can be no satisfactory explanation or rationalization of happiness (or for that matter beauty). The secret of how to be happy cannot be uncovered by theory. Happiness can only be discovered by practice, in the process of living.

Ethics as an enquiry into the meaning of life

Beauty, happiness, goodness and meaningfulness – for Wittgenstein all these words hang together, pointing towards a common, if fuzzy reality, or if you will, superreality. Ethics and aesthetics are one, Wittgenstein decreed in his *Tractatus*, without making any effort to explain why he thought that. Only once in his work, more than a decade later, he became more explicit. In November 1930, Wittgenstein gave an invited talk on ethics to the Cambridge Heretics Society. The lecture is short – only ten pages long in the published version – but very revealing. Following G.E. Moore, he now defines ethics as 'the general enquiry into what is good', which for him includes what is normally called 'aesthetics', but goes far beyond it: 'Instead of saying "Ethics is the enquiry into what is good" I could have said "Ethics is the enquiry into what is valuable, or, into what is really important", or I could have said "Ethics is the enquiry into the meaning of life, or into what makes life worth living, or into the right way of living"' (LE, 43–4). Now, as Wittgenstein goes on to explain, there is a perfectly good sense in which we use these and similar expressions. We may for instance say that so and so is a *good* tennis player, or that it is *important* for me to do certain things, or that a particular way of doing things is the *right* way. In such contexts the meaning of those expressions is clear. They relate to a particular given purpose, and we could always have different purposes, in which case what used to be important may no longer be important or what used to be right may now be wrong. Values of a sort seem to be articulated here, but a closer look teaches us that those values are actually nothing but facts. Being a good tennis player for instance means being able to do certain things (e.g. hit the ball very hard and on target and as a consequence win matches against a vast majority of other players). That someone is able to do these things is a fact. Similarly, if someone says that a road is the right one, what they mean is that if you want to go to a certain place, then this is the road that will bring you there, or bring you there fastest, or something to that effect. This too, if true, is a fact. Wittgenstein calls this the relative or trivial use of value judgements. (As he put it in the *Tractatus*, such values are values that have no value.) However, there is also a non-trivial, absolute use, which is the *ethical* use and which is much harder to understand, because in order to understand it, we need to go beyond the facts of the world. Echoing David Hume, Wittgenstein points out that as *facts* a 'murder will be on exactly the same level as any other event, for instance, the falling of a stone' (LE, 45). And nothing we could possibly say can explain what makes the former *wrong* in an absolute sense. This is why there can be no science of ethics. 'Ethics, if it is anything, is supernatural, and our words will only express facts' (LE, 46). Accordingly, we cannot really make sense of value judgements when they are meant to be *not* relative, for instance, when someone declares that a particular action is the right one for everybody at all times and independent of all circumstances.

> Now let us see what we could possibly mean by the expression 'The, absolutely, right road'. I think it would be one which everybody, independent of his tastes and inclinations, would, *necessarily*, bring about or feel guilty for not bringing about. And I want to say that such a state is a chimera. No state of affairs has in itself, what I would like to call, the coercive power of an absolute judge. (LE, 46)

It seems to follow from this that whether something is right or wrong, important or unimportant, meaningful or meaningless depends on, among other things, who we are. Actions and generally our ways of living are not right or wrong per se; they are right or wrong *for me* or right or wrong *for you*. In other words, there is no *one* way to live one's life: perhaps one way is right for you and a very different one is right for me.

And yet, once again Wittgenstein is reluctant to completely abandon the notion of the absolute good or an absolute value. Instead, as a reader and admirer of William James's *Varieties of Religious Experience* (SD, 182), he recalls and invokes certain *experiences* that for him indicate or signal some sort of absolute value, hoping that others had similar experiences to find some common ground (LE, 47). One such experience is sheer wonder at the existence of the world: 'I believe the best way of describing it is to say that when I have it I *wonder at the existence of the world*. And I am then inclined to use such phrases as "How extraordinary that the world should exist".' Another experience that evokes a sense of absolute value is 'the experience of feeling absolutely safe', which is 'the state of mind in which one is inclined to say "I am safe, nothing can injure me whatever happens".' What these two experiences have in common is that, on the face of it, neither makes any sense. I can wonder at things that I can conceive to be different (like, say, the astonishing size of a dog), but the world is not something I can imagine not existing. And I can feel safe from being run over by a car when I am in a house, but to say that I am safe *whatever happens* appears to be a misuse of the word 'safe'. But it is not just particular statements such as these that suffer from a misuse of words: it is *all* ethical and religious claims that do (LE, 48). And not only do such statements make no real sense, we cannot find anything approaching an absolute value in the underlying experience either, because those experiences are themselves certain *facts* in the world and as such can only ever have relative value. (They may be good for something, but they cannot be good in themselves.) So we seem to end up with a paradox, which Wittgenstein says is the main point of his paper: 'It is the paradox that an experience, a fact, should seem to have absolute value' (LE, 49).

A scientist or scientifically minded person will of course explain the paradox away, or if she cannot do that, she will still assume it can in principle be explained, namely, if we had knowledge of all the facts. We could also express this by saying that there are no *miracles* in science, not because science has proved that there *are* no miracles but because the scientific way of looking at things does not allow for anything to be understood as a miracle (viz. not as something that has not been understood *yet* but as something that simply *cannot* be understood). For Wittgenstein, however, the experience he described earlier, the experience of wondering at the existence of the world, is best described as 'the experience of seeing the world as a miracle' (LE, 50). The miraculous is of course, by its very nature, also something that we cannot talk about in a way that makes sense, and we cannot do this *not* because we have not quite figured out yet how to but because it is just not possible.

I see now that these nonsensical expressions were not nonsensical because I had not yet found the correct expressions, but that their nonsensicality was their very essence. For all I wanted to do with them was just *to go beyond* the world and that is to say beyond significant language. My whole tendency and I believe the tendency of all men who ever tried to write or talk ethics or religion was to run against the boundaries of language. This running against the walls of our cage is perfectly, absolutely, hopeless. – Ethics, so far as it springs from the desire to say something about the ultimate meaning of life, the absolute good, the absolute valuable can be no science. What it says does not add to our knowledge in any sense. But it is a document of a tendency in the human mind which I personally cannot help respecting deeply and I would not for my life ridicule it. (LE, 51)

Language as a toolbox

The younger Wittgenstein was convinced that we cannot talk meaningfully about ethical issues, which for him ultimately meant that we cannot talk meaningfully about the meaning of life, or even meaning *in* life. That is why we have to remain silent about it. However, the later Wittgenstein eventually came to understand that language did not quite work the way he initially thought it did. He had always thought of philosophy, or at any rate his own philosophy, as 'a battle against the bewitchment of our intelligence by means of language' (PI, I.10), but during the time he wrote the *Tractatus* and still when he gave his 'Lecture on Ethics' he thought our bewitchment consisted mainly in our inability to realize that certain words we use and certain statements we make don't really mean anything at all, in the sense that they do not represent anything real and there is no natural fact that corresponds to them. The 'subject' is one example, 'time' another, but also and perhaps most importantly ethical (which includes supposedly aesthetic) concepts such as 'goodness', 'beauty' or 'meaning'. All talk about meaning, then, is meaningless, even though it may be indicative of a stubborn tendency in the human mind that Wittgenstein himself, as he says, 'cannot help respecting deeply'.

However, the whole argument still assumes that words stand for something, some external reality that they 'picture', as the young Wittgenstein thought when he wrote the *Tractatus*. Later he realized, however, that this is not how language works at all. Words are not pictures of reality. They are tools: we *do* things with them. When I use for instance the word 'chair', I normally use it in a particular life context. I may ask people to sit on one, or ask someone to get one, or I talk about its price when I want to buy one, etc. I am very rarely in a situation where I use the word 'chair' simply to represent a particular kind of object, nor do I normally worry about its existence or its exact nature. Chairs are part of our life world: we sit on them, stand on them, topple them, paint them, break them and so on, and through all this we never stop to wonder *if* they are and *what* they are because that is taken for granted and we have no good reason to concern ourselves with these questions. Accordingly, what the word 'chair' *means* depends on the context in which the word is used, or more precisely, what it means *is* nothing but the way it is used in a given context, and since it can be used in different ways in different contexts, it can mean all sorts of different things, and there is not necessarily any particular characteristic that all those different uses have in common. In a series of lectures delivered to students at Cambridge University in 1938 Wittgenstein says: 'I have often compared language to a tool chest, containing a hammer, chisel, matches, nails, screws, glue. It is not a chance that all these things have been put together – but there are important differences between the different tools – they are used in a family of ways – though nothing could be more different than glue and chisel' (LC, 1).

Wittgenstein does not apply this new way of thinking about language directly to questions regarding the role of ethical propositions, and specifically the question of meaningfulness (the meaning *of* life and meaning *in* life), but the implications are clear enough: in order to understand what we mean when we talk about things like 'meaningfulness', we need to ask what the function of words like 'meaningful' and 'meaningless' is, that is, how they are actually being *used* in a variety of different contexts. 'The meaning of a word is its use in language' (PI, I.43). The only context we can safely ignore here is the *philosophical* context, which is misleading precisely because it tends to take words out of their natural environment. Instead, we must bring the words whose meaning we want to understand back from their metaphysical use to their everyday use (PI, I.116). Accordingly, we can understand propositions that in one way or another assert meaninglessness (such as 'this meant nothing to me', 'he is wasting his life away playing those mindless games', or 'all this seemed so pointless at the time') when we understand how it is *normally* used in a conversation. When do we say things like that? In what circumstances? And why do we say them? What are we involved in *doing* when we say them? 'In order to get clear about aesthetic words you have to describe ways of living' (LC, 11). The same can be said about all ethical terms (of which aesthetic words are either a subclass or from which they cannot be sharply distinguished): we learn to understand them by studying (or even better: practising) the ways of living which they are embedded in, which is to say that within those ways of living those words actually, contrary to Wittgenstein's initial assessment in the *Tractatus*, *do* have meaning, or more likely multiple (possibly only very loosely connected) meanings. When asking for what reason we call meaningful what someone does, we should not assume that there must be *one* distinct and particular reason. There might be all sorts of *different* reasons (cf. LC, 50). The best we can reasonably hope to find is some kind of 'family resemblance' between the different uses of the term (PI, I.67). In other words, there may be certain similarities, but no element that is common to all of them. This should not be seen as a problem, though. Clearly it is misguided to look for a definition if what we seek to define does in fact not have any sharp boundaries, and this is always the case in ethics or aesthetics. How for instance did we learn the meaning of the word 'good'? The answer is, not at one particular time, by being given a definition, but bit by bit, namely, by gradually being introduced to different uses of the word, resulting in the creation of a 'family of meanings' (PI, I.77). We must not forget that the words we use are, after all, only one aspect in a variety of complex activities that also comprise non-verbal elements, such as gestures, all of which contribute to the meaning that those words have in *that* situation. It is this whole complex activity that has meaning and that gives its particular meaning to the instances of language use that are part of it. 'An expression has meaning only in the stream of life' (Monk, 556). That meaning shows in what we do and the way we live (cf. LC, 54).

Of course that also means that we still cannot really *say* what that meaning is. What shows is precisely what cannot be said. There is simply too much going on in any given situation, and things are connected in intricate ways with an environment that stretches indefinitely back into the past and forward into the future. Thus what happens now has the significance it has only in a specific spatio-temporal environment, which includes what happened before and what will happen after – just as 'a smiling mouth only *smiles* in a human face' (PI, I.583). That smile can only be experienced and understood *as* a smile in the context of that face and the situation in which we encounter it. And the same is true for our experience of meaning in life. If we try to remove it from that context and understand it in isolation, asking what particular *fact* the word actually stands for, the meaning at once disappears and it again seems as if we did not really know what we are talking about. St Augustine famously remarked about time that he knew what it was when nobody asked him, but that as soon as he was asked he no longer knew it, for it then turned out that he was unable to *say* what it was. Wittgenstein cites the case of a musical instrument whose sound we know without being able to *say* how it sounds (PI, I.78). Obviously that does not make the sound any less real. Perhaps experiencing an activity or an experience as 'meaningful' or 'meaningless' is similar to hearing a sound. (Again: ethics and aesthetics are one!) We may then well know whether a certain life (or a certain moment or period in a life) is meaningful or meaningless, especially when that life is our own, without being able to say exactly what makes it so.

The things we cannot doubt

In 1949, not long before his death, Wittgenstein visited the United States to stay for a while in Ithaca at the house of his erstwhile student, the philosopher Normal Malcolm, who got him interested in G.E. Moore's 'Defence of Common Sense' and particularly in Moore's assertion that he *knew* certain things such as that he had never been on the moon or that he had two hands. Wittgenstein then spent the last one and a half years of his life engaging with Moore's assertion and thinking about what it means to know something and whether we can ever be justified in claiming that we do. The results were published in 1969 under the title *On Certainty*. Some of what Wittgenstein says here we are already familiar with from his *Philosophical Investigations*: that questions of existence are often difficult to answer, and that we are rarely in situations where it makes sense to ask them. Words are linked to certain activities. We learn words by making those links. 'Children do not learn that books exist, that armchairs exist, and so on. Instead, they learn to fetch books, to sit in armchairs and so on' (OC, 476).

Once again, Wittgenstein did not directly apply this insight to ethical propositions and the question of meaning in life, so we must do it for him: just as children do not learn that books and armchairs exist, but how to use them, they may not learn either that there *is* meaning in the world. Rather, what they learn is how to engage in meaningful activities or to do something with their lives that is widely regarded (and will hopefully be experienced by them) as 'meaningful'. Talk about meaning is part of a particular 'language game' that we have been trained to play, which as such is neither reasonable nor unreasonable. It just *is* (like life itself) (OC, 559), and we play it whether we want to or not. Playing that game is part of our life and, contrary to what the word 'game' may suggest, deadly serious. As a result, we 'know' that some things matter and others don't. Yet we are being taught that they matter not by being told that they do but by being introduced to and inducted into ways of living in which certain things matter and others don't, or some things matter more than others. We then live in a certain way and if we are lucky we experience what we do and how we live as 'meaningful', without ever thinking much about it or wondering what it actually means for something to be meaningful or whether anything we do is *really* meaningful, such as developing certain interests, following a particular career path, finding a partner and having children and just generally living our lives as best we can. 'Certain doubts', Wittgenstein writes, 'the reasonable man has *not*' (OC, 220), and doubts about whether what we do is 'meaningful' may well be among them, at least if those doubts do not concern particular activities that we may actually give up and replace with more meaningful ones, but the *very existence of meaning*. We *can* of course come to doubt that there is anything at all that matters. We can come to believe that *everything* we do and everything we could possibly do is utterly pointless, that nothing we do 'means' anything. But if we do that, the foundations of our world are crumbling just as much as they would if we started to doubt the existence of external objects. It may make sense in certain situations to doubt that *this* particular object is an armchair or a book, but if I start doubting that there actually *are* chairs or books, then I am in deep trouble because it makes living so much harder, if not downright impossible. And there is no need to have any kind of proof that chairs and books really do exist. Once I have reached a stage where I feel I *need* such proof I am already lost. There are some things whose existence we simply have to take for granted if we want to go on living, or for that matter, if we want to go on making sense of life: 'The ground of well-grounded belief is ungrounded belief' (OC, 253). We can doubt some things, but not all things. 'My *life* consists in my willingness to accept certain things' (OC, 344).

Yet there is more to my life than books and armchairs and other material things. There is more to my life than the mere facts of it. My life also consists in my willingness to accept that it generally *does* matter what I do, that not everything is utterly pointless. I don't need any proof for this either. I can and indeed must take it for granted. I may occasionally wonder whether this *particular* activity I am engaged in right now is actually 'meaningful', but it would be entirely unreasonable for me to think that *nothing* I do or could possibly do is in any way meaningful. Of course, if somebody asked me, 'Are you really *sure* that any of the things you do are meaningful / matter / have a point / have some absolute value?', 'Do you *know* that they do?' then I will falter, unable to confirm that I cannot *possibly* be mistaken. However, the same happens when somebody asks me whether I actually *know* that there are books and armchairs in the world and that there is no way I could be wrong about that. I can only say that if I don't know *that*, then I don't *know* anything at all. 'It is as if the "I know" does not go well with a metaphysical emphasis' (OC, 482). Yet just as it still makes perfect sense for me to continue to live as if I knew that there are external objects, it also makes sense to simply assume that my life can be, under suitable conditions, meaningful. And if a philosopher comes along and tells me that there really is no such thing as 'meaning' in the world and that all talk about meaning is itself meaningless, then I can tell them that they have understood neither language nor life, and I would be well advised not to take their concerns seriously. 'One might simply say "What nonsense!" to someone who raised objections to propositions that are beyond doubt' (OC, 495).

Ultimately, it is just as pointless to worry about meaning as it is to worry about death. Death will come no matter what, but it is not part of our world. Meaning, on the other hand (or more precisely thinking and talking about what we do and what happens to us in terms of meaning or its absence), is very much part of our world, and it won't go away no matter what. 'I can die in one hour, I can die in two hours, I can die in a month or in a few years. I cannot know this and cannot do anything about it: such is this life. So how do I have to live to exist in every moment? Living in the good and the beautiful until life stops on its own' (SD, 7.10.14).

CHAPTER TEN

The benign indifference of the world
Albert Camus (1913–1960)

The absurd

'Cold, fathomless depths of sky glimmered overhead, and near the hilltops stars shone hard as flints', writes Albert Camus in his novel *The Plague* (P, 270), published in 1947, shortly after the long war that plunged the whole of Europe into turmoil and left many millions dead and millions displaced. For many the experience of that war, of the terrors unleashed in it, had metaphysical implications. Camus was one of them. There must be something deeply wrong with a world in which such things were possible. Camus's words describe a world that is unresponsive to our human needs and wants, our ambitions and desires: cold and hard, without compassion, forbidding, unforgiving, unsupportive and in the end utterly alien. Things happen in it for no good reason, both bad things and good things, equally random (but the fact that there is good in this world, too, does not make the bad any more bearable – if anything, it makes it worse). How can life lived in such a world be anything other than, as Shakespeare had it, 'a tale told by an idiot, full of sound and fury, signifying nothing'?

The experience of an absence of meaning in the world, the ultimate pointlessness of it all, is the starting point, the root, of

Camus's philosophy. While we are constituted in such a way that we yearn for meaning, yearn to *make sense* of it all, the universe refuses to comply. We want to understand why we are here and how we fit in, what the point is of our existence, of our sufferings and strivings, but no matter how hard we try to find an answer to these questions, the world in which we find ourselves gives us no clue and remains silent on the matter. Even if there *is* a meaning somewhere out there, we are clearly unable to fathom it, and a meaning that we have no knowledge of and that cannot be grasped is as good as non-existent. 'I don't know whether this world has a meaning that transcends it', writes Camus in *The Myth of Sisyphus* (1942). 'But I know that I do not know that meaning and that it is impossible for me just now to know it. What can a meaning outside my condition mean to me? I can understand only in human terms' (S, 533). Meaning is here conceived not as something that by necessity had to *surpass* human understanding (as Wittgenstein argued), but on the contrary as a function of human understanding. What lies beyond our understanding cannot make life meaningful for us. True, or relevant, meaning must be *accessible* to us.

But meaning requires more than just understanding. We also want to be happy, indeed we feel that we *deserve* to be happy, but the way the world is organized makes sure that our happiness, if we are lucky enough to find some, is bound to pass. In this world, suffering is almost unavoidable. And in the end, not very far from now, death will put an end to all our aspirations. Our life, which we value so much, will be taken away from us through no fault of our own and in that sense for no good reason. And then all that seemed to matter a great deal to us while we were still alive not only ceases to matter, but reveals itself as having never really mattered in the first place. It was all, ultimately, for nothing. This is more than just deeply unsatisfying. It is unfair, and as such intolerable. It cannot be accepted. It must provoke moral outrage. And for the philosopher it raises the question how we can and should deal with this apparent pointlessness, both theoretically and practically: What does the fact that life appears to have no meaning, that the universe is irrational, unpredictable and overshadowed by death, mean for us, and what is the appropriate course of action in the face of this 'unintelligible and limited universe' (S, 509) and our own 'unjust and incomprehensible condition' (R, 16)?

The experience of the mismatch between what we, as human beings, want (and cannot help wanting) and what we get (and can ever hope to get) is what Camus calls the *absurd*. 'This world in itself is not reasonable, that is all that can be said. But what is absurd is the confrontation of this irrational and the wild longing for clarity whose call echoes in the human heart. The absurd depends as much on man as on the world' (S, 509). If we were not what we are, if there were no tension, no conflict between what we are and what the world is (the world that is supposed to be *our* world and that is our *only* world), then the absurd would not exist: 'Man stands face to face with the irrational. He feels within him his longing for happiness and for reason. The absurd is born of this confrontation between the human need and the unreasonable silence of the world' (S, 515).

Yet the world is only unreasonable in the sense that it does not, unlike us, show any preference for any particular state of being, that it does not care who lives and who dies, whether there is suffering or happiness, whether good prevails in the end or evil, *while we do*. There is no direction, no purpose, no reliability (anything can happen at any time; we may die senselessly, like Camus himself, in a car accident tomorrow), no good or evil, nothing that is valued more than anything else. It is, in other words, unreasonable in the sense that it is not like us at all and, consequently, not what we want and need it to be: a world that chimes with our being, a home. In 'a universe suddenly divested of illusions and lights, man feels an alien, a stranger' (S, 497). Everything that happens in that universe may happen for a reason in the sense that there is always something or other that has caused it to be what it is, so that it couldn't really be any other way. But efficient causes are not the kind of reason that we need in order to make sense of the world, to feel properly at home in it. Caligula – the seemingly mad Roman emperor whom Camus portrays in his eponymous play (published in 1944), who does seemingly mad, incongruent things and who has killed people at random – appears perfectly reasonable to himself. After realizing that from the point of view of the universe nothing really matters, he decides to 'push absurdity to its logical conclusion' (C, 61) and to henceforth follow the logic of perfect equivalence that the universe, for all we know, follows throughout. Unfortunately, this logic is inhuman. It makes life unbearable. Caligula does not consistently punish the bad and reward the good, which we could understand, or hurt his enemies and benefit his friends, which we could also understand. He is just as likely to do the opposite. It makes no (human) sense. He is predictably unpredictable, reliably unreliable, consistently inconsistent, just like the universe, and deliberately so. 'I've made myself into fate. I've put on the blank, moronic mask of god' (C, 53). Since he cannot make the universe more human, Caligula makes himself as inhuman as possible. He is a modern Stoic, determined to live in accordance with nature, to merge with the logos of the world. This is unreasonable, and it is not. If nothing really matters (including his own well-being and survival), then it is rational, or at least not in any way irrational, to act as he does. But since there is no discernible reason for him to perform any *particular* action, to do this rather than that, no particular action that he performs is reasonable. We cannot understand why he does what he does, except in the most general terms: he does it because he can, because there is no reason not to, because there is nothing that prevents him from doing it, but that can never be enough for us.

That is why in the end Caligula is assassinated, killed by those closest to him. He knows it is going to happen, that it cannot be otherwise because human beings cannot live under such tyranny. Not so much because it makes people suffer and die, but because it makes them do so for no good reason. As the Praetorian Cherea, who leads the plot against Caligula's life, puts it, 'To see life itself being drained of its meaning, to see it rendered absurd, that is unbearable. Life must make sense!' (C, 25). That is why Caligula needs to go: to restore meaning to the world, or at least to the human world – that part of the world that humans can create. Caligula does not mind being killed, does nothing to prevent it. Nothing matters, including whether he himself lives or dies. To the very end he remains true to his role as a moronic God, a faithful representative of an indifferent Universe, a blind, undiscerning fate. And by representing blind fate as a human tyrant, Camus makes us realize how unbearable life in a universe governed by such fate really is.

Yet while Caligula, the human tyrant, can be killed, the Universe cannot. *This* tyrant is here to stay. Seeing life drained of its meaning, says Cherea, is unbearable. Life *must* make sense. Except it doesn't, even if there is no real-life Caligula playing his games with us, which was more or less the case when Camus wrote and published his absurdist works (*The Outsider, The Myth of Sisyphus* and *Caligula*). The universe is a cosmic Caligula. So the question is, how can we live with this? And can we live with it at all? To give an answer to these questions is the task that Camus sets himself in *The Myth of Sisyphus*. Suicide, he says there, is the 'one truly philosophical problem', meaning that more than anything else we need to figure out whether in a world that is completely devoid of meaning, as this one seems to be, it is really worth carrying on with life, or if it would not be better to spare ourselves the trouble and the inevitable heart-ache, all the frustrations and disappointments of life, and just have done with it. This is 'the fundamental question of philosophy': 'whether life is or is not worth living' (S, 495).

Freedom

So does life need to have a meaning to be lived, or at any rate to be *worth* living? David Bellos, in his introduction to the Everyman's Library edition of Camus's *The Plague* (and other writings), chides Camus for his alleged belief that an absurd world, that is one that lacks a God and in which, consequently, nothing has any meaning (beyond itself), is somehow deficient. If everything we did had 'meaning', he argues, life would be pretty much unbearable:

> Things would surely be far worse if the opposite were the case. If the world were not at all absurd, in Camus's sense, then things in general and acts in particular would be endowed irrevocably with 'meaning'. And that would make the world a very strange and inhuman place indeed. Every cup of tea, broken shoelace, premature death, and outbreak of slaughter would be 'meaningful', that is to say fully explicable in terms of a higher order, and thus necessary. Under such conditions, human life, which characteristically involves imponderable choices, rough guesses, effort, and surprise, would surely seem quite futile, since no matter what a person did, it would fit in with a higher scheme by the very fact of having been done. A necessary world thus seems to many readers (myself included) as rather more absurd than one in which meanings are not given. (Bellos, XV)

This sounds pretty convincing. However, the whole argument rests on a conception of meaningfulness that equates meaning with complete explicability and necessity, and I am not sure that we *have* to understand (objective?) meaningfulness in those terms, and I doubt that Camus understood it that way. Is a meaningful life necessarily one in which there is an explanation, a good reason, for everything that happens and everything we do? Is there no scope in a meaningful life for chance and choice? Can our lives only be meaningful if the universe is deterministic, if human freedom is an illusion? Surely that was not Camus's view. If the universe had to be deterministic to be meaningful, then it would indeed be strange if we lamented the lack of meaning. However, Bellos himself seems to acknowledge the possibility of understanding meaning in a different, non-deterministic way when he argues that human life would appear 'rather more absurd' and would 'surely seem quite futile' if everything we did 'fit in with a higher scheme'. A life that is *not* absurd and *not* futile – that is more or less what we mean by a meaningful life. So the question is what makes a life not futile, not absurd. I guess that most people would agree that we at least have to be able to make our own choices, which also means that there must be the possibility of failure, of *not* doing the right thing. If things turned out to be fine no matter what we did, then there doesn't seem to be much point in doing it in the first place. That doesn't mean that the freedom to make our own choices is in itself sufficient to make our lives meaningful. Perhaps there is something else required, but that something does not have to be a divine plan or any other kind of 'higher scheme'. It is also not clear why it should be the case that a life can only be meaningful if *everything* matters in it, every cup of tea we drink, every shoelace that breaks. Why can there not be things in our lives that do not matter much or do not matter at all, pockets of indifference as it were, while others matter a great deal ('outbreaks of slaughter' for instance and how we react to them)?

This is pretty much the conclusion that Camus himself reached. When he lamented the lack of objective meaning in the universe, he did indeed deplore the apparent absence of a higher power in the universe that not only makes sure that things happen for a reason, but that also is responsive to and considerate of our needs and wants, hopes and fears. Basically, what we desire is someone out there who looks out for us and who makes sure everything will turn out well, a loving, all-powerful cosmic father or mother. Definitely not a Caligula. The realization that there is in fact no one there, that the universe does not care whether we live or die, experience joy or suffering, flourish or wither, that we are, for all we know, completely alone, cosmic orphans, that nobody will save us, is bound to hit us hard. However, Camus knew very well that the absence of a caring, parental power in the universe, its utter indifference to us, can also be quite liberating. Camus's answer to the question whether life needs a meaning to be worth living is, ultimately, a very clear no. In fact, he says, 'it will be lived all the better if it has no meaning' (S, 535). The reason for this is obvious: the lack of a preset meaning takes the pressure and the shackles off us. If there is no one way our lives are *meant* to be lived, then we are free to live them any way we please and how *we* think we should live them. 'If God exists, all depends on him and we can do nothing against his will. If he does not exist, everything depends on us' (S, 580). So there is some bad news and some good news here. The bad news is that the universe does not care whether we live or die and what we do or do not do. And the good news is that the universe does not care whether we live or die and what we do or do not do. In other words, its 'hostility' is entirely passive: it does not help and support us, but nor is it out to get us. There is no malignity in its indifference to us, to our needs and wants. In that sense (and in that sense only) it is benign. Camus's Caligula talks about 'the gift of meaninglessness' (C, 20), and he is not wrong. In some sense meaninglessness certainly is a gift, something that benefits us, that gives us scope to write our own history: 'If the absurd cancels all my chances of eternal freedom, it restores and magnifies, on the other hand, my freedom of action. That privation of hope and future means an increase in man's availability' (S, 538). Our confrontation with the absurd leaves us no option but to become creative, to give the world what it lacks. The absurd creator, Camus writes, 'must give the void its colours' (S, 585). The world is indeed empty, but if it were full already, then there would be nothing left for us to do (except perhaps to admire the handiwork of the divine Creator, which is ultimately not very satisfying).

So we are free, which is, presumably, good. But what should we do with our freedom? In the *first* instance, Camus suggests, our goal should be to get as much out of life as possible: to live our life and to live it to the fullest, without any hope (that it is going to last), but also without regrets. To make the best of what has been given to us for the time that it is given to us. Not to live in abstract ideas, to pursue intellectual pipe-dreams, but to immerse ourselves in the concrete experience of the world, in everything that is undeniably real and there for the taking, that we can have and do have here and now, in sounds and smells and sights and the accompanying feelings, and in our being keenly aware of all this: 'The body, affection, creation, action, human nobility will then resume their places in this mad world. At last man will again find there the wine of the absurd and the bread of indifference on which he feeds his greatness' (S, 535). We find meaning in life by living it, here and now, and by savouring it. What life means in an absurd universe is 'nothing else for the moment but indifference to the future and a desire to use up everything that is given' (S, 541). What will happen tomorrow is not in our hands. *Anything* can happen in an unpredictable, unreasonable universe. That is why the 'present and the succession of presents before a constantly conscious soul is the ideal of the absurd man' (S, 544).

So what?

In Camus's work, this ideal is initially (though incompletely) embodied in Meursault, the main protagonist in *The Outsider*. Meursault is strange to us because he is principally an observer, not a participant. He observes his own actions as if they were things happening to him, and what is happening to him as if it was happening to somebody else, all with a mild, rather detached curiosity. He does not act, but only reacts. He takes everything as it comes, resists nothing (except the demand to explain himself). He does not have any moral principles, beliefs or convictions, no character, no distinctive self. There is nothing in him that would forbid or prevent him from doing something. It is thus just as likely that he kills someone as that he does not. In that respect, however, Meursault is not very different from other people. He is a modern everyman, because what Camus calls 'the primitive hostility of the world' (S, 504) is not confined to the outside world. 'Men, too, secrete the inhuman' (S, 504), which means that we, too, are strangers to each other, and even to ourselves. We frequently do things we cannot justify, and fail to fully understand why we are doing them. We don't really understand each other, or ourselves. All we get to know is the facts, that what actually happened, but it seems that what happened could just as well not have happened. 'I'd lived in a certain way', says Meursault, 'and I could just as well have lived in a different way. I'd done this and I hadn't done that. I hadn't done one thing whereas I had done another. So what?' (O, 111). To some extent this is true for all of us. There is ultimately no logic, no reason behind our actions. There is no inner necessity. This is why I shall 'for ever ... be a stranger to myself' (S, 508).

The Outsider emphasizes the general unpredictability and opaqueness of the world, which includes the people in it. Anything can happen at any time, for no good reason. Anyone can do anything at any time, for no good reason. Meursault didn't expect to end up in prison, and he finds that curious: 'As if a familiar journey under a summer sky could as easily end in prison as in innocent sleep' (O, 90). Nor had he ever planned to kill an unnamed Arab on the beach, or anyone else for that matter. He never knew he had it in him. It just happened. Now, after the fact and facing the legal consequences, he wishes he had shown more interest in executions: 'You should always take an interest in these things. You never know what might happen' (O, 100). This unpredictability in the course of one's own life, however, also means that there is always a chance to change direction, at least as long as we are alive. The openness of being (as Heidegger called it) is both scary (because you cannot rely on things staying as they are) and full of opportunities for change (so that *we* may be able to change them, too). Only death cuts off all possibilities. It is the only thing predictable and also what robs us off the unpredictable. 'I could see that what was wrong with the guillotine was that you had no chance at all, absolutely none. In fact, it had been decided once and for all that the patient would die' (O, 102/3).

But Meursault is no rebel. He has no interest in changing the direction his life is taking. He remains detached, almost indifferent, even in the face of his own imminent death through the hand of the executioner. Death is, he reasons, not very important if you think about it. He knows that if his appeal gets rejected, he will have to die, but since he does not care very much about his life, he does not care very much about his death either. If he has to die now (that is in the near future, which is not quite *now* yet), he will have to die 'sooner than other people, obviously. But everybody knows that life isn't worth living. And when it came down to it, I wasn't unaware of the fact that it doesn't matter very much whether you die at thirty or at seventy. ... Given that you've got to die, it obviously doesn't matter exactly how or when' (O, 105).

Since we are all going to die, some sooner, some later, nothing matters in the end, and everything that happens is equally important, equally indifferent. Nothing is more valuable than anything else, which, incidentally, implies that nothing is *less* valuable than anything else either: 'There were only privileged people. The others too would be condemned one day. He too would be condemned. What did it matter if he was accused of murder and then executed for not crying at his mother's funeral? Salamano's dog was worth just as much as his wife' (O, 112).

Meursault feels liberated by his insight in the universe's radical egalitarianism. When he is asked to explain himself, to justify his actions, he angrily refuses. There is nothing to explain, nothing to understand. When Meursault refuses to accept responsibility, defying society's demands to do so, he makes the universe's indifference his own. He is no longer merely indifferent, but has now come to be indifferent towards his own indifference. His defiant 'So what?' (which echoes Tolstoy) marks the moment when he actively embraces it. And by abandoning all concern (for both others and himself), all hope for the future, all hope for salvation, he finds a strange kind of happiness:

> As if this great outburst of anger had purged all my ills, killed all my hopes, I looked up at the mass of signs and stars in the night sky and laid myself open for the first time to the benign indifference of the world. And finding it so much like myself, in fact so fraternal, I realized that I'd been happy, and that I was still happy. (O, 113)

When the universe is free of meaning, then we are free of the need to align our lives with it. We can give up looking because there is nothing to be found. Meursault takes this realization as his clue to make the best of all things, irrespective of the circumstances. He should feel unhappy in prison, he thinks, but he is fine really. On reflection, he believes he could find things to sustain his interest even if he were forced to live in a hollow tree trunk 'with nothing to do but look up at the bit of sky overhead': 'I'd have looked forward to seeing birds fly past or clouds run together' (O, 71). He should be unhappy (we think, given the circumstances), but he is not.

> I could spend hours doing nothing but listing the things in my room. And the more I thought about it the more things I dug out of my memory that I hadn't noticed before or that I'd forgotten about. I realized then that a man who's only lived for a day could easily live for a hundred years in a prison. He'd have enough memories not to get bored. (O, 73)

This claim is, of course, hardly credible. It is not humanly possible to be so indifferent to one's own circumstances. (We would need some serious cognitive and emotional enhancement for it to become possible.) I don't think Camus believed it was possible either, nor do I think that he meant to advise us to adopt Meursault's attitude to life (and death). Camus was not the kind of person who would seriously think that happiness can be found just as easily behind prison walls, let alone on the death row, as anywhere else. All things considered, Meursault is *not* the absurd hero that Camus is looking for, precisely because he is too easily satisfied. By mirroring the universe's indifference to all human affairs, including human suffering, by coming to terms with the fate that has been imposed on him, he actually fraternizes with the enemy. In the end he persuades himself that he is fine with what happens to him, but he shouldn't. Because it is not fine. It is, in fact, an outrage. Meursault provides us with one answer to the question how we should live in the face of the absurd (just as Caligula provides us with another), but it is not yet the right answer. As an ideal, Meursault is deficient because he fails to keep the absurd (i.e. the tension between what we desire and we can ever hope to get) alive. However, what we *can* learn from Meursault is that there is a lot of good to be found even in a universe devoid of meaning, stuff that makes life worth living despite its ultimate pointlessness, like our ability to see 'birds fly past or clouds run together' or quite simply the experience of being alive. Yet *The Outsider*, with its laconic, deliberately non-lyrical style, gives us only glimpses of what makes life good. We get a better, more vivid picture in Camus's late, unfinished (and actually quite wonderful) novel *The First Man* (which was first published in 1994), for instance, when the protagonist Jacques Cormery remembers his childhood in a poor neighbourhood of Algiers after the First World War, recalling the way he played with the other children:

> The sea was gentle and warm, the sun fell lightly on their soaked heads, and the glory of the light filled their young bodies with a joy that made them cry out incessantly. They reigned over life and over the sea, and, like nobles certain that their riches were limitless, they heedlessly consumed the most gorgeous of this world's offerings. (FM, 40–1)

Those children lived in the present moment, and it was enough for them. In the grand scheme of things their lives may have been pointless, and they may not have had much of a future, but what they had, at the time, was still everything that makes a life worth living.

Defending life

Meursault, in *The Outsider*, is a murderer. He kills a man, not for any good reason (in fact, not even for a bad reason), and without remorse. And why should he feel remorse? If ultimately nothing matters, then people's lives do not matter either. They will end anyway, some sooner, some later. No matter what we do, the outcome is always the same. So why bother? Why try to protect something that cannot be protected? In *The Myth of Sisyphus*, Camus contemplates the question whether life is still worth living even if it is pointless and does not make any sense at all. He comes to the conclusion that, despite all, it is indeed still worth living and that, consequently, suicide is the wrong response to the absurd. In *The Rebel*, published nine years after *Sisyphus* (in 1951), the guiding question is whether life is still worth respecting and defending, or in other words whether we still, in an absurd world, have any reason not to kill people. On the face of it, it may well seem that we do not. If nothing matters, if nothing we do is more important than anything else, if the universe does not make any distinctions between good and bad, permissible and impermissible, then it is difficult to see why we should not kill people if it suits us. If nothing is *im*permissible, then it seems only reasonable to conclude that everything is permissible, including murder:

> The sense of the absurd, when one first undertakes to deduce a rule of action from it, makes murder seem a matter of indifference, hence, permissible. If one believes in nothing, if nothing makes sense, if we can assert no value whatsoever, everything is permissible and nothing is important. There is no pro or con; the murderer is neither right nor wrong. One is free to stoke the crematory fires, or to give one's life to the care of lepers. Wickedness and virtue are just accident or whim. (R, 13)

Yet since we want to live, and to live well, we have reason to prolong and protect our own existence and to do whatever needs to be done to support those goals. The only thing that matters then is who keeps the upper hand, who gains the most power and uses it most effectively, who is master and who is slave. Or more precisely, the only thing that matters is that *I* end up being the master, and *you* end up being the slave. In a meaningless world the only thing that makes sense is thus a complete, Nietzschean affirmation of my own being.

Or so it may seem. In *The Rebel*, Camus insists that this kind of aggressive and self-serving nihilism constitutes in fact a grave misunderstanding of the absurd. It is quite simply inconsistent. What the 'absurdist analysis' really leads to, when properly thought through, is actually a *condemnation* of all killing. For Camus, the rejection of suicide entails the rejection of murder. Both must be seen as mistaken responses to the absurd, and for exactly the same reason. The experience of the absurd is not nihilistic, quite the opposite. The mark of nihilism is indifference to life, but the absurd is born out of the clash between the indifference that we encounter in the structure of the world and our own desperate desire to live, and to live well. The point is that *we* are not indifferent to life, certainly not to our own. This is why the coldness of the universe is so offensive. We want to live, but the world doesn't care. It may not make a difference to the universe whether we live or die, prosper or perish, but to *us* it makes a huge difference. When we are being confronted with the indifference of the universe we do not suddenly discover that life is actually worthless. On the contrary, it is only then that we become fully aware how precious life is and, consequently, how *wrong* it is to have it taken away from us. Yet if I appreciate my being alive, if I know from my own experience as a living being that being alive is good, then I need to assume that everybody else's being alive is good too. It is *life* that is good and worth protecting and promoting, not merely *my* life. We thus recognize, reasons Camus, 'life as the single necessary good' (R, 14). The experience of the absurd precedes and triggers that insight. We know that life is good because we know that it is bad to have it mistreated and destroyed, and we know that this is bad because we cannot help resenting and rebelling against a universe (as well as against any other power in the world) that does, or is bound to, inflict such badness on us sooner or later. Yet since I experience the violation of (my) life not only as bad but also as *wrong*, I can only conclude that it is not only wrong for others to violate my life but also wrong for me to violate their life, or in other words that other people, too, have the right to live: 'The moment we recognize the impossibility of absolute negation (and living is a manner of recognizing this) the very first thing that cannot be denied is the right of others to live' (R, 15).[1]

Defending that right against the universe's relentless onslaught of meaninglessness (which often occurs by means of other humans) is, paradoxically, what gives meaning to our lives. Where everything is, ultimately, pointless, we can make a point, and that is a lot better than nothing. When the world tells us that nothing matters, we are free to reply that it does! And because we are, and only because we are, things do matter, and continue to do so as long as they matter to us and as long as we act accordingly. In a meaningless world *we* create meaning by refusing to accept meaninglessness as the last word, which does not mean that we cling to the illusion that what happens in the world is meaningful, but rather that we refuse to make our peace with the fact that it is not. There is, then, 'something that still has meaning', and that is us, human beings able and courageous enough to fight back, us, the force that 'ultimately cancels all tyrants and gods' (LGF, 14). 'For a long time', Camus writes in his *Letters to a German Friend* (written in 1943 and 1944),

we both thought that this world had no ultimate meaning and that consequently we were cheated. I still think so in a way. But I came to different conclusions from the ones you used to talk about, which, for so many years now, you have been trying to introduce into history. ... You never believed in the meaning of this world, and you therefore deduced the idea that everything was equivalent and that good and evil could be defined according to one's wishes. You supposed that in the absence of any human or divine code the only values were those of the animal world – in other words, violence and cunning. Hence you concluded that man was negligible and that his soul could be killed, that in the maddest of histories the only pursuit for the individual was the adventure of power and his only morality, the realism of conquests. And, to tell the truth, I, believing I thought as you did, saw no valid argument to answer you except a fierce love of justice which, after all, seemed to me as unreasonable as the most sudden passion. Where lay the difference? Simply that you readily accepted despair and I never yielded to it. Simply that you saw the injustice of our condition to the point of being willing to add to it, whereas it seemed to me that man must exalt justice in order to fight against eternal injustice, create happiness in order to protest against the universe of unhappiness. ... Because you were tired of fighting heaven, you relaxed in that exhausting adventure in which you had to mutilate souls and destroy the world. In short, you chose injustice and sided with the gods. Your logic was merely apparent. I, on the contrary, chose justice in order to remain faithful to the world. I continue to believe that this world has no ultimate meaning. But I know that something in it has a meaning and that is man, because he is the only creature to insist on having one. This world has at least the truth of man, and our task is to provide its justifications against fate itself. And it has no justification but man; hence he must be saved if we want to save the idea we have of life. (LGF, 28)

Rebellion and solidarity

There may be no good, rationally compelling reason to defend life and to protest against injustice, to care about things and especially to care about other people and what happens to them. We know, after all, that ultimately it is highly unlikely to make any difference. Whatever we do, the best we can hope for is that we manage to postpone the inevitable for a little while. Yet fight we must, because it is in our nature to do so. It is what our love of justice and our hatred of injustice commands us to do. We don't really have a choice in the matter. Camus calls this 'rebellion'.

Rebellion is what *The Plague* is all about. The main protagonist and narrator, Bernard Rieux, is a doctor who, when a deadly infectious disease hits the Algerian city of Oran where he lives, tirelessly works to alleviate the suffering of the victims, without any concern for his own well-being and knowing very well that there is little if any chance for him to actually cure anyone. When his friend Tarrou asks him why he is so committed, considering he does not believe in God and it all seems so pointless, he replies that if there actually were a God, then we could trust him to take care of the situation. But since there is not, whatever needs to be done needs to be done by us. In the end, to be 'fighting against creation as he found it' (P, 114) just seems right to him. Rieux cannot really explain why that is. He doesn't know. All he knows is that people are suffering, which calls for an immediate response, irrespective of causes or consequences, and that he can help, if only by making it a little easier for them and by simply being there for them. This is not the *reasonable* thing to do. It is simply what the situation requires.

> And then I had to see people die. Did you know that there are some who refuse to die? Have you ever heard a woman scream 'Never!' with her last gasp? Well, I have. And then I saw that I could never get hardened to it. I was young then, and I was outraged against the whole scheme of things, or so I thought. Subsequently, I grew more modest. Only, I've never managed to get used to seeing people die. That's all I know. (P, 115)

It is less a strength than a weakness that guides Rieux's actions, an inability to accept things for what they are, a lack of, if you will, realism. But the weakness turns into a moral strength when it sparks the resolve to 'struggle with all our might against death'[2] and to do so without the hope that God is on our side. When Tarrou points out that none of our apparent victories against death will ever be lasting, Rieux insists that this is no reason to give up the fight. The fight is worth fighting, despite it being a 'never-ending defeat' (P, 115). Rieux does not think that this makes him a hero. What drives Rieux's defiance is not, he says, heroism, but merely 'common decency' (P, 147). It is, in other words, something that every decent person would do (or should do). It is the *obvious* thing to do. The alternative is almost unthinkable. 'Until my dying day', says Rieux (echoing Dostoyevsky's Ivan Karamazov), 'I shall refuse to love a scheme of things in which children are put to torture' (P, 192). It would indeed be preposterous to suggest that we might actually *love* such a scheme. Hate or, more practically, resistance and rebellion seem the only appropriate response here.

However, it is also important to remember what we are actually fighting for and what it is that stands in need of being defended. The fight is not its own end. It is a means to protect and preserve that which makes life worth living in the first place. The pleasures that life offers are important, especially the pleasure that comes from loving relationships with other people. The rebellion is not only *against* something but also, and more importantly, *for* something. As Tarrou reminds Rieux, 'Of course a man should fight for the victims, but, if he ceases caring for anything outside that, what's the use of his fighting?' (P, 226). Rieux knows that Tarrou is right. He knows that a 'loveless world is a dead world' and that when all is said and done 'all one craves for is a loved face, the warmth and wonder of a loving heart' (P, 231). Happy are those who do not ask for more because that love is something we can, if we are lucky, actually get in this life. Our 'homeland' lies 'in the waves of the sea, under free skies, and in the custody of love' (P, 263), and if we have that, we have the best that life has to offer (P, 264). And we don't have to wonder what such things, along with suffering and relief, 'mean' and whether they 'mean' anything at all. Its 'meaning' is not relevant (P, 263).

Rieux is what neither Meursault nor Caligula managed to be. He is the *rebel* that the absurd demands. His response alone is appropriate. He says no, but his 'no' roots in a fundamental and indeed foundational 'yes': 'He rebels because he categorically refuses to submit to conditions that he considers intolerable and also because he is confusedly convinced that his position is justified' (R, 19). Rieux fights against the plague because he stands in for life and consequently for the right of people to live and to not suffer, and in doing so, he also stands in for human solidarity. Through his actions he demonstrates his belief in something that we all share, some common human nature that is still worth protecting. For Camus, rebellion and solidarity are tied together. As (felt) solidarity gives rise to rebellion, rebellion realizes itself in (practiced) solidarity. Any rebellion that spurns or sacrifices human solidarity or ends up doing so (like the Russian Revolution) is not really rebellion at all. Real rebellion 'lures the individual from his solitude. Rebellion is the common ground on which every man bases his first values. I *rebel* – therefore we *exist*' (R, 28).

I rebel, therefore *we* exist – this is Camus's remarkable new cogito, the epistemological foundation that allows us to rebuild a subjectively meaningful human world out of the ruins of a shattered and discredited objectively meaningful *cosmos*. Meursault's world, in *The Outsider*, is still Cartesian. It shows us an ego alone with his thinking, a self that when confronted with an absurd world only withdraws deeper into itself. For that self, there is no way out, no way to escape its existential solitude and to reclaim possession of the world. Rieux on the other hand steps out of the narrow boundaries of the self by tying his own fate firmly to the common fate of humanity and by replacing thought (observation and reflection) with affirmative action. Like Ivan Karamasov (whom Camus discusses in *The Rebel*) he refuses to save himself as long as there are others who are not saved. It is everyone or no one for him. Foregoing his own possible salvation out of compassion, he thus commits to 'a kind of metaphysical Don Quixotism' (R, 51), which holds that even if it is all for nothing, it is still better than the alternative, which is the acceptance of injustice (be it metaphysical or political). The tension (between the goal pursued and the impossibility to achieve it) must be borne (rather than solved by a revolution that chooses tyranny and servitude).

Death and limits

But what if that which to Camus seemed still impossible suddenly became possible? What if the goal *could* be achieved and the tension resolved? What if human suffering could be ended and even death be conquered? More than half a century has passed since Camus's fatal car accident, and there are scientists today who believe it is only a matter of time before we figure out how to halt and possibly reverse human ageing and thus to conquer, if not death, then at least the *necessity* to die. Death, transhumanists keep telling us, is 'the greatest evil'[3], which is why we need to do everything in our power to fight and eventually defeat it. Like Camus, transhumanists recommend rebellion against the supposedly natural order of things, which they, too, regard as fundamentally unjust. These similarities make me wonder whether, given his premises, Camus would have approved of the transhumanist agenda and especially the goal of radical life extension. Initially it may certainly seem that way. Metaphysical rebellion, Camus writes, 'is the means by which a man protests against his condition and against the whole of creation. It is metaphysical because it disputes the ends of man and of creation' (R, 29). And we are right to protest against those conditions because they really are intolerable. 'Metaphysical rebellion is the justified claim of a desire for unity against the suffering of life and death – in that it protests against the incompleteness of human life, expressed by death, and its dispersion, expressed by evil' (R, 30). Ultimately, then, metaphysical rebellion is a rebellion against death. 'Human insurrection, in its exalted and tragic forms, is only, and can only be, a prolonged protest against death, a violent accusation against the universal death penalty' (R, 72).

Now, if we protest against the 'universal death penalty', that is, human mortality, then it seems that what we are asking for instead is immortality, and that, consequently, immortality is what we should strive for if we can get it. A bit surprisingly, however, Camus does not seem to see it that way. He uses a line from Pindar as an epigraph to his *Myth of Sisyphus*: 'O my soul, do not aspire to immortal life, but exhaust the limits of the possible' (S, 493). This is odd because it is not easy to understand how the rebel can both rebel against death and not aspire to immortal life. The reason for this has something to do with the distinction Camus draws between rebellion and revolution. In order to abolish (necessary) death, we would need a revolution. Revolutions, however, always require violence, always require oppression, always require death. They thus tend to betray the rebellion that initially gave rise to them. Camus finds a vivid demonstration of this betrayal in the two major revolutions of his own time: Fascism (i.e. German National Socialism) and Marxism (i.e. Soviet communism). While Fascism wanted 'to establish the advent of the Nietzschean superman', requiring its supporters to assume godlike powers 'of life or death over others', Marxism aimed 'at liberating all men by provisionally enslaving them all' (R, 212). The impulse that leads to those revolutions is justified, but the power that is needed to follow through with it, will always, by necessity, be used against those (or at least some of those) it is meant to benefit. 'If men kill one another, it is because they reject mortality and desire immortality for all men' (R, 213).

Transhumanism demands a revolution in Camus's sense, not a rebellion. Transhumanists want to do away with limits and want the total freedom that has been denied to us as mere humans. Camus sees a contradiction in the attempt to realize those goals because total freedom is precisely what rebellion puts up for trial.

> The object of its attack is exactly the unlimited power which authorizes a superior to violate the forbidden frontier. Far from demanding general independence, the rebel wants it to be recognized that freedom has its limits everywhere a human being is to be found – the limit being precisely that human being's power to rebel. ... The rebel demands undoubtedly a certain degree of freedom for himself; but in no case, if he is consistent, does he demand the right to destroy the existence and the freedom of others. He humiliates no one. The freedom he claims, he claims for all; the freedom he refuses, he forbids everyone to enjoy. He is not only the slave against the master, but also man against the world of master and slave. (R, 248)

Because absolute freedom is, in practical terms, nothing but 'the right of the strongest to dominate' (R, 251), the rebel wants to see freedom tempered by justice, but also, and equally, justice tempered by freedom. 'Absolute freedom mocks at justice. Absolute justice denies freedom. To be fruitful, the two ideas must find their limits in one another' (R, 255). The revolutionary does not recognize this need to balance freedom with justice. 'I've finally understood', says Caligula in Camus's play, 'what absolute power is for. It gives the impossible a chance to exist. Freedom has no boundaries anymore' (C, 17), to which his mistress Caesonia, who is far more sensible than the emperor, replies, 'The possible deserves its chance as well' (C, 19). In the end, Camus is a champion of the possible who recognized the value of freedom and justice, but also the value of there being limits to both. 'If ... rebellion could found a philosophy it would be a philosophy of limits' (R, 253). Unlike the revolutionary's, the rebel's goal is not to overturn the human condition, even though he recognizes it as unjust, but to serve justice by not adding to its injustice and to support happiness in a world that has so much potential for misery (R, 249). The rebel, who 'does not ask for life, but for reasons for living' (or, in other words, for a *meaningful* existence) (R, 73), fights not to create a better future but to preserve and protect what is good in the present. He is, in other words, at heart a conservative, urging us not to kill and die 'in order to produce the being that we are not' but instead to 'live and let live in order to create what we are' (R, 218).

Transhumanists believe that this world is bad, which is why we need to build ourselves a new one. Naturally, in the process some sacrifices will have to be made.[4] Camus on the other hand believed that the world is not exactly good but full of good things that are worth protecting, promoting and holding onto, and what is bad about it is merely that it is so difficult to do that. It is not that we suffer because we do not really want this world, but we suffer because we feel that the world does not really want us. It is like being rejected by someone we love. Even death, in Camus's understanding, does not seem to be altogether bad, not only because it sets limits to our existence (and thus to our freedom and power, which is good) but also because it somehow completes our existence, like the ending of a (hopefully good) story that has been fully told and which then gives meaning to the whole.

> The contradiction is this: man rejects the world as it is, without accepting the necessity of escaping it. In fact, men cling to the world and by far the greater majority do not want to abandon it. Far from always wanting to forget it, they suffer, on the contrary, from not being able to possess it completely enough, strangers to the world they live in and exiled from their own country. Except for vivid moments of fulfilment, all reality for them is incomplete. ... To know the whereabouts of the orifice, to control the course of the river, to understand life, at last, as destiny – these are their true aspirations. But this vision, which in the realm of consciousness at least will reconcile them with themselves, can only appear, if it ever does appear, at the fugitive moment which is death, and in which everything is consummated. In order to exist just once in the world, it is necessary never again to exist. (R, 226)

Far from rejecting the world as a bad place and life as an endless progression of miseries (in the manner of Schopenhauer, or more recently David Benatar), Camus's rebellion is inspired and supported by 'a ravenous appetite for life' (FM, 215), for beauty, the pleasures of the senses and the warmth of human bodies and human love. It is this 'mad passion for living' (FM, 219) that, in moments of keenly felt loss, makes him wish that things could stay as they are, that time was not real, that we could 'flee to a country where no one would grow old or die, where beauty was imperishable, where life would always be wild and radiant' (FM, 220), while knowing very well that this is not possible, and never will be (whatever transhumanists might say). That ideal country does not and cannot exist. Camus's metaphysical rebellion, therefore, largely plays out as a *political* rebellion, as a fight against those forces that are inimical to life, that *add* to the injustice of the world – all the various kinds of human dictators and tyrants, the Caligulas of this world, including the revolutionaries that are only too willing to sacrifice the individual for an alleged greater good, and the present for an uncertain, but allegedly much better future: 'The only original rule of life today: to learn to live and to die, and in order to be a man, to refuse to be god' (R, 269).

Camus's last, unfinished novel, *The First Man*, ends with a conciliatory note. Jacques Cormery, the main protagonist (who can easily be identified with Camus), now feels old age approaching (despite being only forty years old). Although he still mourns the inevitable eventual loss of everything that makes life good, he seems to be willing to at least try to make peace with human mortality. There is even a hint of gratitude:

> Today he felt life, youth, people slipping away from him, without being able to hold on to any of them, left with the blind hope that this obscure force that for so many years had raised him above the daily routine, nourished him unstintingly, and been equal to the most difficult circumstances – that, as it had with endless generosity given him reason to live, it would also give him reason to grow old and die without rebellion. (FM, 221)

POSTLUDE

It is commonly expected that the author of a philosophical book end the same with a proper conclusion in which he or she tells the reader what they have done and what they hope to have achieved. I am afraid I have to disappoint that expectation, because I don't have a conclusion. The reader may have noticed that none of the ten chapters in the book has had one. There are no summaries of what was said previously, no final assessments, no convenient provision of the gist of the matter, no wrapping up. Readers can draw their own conclusions if they wish to, and there are certainly lessons to be learnt from each of these chapters, but for me they, as well as the book as a whole, are more like musical compositions. You should get a sense of aesthetic satisfaction out of them. Of course the material used are not sounds but words and the ideas and images they create and convey. Some of these I hope will linger in the reader's mind, like segments of a melody, perhaps subtly changing and enriching the way we look at the world and understand our own life in it, perhaps also affecting the way we live it. Yet the ultimate question, whatever that is, remains unanswered. Life, just like this book, refuses to provide us with a pithy conclusion. At some random moment in the past we came into existence, and we will go out of it at some equally random moment in the future. And when we do, we will most likely still have no clue what it was all about. But if we are lucky, we will at least feel that we lived our life well, or well enough, that at least some of what we did and some of what we had was worth the trouble, that we made it count, that it was not a complete waste of time.

And since we are not quite there yet, it's not too late to make it count. If you remember anything from this book, remember this: whether life is worth living depends mostly on the liver.

NOTES

Chapter 1

1 The exception being moral purposes.
2 The German language helpfully distinguishes between the body as a material object (Körper) and body as lived experience (Leib). Today, the distinction between *Körper* and *Leib* has become quite common in certain areas of contemporary philosophy, usually in reference to the phenomenological tradition and especially the work of Merleau-Ponty. Schopenhauer, however, was the one who introduced the distinction, and should be recognized as the first philosopher of the lived body.
3 It can only ever be a description and not, properly speaking, an *explanation* because the existence and the nature of the will cannot be explained. It cannot be explained because it is groundless. The law of causality does not apply to it. Causal relations only exist in the realm of representation.
4 Schopenhauer is quoting from Goethe's poem 'Die Grenzen des Menschen' (The Limits of Humanity).
5 The phrase seems to have originated in the practice of using oars on sailing ships when there was not enough wind for the ship to move without human help.

Chapter 2

1 The fragmentary, writes Kierkegaard in *Either/Or*, is 'a characteristic of all human striving' (E/O, 150).
2 Kierkegaard spent the last two years of his life in a full-blown war against the Danish state church, accusing everyone who had anything to say in the matter of having betrayed Christianity, of having 'tricked God out of' it. The church did not take those attacks well. Some thought of Kierkegaard as the devil incarnate, the Antichrist, and with good reason: no atheist could have been a more fervent critic, a more hostile and unforgiving enemy, than the Christian Kierkegaard.

3   One should note that Kierkegaard did *not* used to think of himself as a Christian in this true sense. One should also note, however, that towards the end of his life, such an 'inward appropriation' was no longer enough for Kierkegaard. He became obsessed with the idea that true Christians had to be 'witnesses to the truth', which basically meant that they had to become martyrs and sacrifice their well-being and even life to the cause of Christianity, and Kierkegaard did his best to become such a martyr. It appears that in those last years he saw himself as a (and perhaps the only remaining) witness to the truth, persecuted by the authorities. However, it would be more accurate to say that it was Kierkegaard who did the persecuting.

4   'Of all the ridiculous things in the world what strikes me as the most ridiculous of all is being busy in the world, to be a man quick to his meals and quick to his work' (E/O, 46).

5   See Kierkegaard's last entry in his journals.

6   'If you cannot reach the point of seeing the aesthetic, the ethical, the religious as the three great allies, if you do not know how to preserve the unity of the different expressions everything acquires within these different spheres, then life is without meaning' (E/O, 469).

7   There is a certain irony in Kierkegaard's (or Vilhelm's) praise of unification and stern warning against becoming a multitude, given that Kierkegaard himself used a number of fictional personas to present his views to the public.

8   The 'crowd', in Kierkegaard, is clearly a precursor of Heidegger's 'Man' (or, as it is often, rather awkwardly, translated into English, 'the they').

9   Cited in Garff (2005, 765). The quotation is from *The Moment*, the single-authored polemical journal that Kierkegaard published during the last year of his life (1855) to support and popularize his sustained attack on institutionalized Christianity.

10 These are of course not Kierkegaard's examples. The ones he uses are a man wanting to become Caesar and a young girl who cannot be with the man of her dreams.

11 Hannay translates the Danish *lykke* as 'good fortune', but as he himself admits in a footnote, 'happiness' suits the context better.

12 Cited in Garff (2005, 547).

Chapter 3

1   For more on the religious dimensions of the Great Exhibition see Cantor (2011).

Chapter 4

1 In Victor Hugo's *Notre Dame de Paris*.
2 I am assuming that Dostoyevsky took this idea from Schopenhauer.
3 Dostoyevsky himself provides an excellent, very readable and moving account of his time in Siberia in his semi-fictional *Memoirs from the House of the Dead* (MHD). Compare also ch. 16 ('Monsters in their Misery') of Joseph Frank's *Dostoevsky. A Writer in His Time*.
4 Cf. Frank (2010, 549–50).
5 William James uses the same image in 'The Moral Philosopher and the Moral Life':

> If the hypothesis were offered us of a world in which Messrs. Fourier's and Bellamy's and Morris's utopias should all be outdone, and millions kept permanently happy on the one simple condition that a certain lost soul on the far-off edge of things should lead a life of lonely torture, what except a specifical and independent sort of emotion can it be which would make us immediately feel, even though an impulse arose within us to clutch at the happiness so offered, how hideous a thing would be its enjoyment when deliberately accepted as the fruit of such a bargain?

Ursula K. Le Guin, too, takes this up in her story *The Ones Who Walk Away from Omelas*.

Chapter 5

1 This terrible dragon is later revived in Bostrom (2005).
2 I am not sure what this beast is supposed to represent. What is it we are trying to escape from, so that we end up in this unfortunate situation? The non-existence before conception perhaps?
3 As described in Chapter 1 of this book, Schopenhauer argued that even the best of lives is still pretty miserable, plagued by all kinds of unavoidable suffering and that not having been born is by far the better option. He even argued that suffering is the very purpose of life.
4 We don't need to understand this as an endorsement of the traditional Christian view of a life after death, that is, a continued existence of the personal soul. In Tolstoy's last novel, *Resurrection*, an alternative is suggested:

> He never thought about future life, always bearing in the depth of his soul the firm and quiet conviction inherited from

> his forefathers, and common to all labourers on the land, that just as in the world of plants and animals nothing ceases to exist, but continually changes its form, the manure into grain, the grain into a food, the tadpole into a frog, the caterpillar into a butterfly, the acorn into an oak, so man also does not perish, but only undergoes a change. He believed in this, and therefore always looked death straight in the face. (R, 413)

Death, then, is just a change of form. Life goes on in a different form. Therefore, death is not to fear. Those who work with the land, and who live off it, understand this.

5 Here the term seems appropriate to me. Cf. Campbell and Nyholm (2015).

6 Which is to say, the God that he finds in himself: the voice of his consciousness.

Chapter 6

1 Nietzsche, who certainly felt differently, did not commit himself, but he nonetheless ended up spending the last eleven years of his life in a mentally deranged state after breaking down in the streets of Turin in 1889.

2 This argument is a bit confusing because it seems to rely on the assumption that the value of creating is not one of those values that have been created by us. But *all* values are supposed to have been created by us, in which case we seem to have no better reason to value creation than to value any of the other things that we would have to destroy in order to be able to create. In any case, it seems that Nietzsche later abandons his claim that there are no objective values in nature. In *The Antichrist* (1888) he writes that every demand that originates in an 'instinct of life' has its value in itself (II, 1188), which allows us to understand how what we conceive of as evil (meaning it has negative subjective value) may in fact be part of the good (having positive objective value).

3 What elicits disgust is the dishonesty of a society whose people pretend to believe in the Christian God without living their life accordingly (II, 1200) and without really believing what they say they believe. People *know* it's all a lie (II, 1199), and still talk as if it wasn't. That dishonesty is what makes it, in Nietzsche's view, *indecent* to be a Christian these days.

4 Nietzsche knew what he was talking about. His ability to intensely feel the suffering of others must have been well developed, given that it was indeed his pity for a maltreated horse that in the end proved

too much for him. It caused a mental breakdown from which he never recovered.

5 Nietzsche shrewdly notes that pessimism is a philosophy that is popular not in times when life is truly hard but in times where life is easy, which is when the 'inevitable mosquito bites of soul and body' begin to appear unbearable. In times where there is no real pain, we start to suffer from mere ideas (II, 71). (This is why today we have David Benatar.) Nietzsche also points out that optimism is just as decadent as pessimism (II, 1155).

6 Nietzsche insists that we are body and nothing else (II, 300) and that body has its own reason that we would be well advised to follow. This includes our sexual desires, which should be pursued without guilt or remorse. Sex is innocent, pure and good. It is simply an expression of the will to create (II, 378) and an affirmation of life and self (II, 1106).

7 Accordingly, the greatest progress would result from the sacrifice of our whole species to bring about the arrival of a new, higher species.

8 Your cat, for instance, is actually the *same* cat that has already lived countless times before in the guise of various seemingly different cats. It just *appears* to be different.

Chapter 7

1 As it happens, James did believe that free will makes a difference: it allows for the possibility of change, or more precisely, that things may improve. It is, as James puts it, a "doctrine of relief" (P, 56).

2 If for instance you don't have the money to pay for an expensive surgery that would save your child's life and you decide to kill yourself, so your wife can cash in on your life insurance policy to pay for the operation, then this does not show that you find your life not worth living. It merely shows that you love your child more than yourself. This would qualify as a good reason.

3 If we need a reason to go on living, we already have a problem, just like the man who needs a moral reason to feel justified to save his wife instead of two strangers. In both cases, we are having, as Bernard Williams put it in his book *Moral Luck* (1981, 18), 'one thought too many'. According to Williams, deep attachments to other people give substance to life, and without such a substance, nothing makes any sense, including abstract moral principles. For James, what grounds our experience of living a meaningful life is a deep attachment to the world. Reasons to live are secondary and powerless without that attachment.

4 Wolf (2010).

5 This echoes Mill's argument in Utilitarianism regarding what is desirable: that which is universally desired for its own sake. We should read this as an application of the pragmatist method rather than a naturalistic fallacy.

6 Pierre is the central character in *War and Peace*. James read Tolstoy's *Confessions* in 1888, and first *War and Peace* and then *Anna Karenina* in the summer of 1896 (Richardson 2007, 284, 366–7).

7 This is of course an idealization: most people combine elements of both temperaments. James is one of them.

8 There *are* no objective, mind-independent facts. For James, mind is not a mirror of reality, but its co-creator.

9 It seems that James was not too familiar with his contemporary Nietzsche's works (James was two years older than Nietzsche) since he tags him as a pessimist, lumping him together with Schopenhauer. As we saw in the previous chapter, this is a serious misunderstanding of what Nietzsche was trying to do.

10 As for James himself, he seems to have been a mixture of all those different temperaments he describes. As one of his biographers, Robert D. Richardson, notes, 'In some intricate way, James appears to have been, at bottom, both healthy-minded and a sick soul, both tender and tough-minded' (Richardson 2007, 473).

11 The idea that it all depends on the liver also references the humoralist understanding of the temperaments in ancient medicine, where the sanguine temperament (James's healthy-minded) was thought to be connected to the blood (which was believed to be produced by the liver), and the melancholic temperament (James's sick souls) connected to black bile (*melaina chole*) produced by the gall bladder.

12 I couldn't find any data about suicide rates in the United States in the late 1900s, but according to latest figures provided by the American Foundation for Suicide Prevention each year more than 44,000 Americans die by suicide. https://afsp.org/about-suicide/suicide-statistics/, accessed February 2017.

13 James seems to have taken the distinction between the midnight view and the daylight view from the German physicist and philosopher Gustav Theodor Fechner. James describes the daylight view as the view that 'the whole universe in its different spans and wave–lengths, exclusions and envelopments, is everywhere alive and conscious' (PU, 149).

14 In his last public talk, 'The Moral Equivalent of War' (MS, 265–96), James argues that those impulses are so much part of human nature that a civil, peaceful society needs to find ways to accommodate them and provide opportunities to express them and develop the matching 'manly virtues'.

15 This foreshadows Albert Camus, who develops the idea in his
    concept of rebellion, which we will analyse in the last chapter of
    this book.

Chapter 8

1 'Ideal' in the Platonic sense, where 'ideal' does not mean the opposite
   of real, but on the contrary something like 'truly real' or 'fully real'.
   The ideal is more real than what is commonly perceived as real.

Chapter 9

1 The *Tractatus* was eventually published in 1921 in another journal,
   the *Annalen der Naturphilosophie*, and a year later in English
   translation by Kegan Paul.

Chapter 10

1 I don't know whether Camus was familiar with the work of Albert
   Schweitzer, but his argument here is very similar to the one that
   Schweitzer uses to establish what he thinks of as the 'first principle
   of morality', namely, that promoting life is good, and impeding life is
   bad. For Schweitzer this follows from the most fundamental human
   experience, the recognition that 'I am life that wants to live among
   life that wants to live' (which, in Schweitzer's work replaces the
   Cartesian cogito as foundational fact) (Schweitzer 1923, 239).
2 'Do not go gentle into that good night, ... Rage, rage against the
   dying of the light', wrote the Welsh poet Dylan Thomas in 1947, the
   same year *The Plague* was published.
3 Compare for instance More (1990, 6–12); De Grey and Rae (2007);
   Harris (2007).
4 See for instance Fuller and Lipinska (2014) who argue, very much in
   the revolutionary spirit, that in order to create a better, posthuman
   world, as we must, we need to curtail various human rights, because
   those rights prevent us from getting things done. They are obstacles
   to progress.

SOURCES

Chapter 1: The worst of all possible worlds: Arthur Schopenhauer

Gespr: *Gespräche*. New, extended edition, ed. Arthur Hübscher, Stuttgart-Bad Canstatt, 1971.

HN: *Der handschriftliche Nachlass*, ed. Arthur Hübscher, 5 volumes, Frankfurt/M, 1966–1975.

PP: *Parerga and Paralipomena II*, in: Arthur Schopenhauer, *Werke in fünf Bänden*, ed. Lutker Lütkehaus, Zurich: Haffmans, 1988, vol. 5.

W1: *Die Welt als Wille und Vorstellung I*, in: Arthur Schopenhauer, *Werke in fünf Bänden*, ed. Lutker Lütkehaus, Zurich: Haffmans, 1988, vol. 1.

W2: *Die Welt als Wille und Vorstellung II*, in: Arthur Schopenhauer, *Werke in fünf Bänden*, ed. Lutker Lütkehaus, Zurich: Haffmans, 1988, vol. 2.

Biography: Safranski, Rüdiger, *Schopenhauer and the Wild Years of Philosophy*, Cambridge: Harvard University Press, 1991.

Chapter 2: The despair of not being oneself: Søren Kierkegaard

CUP: Johannes Climacus (Søren Kierkegaard), *Concluding Unscientific Postscript to the Philosophical Crumbs* (1846). Translated by Alastair Hannay, Cambridge: Cambridge University Press, 2009.

EK: *The Essential Kierkegaard*, ed. Howard V. Hong and Edna H. Hong, Princeton: Princeton University Press, 2000.

E/O: Victor Eremita (Søren Kierkegaard), *Either/ Or: A Fragment of Life* (1843). Translated by Alastair Hannay, London: Penguin, 1992.

FT: Johannes de silentio (Søren Kierkegaard), *Fear and Trembling* (1843). Translated by Alastair Hannay, London: Penguin, 1985.

R: Constantine Constantius (Søren Kierkegaard), *Repetition: An Essay in Experimental Psychology* (1843), in: Søren Kierkegaard, *Repetition and Philosophical Crumbs*. Translated by M. G. Piety, Oxford: Oxford University Press, 2009, 1–81.
SD: Anti-Climacus (Søren Kierkegaard), *The Sickness unto Death* (1849). Translated by Alastair Hannay, London: Penguin, 1989.
Biography: Garff, Joakim, *Søren Kierkegaard: A Biography*, Princeton and Oxford: Princeton University Press, 2005.

Chapter 3: The interlinked terrors and wonders of god: Herman Melville

BB: 'Billy Budd, Sailor' (1891), in: Hermann Melville, *Complete Shorter Fiction*, New York: Alfred A. Knopf (Everyman's Library), 1997, 403–78.
BC: 'Benito Cereno' (1855), in: Hermann Melville, *Complete Shorter Fiction*, New York: Alfred A. Knopf (Everyman's Library), 1997, 52–126.
BS: 'Bartleby, the Scrivener' (1853), in: Hermann Melville, *Complete Shorter Fiction*, New York: Alfred A. Knopf (Everyman's Library), 1997, 18–51.
Cantor, Geoffrey (2011), *Religion and the Great Exhibition of 1851*, Oxford: Oxford University Press.
CM: *The Confidence-Man: His Masquerade* (1857), Oxford: Oxford World Classics, 1989.
MD: *Moby-Dick* (1851), Oxford: Oxford University Press (The World's Classics), 1920.
Biography: Robertson-Lorant, Laurie, *Melville: A Biography*, Amherst: University of Massachusetts Press, 1998.

Chapter 4: The hell of no longer being able to love: Fyodor Dostoyevsky

BK: *The Brothers Karamazov* (1880). Translated by Richard Pevear and Larissa Volokhonsky, New York: Alfred A. Knopf (Everyman's Library), 1992.
CP: *Crime and Punishment* (1866). Translated by Richard Pevear and Larissa Volokhonsky, New York: Alfred A. Knopf (Everyman's Library), 1993.

D: *Demons* (1872). Translated by Richard Pevear and Larissa
 Volokhonsky, New York: Alfred A. Knopf (Everyman's Library), 2000.
DRM: 'The Dream of a Ridiculous Man' (1877), in: *A Gentle Creature
 and Other Stories*. Translated by Alan Myers, Oxford: Oxford
 University Press (Oxford World's Classics), 1999, 107–28.
GC: 'A Gentle Creature' (1876), in: *A Gentle Creature and Other Stories*.
 Translated by Alan Myers, Oxford: Oxford University Press (Oxford
 World's Classics), 1999, 59–103.
I: *The Idiot* (1869). Translated by Richard Pevear and Larissa
 Volokhonsky, New York: Alfred A. Knopf (Everyman's Library), 2002.
MHD: *Memoirs from the House of the Dead* (1862). Translated by Jessie
 Coulson, Oxford: Oxford University Press (Oxford World's Classics),
 2001.
NU: *Notes from Underground* (1864). Translated by Richard Pevear
 and Larissa Volokhonsky, New York: Alfred A. Knopf (Everyman's
 Library), 2004.
WN: 'White Nights' (1848), in: *A Gentle Creature and Other Stories*.
 Translated by Alan Myers, Oxford: Oxford University Press (Oxford
 World's Classics), 1999, 3–56.
Biography: Frank, Joseph, *Dostoevsky: A Writer in His Time*, Princeton
 and Oxford: Princeton University Press, 2010.

Chapter 5: The inevitable end of everything: Leo Tolstoy

AK: *Anna Karenina* (1878). Translated by Richard Pevear and Larissa
 Volokhonsky, London: Penguin Classics, 2001.
Bostrom, Nick, 'Fable of the Dragon Tyrant', *Journal of Medical Ethics*
 31/5 (2005): 273–7.
C: *A Confession* (1882). Translated by Jane Kentish, London: Penguin
 Books, 2008.
Campbell, Stephen M. and Sven Nyholm 'Anti-Meaning and Why It
 Matters', *Journal of the American Philosophical Association* 1/4
 (2015): 694–711.
DII: 'The Death of Ivan Ilych' (1886), in: Leo Tolstoy, *Collected Shorter
 Fiction*. Translated by Louise and Aylmer Maude and Nigel J. Cooper,
 New York: Alfred A. Knopf (Everyman's Library), 2001, Vol. 2, 109–71.
KS: 'The Kreutzer Sonata' (1889), in: Leo Tolstoy, *Collected Shorter
 Fiction*. Translated by Louise and Aylmer Maude and Nigel J. Cooper,
 New York: Alfred A. Knopf (Everyman's Library), 2001, Vol. 2,
 241–324.

R: *Resurrection* (1899). Translated by Louise Maude, Ware: Wordsworth Editions, 2014.

WP: *War and Peace* (1869). Translated by Anthony Briggs, London: Penguin Classics, 2005.

Biography: Wilson, A. N., *Tolstoy: A Biography*, New York: W.W. Norton, 1988.

Chapter 6: The joy of living dangerously: Friedrich Nietzsche

Nietzsche, Friedrich, *Werke in drei Bänden* (Works in three volumes), Munich: Carl Hanser, 1966.

Die fröhliche Wissenschaft (The Gay Science), Werke II, 7–274.

Also sprach Zarathustra (Thus Spoke Zarathustra), Werke II, 275–561.

Jenseits von Gut und Böse (Beyond Good and Evil), Werke II, 563–759.

Zur Genealogie der Moral (On the Genealogy of Morality), Werke II, 761–899.

Götzendämmerung (Twilight of Idols), Werke II, 939–1033.

Ecce Homo, Werke II, 1063–159.

Der Anti-Christ (The Antichrist), Werke II, 1161–236.

Biography: Safranski, Rüdiger, *Nietzsche: A Philosophical Biography*, New York: W.W. Norton 2002.

Chapter 7: The dramatic richness of the concrete world: William James

MS: *Memories and Studies*, New York/London/Bombay/Calcutta: Longmans, Green, and Co., 1911.

P: *Pragmatism: A New Name for Some Old Ways of Thinking*, New York/Bombay/Calcutta: Longmans, Green, and Co., 1907.

PU: *A Pluralistic Universe*, New York/London/Bombay/Calcutta: Longmans, Green, and Co., 1909.

TT: *Talks to Teachers on Psychology: And to Students on Some of Life's Ideals*, London/Bombay/Calcutta: Longmans Green and Co., 1899.

VRE: *Varieties of Religious Experience* (1902), New York: Vintage Books/The Library of America, 1990.

WB: *The Will to Believe and Other Essays in Popular Philosophy*, New York/London/Bombay: Longmans Green and Co., 1897.

Williams, Bernard, *Moral Luck*, Cambridge: Cambridge University Press, 1981, 18.

Wolf, Susan, *Meaning in Life and Why It Matters*, Princeton and Oxford: Princeton University Press, 2010.

Biography: Richardson, Robert D., *William James: In the Maelstrom of American Modernism*, Boston/New York: Houghton Mifflin Co., 2007.

Chapter 8: The only life that is really lived: Marcel Proust

Remembrance of Things Past. Translated by C. K. Scott Moncrieff, 3 vols, London: Penguin Classics, 2016.

Biography: Painter, George D., *Marcel Proust: A Biography*, revised and enlarged edition, London: Pimlico, 1996.

Chapter 9: Our hopeless battle against the boundaries of language: Ludwig Wittgenstein

LC: *Lectures and Conversations on Aesthetics, Psychology & Religious Belief*, ed. Cyril Barrett, Oxford: Basil Blackwell, 1966.

LE: *Lecture on Ethics*, eds E. Zamuner, E. V. Di Lascio and D. K. Levy, Chichester: John Wiley & Sons, 2014.

OC: *On Certainty*, eds G. E. M. Anscombe and G. H. von Wright, Oxford: Basil Blackwell, 1969. (Citations refer to the editors' section numbers, not the page numbers.)

SD: *Geheime Tagebücher* (Secret Diaries), ed. Wilhelm Baum, Vienna: Turia & Kant, 1991.

WC: Bouwsma, O. K., *Wittgenstein Conversations 1949–1951*, ed. J. L. Craft and Ronald E. Hustwit, Indianapolis: Hackett Publishing, 1986.

Wittgenstein, Ludwig, *Werkausgabe*, Frankfurt: Suhrkamp, 1989, vol. 1.

  TLP: *Tractatus logico-philosophicus*, 7–85. (Citations refer to Wittgenstein's own numbering of his propositions.)

  D: *Tagebücher 1914–1916* (Diaries), 87–187.

  PI: *Philosophische Untersuchungen* (Philosophical Investigations), 225–580.

Biography: Monk, Ray, *Wittgenstein: The Duty of Genius*, London: Vintage Books, 1991.

Chapter 10: The benign indifference of the world: Albert Camus

Bellos, David, 'Introduction', in: Albert Camus, *The Plague, the Fall, Exile and the Kingdom, and Selected Essays*, London: Everyman's Library, 2004.

C: *Caligula* (1944). In a new translation by David Greig, London: faber and faber, 2003.

De Grey, Aubrey and Michael Rae, *Ending Aging*, New York: St Martin's Press, 2007.

FM: *The First Man*. Translated by David Hapgood, London: Hamish Hamilton, 1995.

Fuller, Steven and Veronika Lipinska, *The Proactionary Imperative: A Foundation for Transhumanism*, Basingstoke: Palgrave Macmillan, 2014.

Harris, John, *Enhancing Evolution: The Ethical Case for Making Better People*, Oxford: Oxford University Press, 2007.

LGF: *Letters to a German Friend* (1943–4). Translated by Justin O'Brien, in: *Albert Camus, Resistance, Rebellion, and Death: Essays*, New York: Vintage International, 1960.

More, Max, 'Transhumanism: Towards a Futurist Philosophy', *Extropy* 6 (1990): 6–12.

O: *The Outsider* (1942). Translated by Joseph Laredo, London: Everyman's Library, 1998.

P: *The Plague* (1947). Translated by Stuart Gilbert, in: Albert Camus, *The Plague, the Fall, Exile and the Kingdom, and Selected Essays*, London: Everyman's Library, 2004, 1–272.

R: *The Rebel* (1951). Translated by Anthony Bower, London: Penguin Books, 1962.

S: *The Myth of Sisyphus* (1942). Translated by Justin O'Brien, in: Albert Camus, *The Plague, the Fall, Exile and the Kingdom, and Selected Essays*, London: Everyman's Library, 2004, 489–605.

Schweitzer, Albert, *Kultur und Ethik. Kulturphilosophie Zweiter Teil*, München: C.H. Becksche Verlagsbuchhandlung, 1923, 239.

Biography: Zaretsky, Robert, *A Life Worth Living: Albert Camus and the Quest for Meaning*, Cambridge: Harvard University Press, 2013.